To Daddy
Happy Father's
Day 2012
Lots of love from
Claudia & Alex
xxx

The Hairy Bikers' Perfect Pies

WEIDENFELD & NICOLSON

We'd like to dedicate *Perfect Pies* to our remarkable team: Lucie, Amanda, Jinny, Kate and especially Justine, who has put her heart and soul into this book.

First published in hardback in Great Britain in 2011 by
Weidenfeld & Nicolson, an imprint of the Orion Publishing Group Ltd
Orion House, 5 Upper St Martin's Lane, London WC2H 9EA
an Hachette UK Company

A CIP catalogue record for this book is available from the British Library.

Photographer: Cristian Barnett
Illustrator: Emma Kelly
Food director: Justine Pattison
Prop stylist: Giuliana Casarotti
Designer: Kate Barr
Editor: Jinny Johnson
Proofreader: Elise See Tai
Indexer: Elizabeth Wiggans
Photographer's assistant: Roy Baron
Food director's assistants: Fran Brown, Lauren Brignell & Jane Gwillim

Printed and bound in China

The Orion Publishing Group's policy is to use papers that are natural, renewable and recyclable and made from wood grown in sustainable forests. The logging and manufacturing processes are expected to conform to the environmental regulations of the country of origin.

www.orionbooks.co.uk

contents

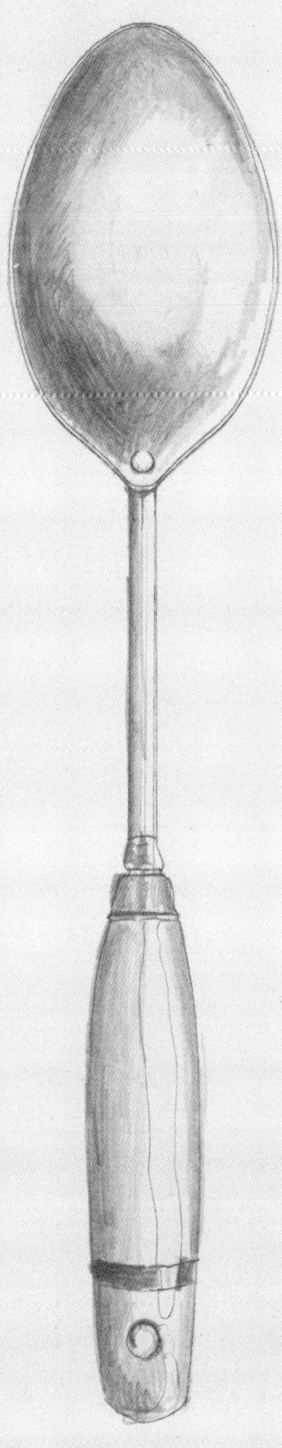

Perfect pie moments

Dave: The smell of the freshly baked pies from the corner shop in Barrow. When I was a lad, I used to eat three meat and potato pies for my dinner every day.

Si: The mince and onion plate pie my mam used to make. Just the thought makes my mouth water.

Dave: Our pie plate. Every home had a plate that was kept for pies – a bit chipped, a bit brown around the edges. I can see it now.

Si: The pies we use to eat at football on a Saturday. Nuclear interior and a cup of Bovril to wash them down.

Dave: My Auntie Marion's bramble tarts – her pastry was like cricket pads but we still gobbled them up!

Si: Getting home on a weekend and finding the house full of the scent of baking pie, then burning my fingers on the pie plate because I was so keen to get my hands on it.

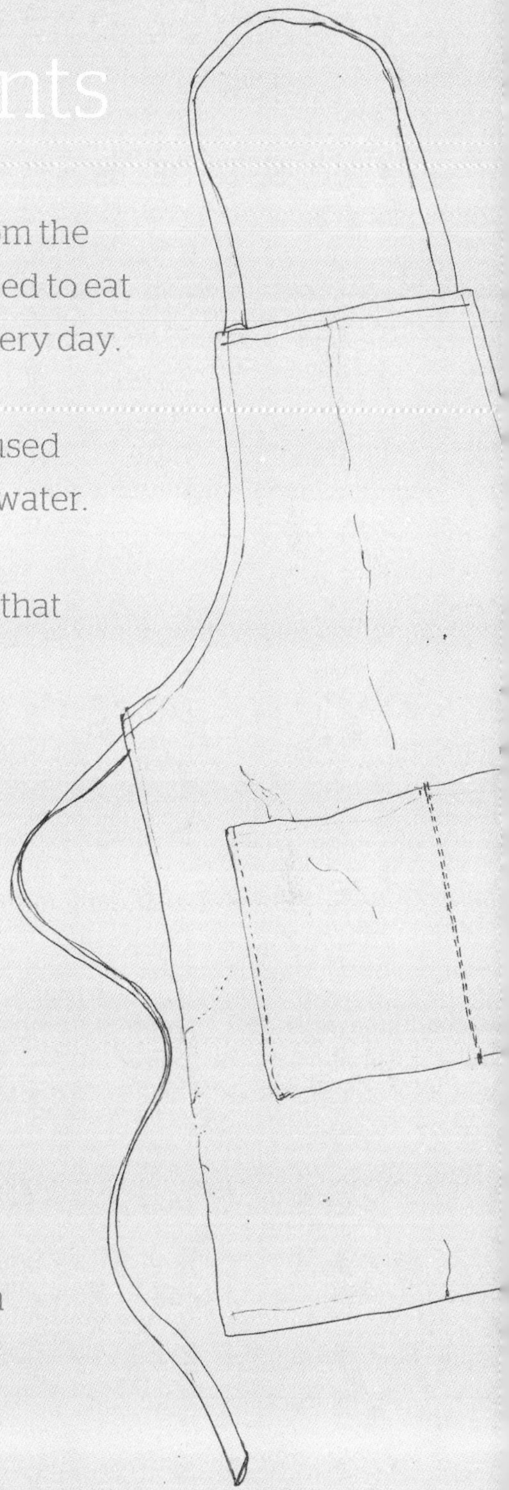

This book is a celebration of our love affair with the pie, so get out your rolling pin and join us. Bring a pie to the table and you'll see smiles all round.

Pies are our passion. We grew up eating pies, we love to cook pies and we eat them with our families now. Pies encased in buttery shortcrust, pies with a light-as-air topping of puff pastry, little tarts and pasties – we love 'em all. There's nothing better than sitting round the table with family and friends and portioning up a pie – a pie is a dish meant for sharing.

The pie started as a way of carrying the filling – a portable feast. Originally the crust wasn't necessarily meant for eating, just for getting the delicious contents to your mouth. Now the pastry can almost be the main event and you can have fun making all sorts of different kinds. Pies know no boundaries and every country has its own version – there are Indian samosas, Argentinian empanadas, French tarts and quiches, to mention but a few.

In this book we've tried to leave no pie unturned and we've included cobblers and crumbles, suet puds and potato-topped pies – everything that we could think of that could possibly be described as a pie. There are lots of the favourites you know and love, such as steak pie, fish pie and apple pie, as well as some new ideas we hope you'll love, and plenty of belting pies for vegetarians – try our roasted vegetable tart and our spicy bean hotpot pie.

When you're having a party, what better to serve than pies? We've put together some cracking recipes for mini pies and tarts that make melting little mouthfuls your friends and family will go mad for. And let's not forget the leftovers. You'll find our pastry recipes are quite generous – always better to have too much pastry than too little – so we've included some ideas for using up those precious scraps, including the fastest fruit pie ever.

Pastry is alchemy and wizardry. Who would have thought you could make a bit of flour, fat and liquid into something so meltingly delicious. And IT'S NOT DIFFICULT! Anyone can do it, so just follow our simple instructions for all the classic pastries from shortcrust to suet and you'll be turning out pies like an expert in no time. If you don't want to make your own, you can make most of these pies with bought pastry – in fact, like many people, we often use bought puff and you can put a pie together with this in double-quick time.

There are plenty of tips about pastry-making throughout this book, but in the last chapter we've put together all the pastry knowledge we've gathered over the years. You'll find the low-down on the best way to make pastry, roll it out, line your tins and decorate your pies. You'll also find some extra-special pastries to try, such as chilli pastry and chocolate pastry.

So, pie lovers everywhere – it's time to roll up your sleeves and start turning out perfect pies. Have fun.

Lots of love

Si & Dave

A few little tips from us:

Weigh all the ingredients carefully and use proper tablespoons and a measuring jug. Try to choose a dish or tin as close as possible to the one recommended in the recipe for best results.

We've made cooking times and oven temperatures as accurate as we possibly can, but all ovens are different. Keep an eye on your pie and be prepared to cook for a longer or shorter time if necessary.

All onions and garlic to be peeled, unless otherwise specified.

We always use free-range eggs. When making pastry it's important to use the size of egg specified in the recipe so you have the right amount of liquid.

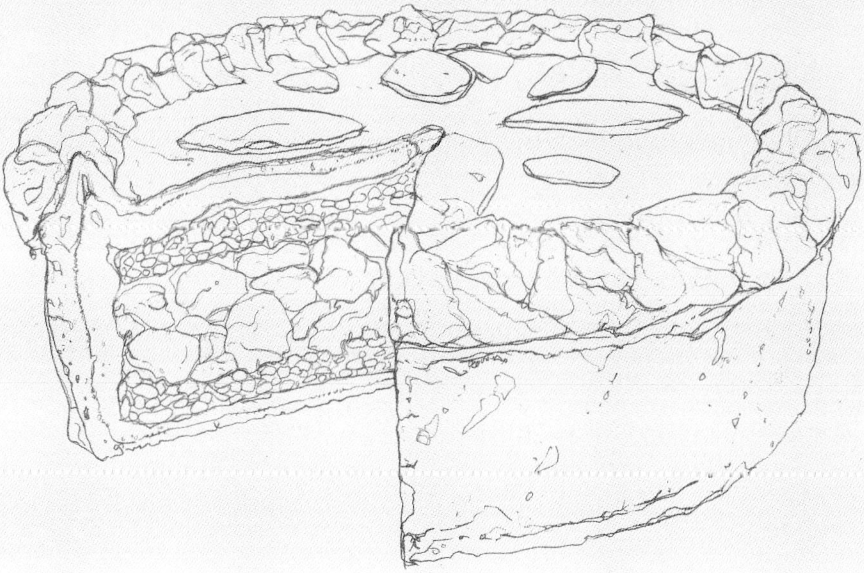
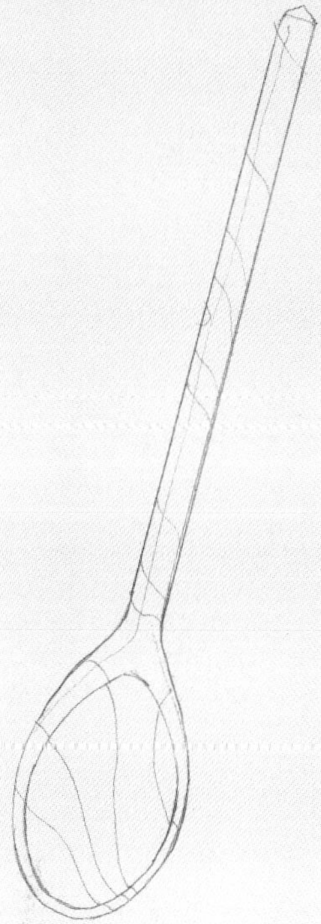

double-crust pies

creamy chicken, ham & leek pie

A fantastic pie for high days and holidays – or for a feast any day of the week. Poaching the chicken keeps it really succulent (see our tip), the leeks add a wonderful sweetness, and it's all encased in crispy, buttery shortcrust pastry.

Serves 4–5

3 boneless, skinless chicken breasts, poached with a stock cube (see below)
250ml cooking liquor (see below)
75g butter
2 slender leeks, trimmed and sliced
2 garlic cloves, crushed
50g plain flour
200ml milk
2–3 tbsp white wine (optional)
150ml double cream
150g thickly carved ham, cut into 2cm chunks
flaked sea salt
freshly ground black pepper

shortcrust pastry
350g plain flour, plus extra for rolling
200g cold butter, cut into cubes
1 large egg, beaten with 1 tbsp water
beaten egg, to glaze

You'll need a 23cm round pie dish

Tip:
Poach the chicken breasts in a pan of 450ml simmering water with a chicken stock cube for 10 minutes. Reserve 250ml of the cooking liquor for making the sauce.

Melt 25g of the butter in a large non-stick saucepan over a low heat. Stir in the leeks and fry gently for 2 minutes, stirring occasionally, until just softened. Add the garlic and cook for 1 minute more, then tip everything into a bowl. Return the pan to the heat and add the remaining butter. Stir in the flour as soon as the butter has melted and cook for 30 seconds, stirring constantly. Add the milk, a little at a time, stirring well between each addition. Gradually add the cooking liquor and the wine, if using, then stir until the sauce is smooth and thick. Bring to a gentle simmer and cook for 3 minutes, while stirring. Season to taste, then remove from the heat and stir in the cream. Pour into a bowl, cover with clingfilm to prevent a skin from forming and leave to cool.

Preheat the oven to 200°C/Fan 180°C/Gas 6 and put a baking tray into the oven to heat. To make the pastry, put the flour and butter in a food processor and blitz on the pulse setting until the mixture resembles breadcrumbs. With the motor running, add the beaten egg and water and blend until the mixture starts to come together in a ball. Weigh the pastry and take off 280g for the lid. Gather the rest of the pastry into a ball and flatten slightly.

Roll the pastry out on a lightly floured surface until it's slightly thicker than a £1 coin and 4cm larger than your pie dish. Lift it gently into the pie dish and press firmly into the base and sides, making sure there are no air bubbles. Leave any excess hanging over the edge. Cut the chicken breasts into 3cm chunks and add to the cooled sauce with the leeks and ham. Tip the filling into the pie dish and brush the rim of the dish with beaten egg.

Roll out the rest of the pastry and use it to cover the pie. Press the edges together to seal, then trim and crimp. Make a small hole in the centre of the pie with a knife tip and brush the top with beaten egg. Bake on the tray in the centre of the oven for 35 minutes or until the pie is golden brown and the filling is piping hot.

deep-filled chicken & mushroom pie

This classic has a shortcrust pastry base, creamy chicken and mushroom filling and a light puff pastry crust. It's surprisingly easy to make and will go down a treat with all the family.

Serves 6

50g butter
1 small onion, finely chopped
1 garlic clove, finely chopped
250g button mushrooms, halved (ideally chestnut mushrooms)
6 boneless, skinless chicken thighs
1 bay leaf
2 tsp freshly chopped thyme leaves or ½ tsp dried thyme
1 chicken stock cube
200ml just-boiled water
50g plain flour
200ml whole milk
4–5 tbsp double or single cream
2–3 tbsp white wine (optional)
flaked sea salt
freshly ground black pepper

shortcrust pastry

200g plain flour, plus extra for rolling
125g cold butter, cut into cubes
1 large egg, beaten with 1 tbsp water

top crust

500g block of ready-made puff pastry

You'll need a 1.2-litre pie dish

To make the shortcrust pastry for the base of the pie, put the flour and butter in a food processor and blitz on the pulse setting until the mixture resembles breadcrumbs. Set aside 2 tablespoons of the beaten egg and water for glazing the pie, then, with the motor running, add the rest to the mixture and process until it starts to come together in a ball. Remove and shape into a slightly flattened ball. Roll out on a lightly floured surface and use to line your pie dish. If you prefer to make your pastry by hand, see page 337.

To make the filling, melt the butter in a large non-stick frying pan over a medium-high heat. Add the onion, garlic and mushrooms and fry for 4–6 minutes, stirring often, until the onion and mushrooms are lightly browned. Cut the chicken into small bite-sized pieces, season with pepper and add them to the pan with the bay leaf and thyme leaves. Cook everything for 4–5 minutes until the meat is no longer pink, turning often. Dissolve the stock cube in the 200ml of just-boiled water.

Stir the flour into the chicken mixture and cook for a few seconds before slowly adding the milk. Gradually stir in the stock and bring to a gentle simmer. Cook for 2 minutes until the sauce is smooth and thick. Season to taste, remove from the heat and stir in the cream and wine, if using. Cover the pan with clingfilm to prevent a skin from forming and set aside to cool. Preheat the oven to 190°C/Fan 170°C/Gas 5.

Spoon the cooled chicken filling into the dish and brush the edges of the pastry with a little beaten egg. Place the puff pastry on a well-floured surface and roll out until it is about 5mm thick and large enough to cover the pie. Place the puff pastry over the pie, trim off the excess and knock up the edges (see page 367). Brush the top with beaten egg. Bake for 40–45 minutes until the crust is puffed up and golden brown and the filling is piping hot.

rabbit & sausage picnic pie

This is the perfect combo of bunny and banger – we love it. If you've never tried rabbit before, this is a good place to start, but you can use chicken thigh meat instead if you prefer.

Serves 6–8

1 tbsp sunflower oil
1 large onion, finely chopped
750g fresh boneless rabbit meat or mixed game
450g herby pork sausages
50g fresh white breadcrumbs
½ tsp ground mace
1 tsp dried thyme
flaked sea salt
freshly ground black pepper

shortcrust pastry
400g plain flour, plus extra for rolling
125g cold butter, cut into cubes
100g cold lard, cut into cubes
6 tbsp water
beaten egg, to glaze

You'll need a dish that's about 20 x 30cm and not too deep

Heat the oil in a large non-stick frying pan and gently fry the onion for 5 minutes until well softened, stirring occasionally. Remove from the heat and leave to cool.

Remove any sinewy bits from the rabbit meat, then use a food processor on the pulse setting to chop the meat finely. Do this in 2 batches to make sure the meat doesn't get over-processed and mushy. Put the meat in a large mixing bowl. If you do not have a food processor, chop the meat by hand as finely as you can.

Squeeze the sausages out of their casings and add to the rabbit. Season well with salt and lots of freshly ground black pepper. Add the cooked onion, breadcrumbs, ground mace and thyme. Mix well together. Preheat the oven to 210°C/Fan 190°C/Gas 6½ for 45 minutes until golden brown.

To make the pastry, put the flour, butter and lard into the bowl of a food processor and blitz on the pulse setting until the mixture resembles breadcrumbs. With the motor running, add the water and process until the mixture is just beginning to come together in a ball. Remove and divide the dough into two-thirds for the base and one-third for the lid, then shape into slightly flattened blocks.

Roll out the larger block of pastry on a lightly floured surface until it is about 4cm larger than the dish you're using. Line the dish, pressing the pastry well into the corners and leaving any excess hanging over the edges. Add the rabbit and sausage filling, patting it well into the corners with a rubber spatula until the mixture is level and evenly spread. Brush the edges with beaten egg.

Roll out the remaining pastry in the same way and lay it over the top of the pie. Press the edges together very firmly. Trim the pastry with a sharp knife until level with the top of the dish and use a fork to help seal the pie and make a decorative edge. Brush with egg or milk to glaze. Bake for 35–45 minutes until the pastry is golden and the filling is cooked. Serve warm or cold.

steak & mushroom pie

Chuck steak is cheap and gives a great flavour in this proper, old-fashioned British pie that everyone knows and loves. Heritage on a plate.

Serves 4–6

750g chuck steak, trimmed of any hard fat or gristle
2–3 tbsp sunflower oil
3 tbsp plain flour
2 medium onions, halved and sliced
2 garlic cloves, finely chopped
150ml red wine
2 tsp Worcestershire sauce
500ml beef stock (made with 1 stock cube)
1 bay leaf
25g butter
250g chestnut mushrooms, wiped and cut in half, or quarters if large
flaked sea salt
freshly ground black pepper

shortcrust pastry
400g plain flour, plus extra for rolling
250g cold butter, cut into cubes
1 large egg, beaten with 2 tbsp cold water
beaten egg, to glaze

You'll need a 23cm round pie dish

Cut the steak into rough 3cm cubes and season well. Heat 1–2 tablespoons of oil in a frying pan and fry the meat over a high heat until browned all over. Do this in 2 batches so you don't overcrowd the pan, adding extra oil if the pan starts to seem dry. Transfer the beef to a flameproof casserole dish as it is browned and then toss it in the flour. Preheat the oven to 150°C/Fan 130°C/Gas 2.

Add another tablespoon of oil to the frying pan and cook the onions and garlic for 5 minutes until golden and soft. Deglaze the frying pan with the wine (or 150ml of water if you don't have any wine) and add the Worcestershire sauce. Bring to the boil, while stirring hard to lift all the sediment from the bottom of the pan.

Pour the gravy over the beef in the casserole dish, then add the stock and bay leaf. Bring everything to the boil on top of the stove. Remove from the heat, cover with a lid and cook in the oven for 1½ hours. Melt the butter in a frying pan and cook the mushrooms for 5 minutes, stirring until lightly browned. Add the mushrooms to the beef, then return the casserole dish to the oven and cook for another 30 minutes. Leave to cool.

To make the pastry, put the flour and butter in a food processor and blitz on the pulse setting until the mixture resembles breadcrumbs. With the motor running, add the beaten egg and water and process until the mixture is just beginning to come together in a ball. Remove and divide the dough into two-thirds for the base and one-third for the lid, then shape into slightly flattened balls. If you prefer to make your pastry by hand, see page 337.

Preheat the oven to 210°C/Fan 190°/Gas 6½. Roll out the larger ball of pastry on a floured surface and use it to line your pie dish. Add the beef and mushroom filling and brush the edges of the pastry with beaten egg. Roll out the remaining pastry for the pie top and carefully lay it over the filling. Trim and crimp the edges, then brush with beaten egg to glaze. Bake for 30 minutes, until the pastry is golden brown and the filling is piping hot.

meat & potato pie

All Northerners have their favourite pies and this is ours. It's more a religion than just a mere tummy filler.

Serves 6

1 large onion, finely diced
2 medium carrots, peeled and diced
2 celery sticks, stringed and finely sliced
500g lean, minced beef
2 tbsp tomato ketchup
2 tbsp brown sauce
1 tbsp Worcestershire sauce
2 tbsp plain flour
½ tsp fine sea salt
360g medium potatoes, preferably Maris Pipers, peeled and cut into 2cm cubes
150ml water
freshly ground black pepper

shortcrust pastry
300g plain flour, plus extra for rolling
150g cold lard or half butter and half lard
a good pinch of fine sea salt
5 tbsp cold water
beaten egg, to glaze

You'll need a 20cm square cake tin that's about 4cm deep

To make the pastry, put the flour, lard and salt in a food processor and blitz on the pulse setting until the mixture resembles breadcrumbs. With the motor running, add the water in a constant stream and process until the mixture is just beginning to come together in a ball. Remove and divide the dough into two-thirds for the base and one-third for the lid, then shape into slightly flattened blocks. Wrap these in clingfilm and chill for 20 minutes. If you prefer to make your pastry by hand, see page 337.

Dry fry the onion, carrots, celery and beef together in a saucepan, over a high heat, until the beef is no longer pink. Stir frequently to break up the meat. Reduce the heat and add the tomato ketchup, brown sauce, Worcestershire sauce, flour and seasoning. Cook for 1 minute, then add the potatoes and water and bring to the boil. Reduce the heat, cover the pan loosely and simmer for 15 minutes until the potatoes are tender. Leave the mixture to cool completely.

Preheat the oven to 200°C/Fan 180°C/Gas 6. Roll out the larger block of pastry on a lightly floured surface, turning it frequently to make a square. Line your cake tin, making sure there's enough pastry to overhang the sides of the tin slightly. Pile in the filling and spread it out evenly, then brush the edges of the pastry with beaten egg.

Roll out the rest of the pastry on a lightly floured surface and place it on top of the pie. Trim off any excess and seal the edges neatly. Using a fork, pierce the top of the pie several times, then brush with beaten egg.

Bake in the preheated oven for 30 minutes until the pie is golden brown. As soon as you remove the pie from the oven, use a knife to carefully loosen the pastry case away from the edge of the tin. Leave the pie to stand for 5 minutes before serving with veg and gravy if you like. (See page 302 for our home-made gravy recipe.)

luscious beef & oyster pies

Oysters were once as cheap as chips and were used as fillers in pies like this. Now a beef and oyster pie is posh enough for a prince. The original surf and turf!

Serves 6

900g stewing beef, trimmed of any hard fat and gristle
2–3 tbsp sunflower oil
3 long shallots, quartered
2 garlic cloves, finely chopped
125g smoked, rindless, streaky bacon rashers, cut into 1cm strips
1 tbsp roughly chopped thyme leaves
2 bay leaves
330ml bottle of Guinness
400ml beef stock (made with 1 stock cube)
12 oysters, freshly shucked
2 tbsp cornflour, blended with 2 tbsp water to make a smooth paste
flaked sea salt
freshly ground black pepper

flaky freezer pastry
600g plain flour, plus extra for rolling
½ tsp fine sea salt
375g butter, frozen for at least 2 hours
325ml cold water
beaten egg, to glaze

You'll need a flameproof casserole and 6 x 200ml pie dishes

Cut the beef into rough 3cm cubes and season. Heat a tablespoon of oil in the frying pan and fry the meat over a high heat. Do this in 3 batches so you don't overcrowd the pan, transferring the meat to a large flameproof casserole dish as it is browned. Add extra oil if the pan seems dry. Add another tablespoon of oil and cook the shallots for 4–5 minutes, then add the garlic and fry for 30 seconds. Add a dash more oil and fry the bacon until slightly browned. Transfer to the casserole dish and add the herbs.

Preheat the oven to 180°C/Fan 160°C/Gas 4. Pour the Guinness into the frying pan and bring to the boil, stirring hard to lift the sediment from the bottom of the pan. Pour this over the beef and add the stock. Cover the dish and place it in the oven for 1½–2 hours or until the beef is tender and the sauce is well reduced. Check the seasoning, then remove from the heat, skim off any surface fat and stir in the cornflour paste. Put the casserole dish on the hob – don't forget that it will be hot – and simmer for 1–2 minutes, stirring, until thickened. Leave to cool.

Preheat the oven to 200°C/Fan 180°/Gas 6. To make the pastry, put the flour and salt in a very large bowl. Grate the butter and stir it into the flour in 3 batches. Gradually add the water – you may not need it all – and stir with a round-bladed knife until the mixture forms a ball. Knead the pastry lightly on a lightly floured surface and set aside 500g for the pie lids.

Divide the rest into 6 portions and roll out each one until about 2cm larger than the dishes you are using. Line the dishes with pastry and pile in the filling, then tuck 2 oysters into each pie. Brush the edges of the pastry with beaten egg. Divide the remaining pastry into 6 and roll out each piece until slightly larger than your dishes. Gently lift the pastry lids over the filling, press the edges firmly to seal, then trim. Brush with beaten egg to glaze. Put the dishes on a baking tray and bake for 25–30 minutes until the pastry is golden brown and filling is bubbling.

game pie

Game on for a game pie. Just right for a yomp in the country or a grand day out at the coast.

Serves 6

1.5kg mixed game meat
500g venison steak
4 tbsp sunflower oil
125g smoked, rindless, streaky bacon rashers, cut in 1cm strips
2 large onions, sliced
1 celery stick, sliced
250g chestnut mushrooms, wiped clean and sliced
55g plain flour
2 bay leaves
500ml red wine
2 tsp finely chopped thyme
500ml beef stock
2 tbsp redcurrant jelly
flaked sea salt
freshly ground black pepper

shortcrust pastry

450g plain flour, plus extra for rolling
2 tsp baking powder
½ tsp salt
60g cold butter, cut into cubes
60g cold lard, cut into cubes
about 120ml water
beaten egg, to glaze

top crust

500g ready-made puff pastry

You'll need a deep 20cm cake tin

To make the pastry, put the flour, baking powder and salt in a bowl and rub in the butter and lard with your fingertips, until the mixture resembles breadcrumbs. Stir in the water to form a dough, then knead lightly. Roll out the pastry on a lightly floured surface and use it to line a deep 20cm cake tin. Prick the base lightly with a fork and chill for 30 minutes.

Cut the game meat and venison steak into rough cubes. Heat the oil in a large frying pan and brown the meat in batches. Take care not to put too much in the pan at once – the meat needs to be sealed, not poached. As the meat is browned, remove it and set aside.

Add the bacon and onions to the same pan and cook until the onions are translucent. Add the celery and the mushrooms and cook for a further 3 minutes. Add the flour and cook for 2 minutes. Now add the bay leaves, red wine, thyme, stock and redcurrant jelly. Season well and simmer gently, uncovered, for about 2 hours or until the meat is tender and melting – exact timing depends on the meat. Leave to cool.

Preheat the oven to 200°C/Fan 180°C/Gas 6. Bake the pastry case blind (see page 358) for 20 minutes. Carefully remove the paper and beans, then return the pastry to the oven for a further 5 minutes.

Once the pastry case is cool, fill it with the cooked meat, packing it well in. Preheat the oven to 180°C/Fan 160°/Gas 4. Roll out the puff pastry to about 5mm thick. Brush around the edge of the shortcrust case with the beaten egg and place the sheet of puff pastry on the top. Crimp around the edges, trim and cut a couple of holes in the top to let the steam out. Decorate the top with any excess pastry. Brush with beaten egg and bake for about 30 minutes until golden. Leave to cool completely before serving.

greek lamb filo pie

Enjoy our big fat Greek pie! If your filo is a little smaller than the size we give, you may need to stagger the layering of the sheets in your tin to give an even coverage.

Serves 6

500g minced lamb
1 medium onion, finely chopped
2 garlic cloves, crushed
1½ tsp dried mint
1 tsp dried oregano
¼ tsp ground cinnamon
200ml red wine
400g can chopped tomatoes
1 tbsp tomato purée
½ tsp caster sugar
2 tbsp plain flour
2 medium aubergines
6 tbsp mild olive oil
200g feta cheese, drained
flaked sea salt
freshly ground black pepper

pastry
100g butter
10 filo pastry sheets (each about 32 x 38cm), thawed if frozen

You'll need a 20 x 30cm baking tin or ovenproof dish – a lasagne dish is fine

Put the lamb, onion, garlic, herbs and cinnamon in a large non-stick frying pan. Fry over a medium heat for 6–8 minutes until the lamb is no longer pink, stirring regularly to break up the meat.

Pour the wine into the pan, then add the tomatoes, tomato purée and sugar. Season well, bring to a gentle simmer and cook for 25 minutes until thick, stirring occasionally. Remove from the heat, check the seasoning, then stir in the flour and leave to cool.

Trim the aubergines and cut them into 1cm slices. Pour 3 tablespoons of the oil into a large non-stick frying pan and place over a medium heat. Fry the aubergine slices in two batches until browned on both sides. Add more oil for the second batch and drain the aubergines on kitchen roll once cooked. Preheat the oven to 200°C/Fan 180°C/Gas 6.

Melt the butter in a saucepan over a low heat. Place a sheet of filo on a board and brush with butter. Top with a second sheet and brush with more butter. Repeat the layers 3 more times until you have a stack of 5 filo sheets. Brush your baking tin with a little butter and line it with the pastry stack, leaving the excess pastry rising up the sides.

Spoon the mince mixture into the dish and spread evenly. Crumble over half the feta and then cover with slightly overlapping slices of aubergine. Crumble over the remaining feta, season with pepper and fold the pastry sides inwards to partly cover the filling.

Make a second stack of 5 filo sheets in the same way as the first. Place over the filling and use a round-bladed knife to tuck the pastry down the sides of the tin to enclose the mince, aubergine and cheese. Score through the top 2 layers of the pastry to make 6 portions. Brush with more butter and garnish with ground pepper. Bake for 40–45 minutes or until the pastry is deep golden brown and the filling is hot.

pork & apple pie
with cider gravy

Pork and apple are a classic flavour combination and make a belter of a pie. Gravy is a must for some pies, and our cider gravy is the perfect partner here.

Serves 6–8

1kg boneless, rindless pork shoulder, cut into 3cm chunks
2 tbsp sunflower oil
3 medium onions, about 300g total weight, halved and sliced
500ml dry cider
1 pork stock cube
150ml cold water
1 fresh bay leaf or 2 dried
16 large fresh sage leaves
400g Bramley cooking apples, peeled, quartered, cored and cut into 2cm chunks
2 tbsp plain flour
2 tbsp cornflour
flaked sea salt
freshly ground black pepper

shortcrust pastry
400g plain flour
100g cold butter, cut into cubes
100g cold lard, cut into cubes
1 large egg, beaten with 1 tbsp of cold water

You'll need a casserole dish and a 23cm springclip cake tin

Season the pork all over generously with salt and pepper. Heat a tablespoon of the oil in a frying pan and fry the meat over a medium-high heat, until browned all over – best to do this in 3 batches so you don't overcrowd the pan. Transfer the meat to a large casserole dish as it is browned.

Add another tablespoon of oil and fry the onions over a medium-high heat until soft and golden. Preheat the oven to 180°C/Fan 160°C/Gas 4. Deglaze the pan with half the dry cider, dissolving a pork stock cube into the cider as soon as it begins to simmer. Stir hard to lift the sediment from the pan. Pour into the casserole dish and add the remaining cider, 150ml of water, 6 whole sage leaves and bay leaf. Cover and cook in the oven for 1½–2 hours, stirring halfway through cooking, or until the pork is very tender.

Carefully tip the pork mixture into a colander over a bowl and allow to drain, then set the cooking liquor aside. Remove the whole sage leaves and bay leaf. Transfer the pork and onions to a bowl and leave to cool. Finely shred the remaining sage leaves, then add the sage and apples to the pork, sprinkle with flour and plenty of seasoning, and toss everything together. Set aside while you prepare the pastry.

To make the pastry, put the flour, butter and lard into a food processor and pulse until the mixture resembles breadcrumbs. Reserve 1 tablespoon of the beaten egg and water for glazing the pie, then, with the motor running, add the rest to the mixture in a constant stream until the dough starts to come together in a ball.

Continued overleaf...

pork & apple pie continued...

Weigh the pastry and set aside 200g for the pie lid. Form the rest of the pastry into a flattish ball. Place on a lightly floured surface and roll it out into a circle about the thickness of a £1 coin, turning the pastry and flouring the surface and rolling pin regularly.

Use the pastry to line the cake tin, leaving the excess overhanging the sides. (There should only be about 2cm of excess pastry. If you have more, it might mean that you've rolled the pastry too thin to support the filling and you'll knead to re-roll it a bit thicker.) Brush the edge with beaten egg.

Add the pork and apple mixture to the tin, spreading it evenly. Roll out the reserved pastry for the lid in the same way as before, place the tin on top and cut around it to make a perfect circle for the lid. Place on top of the filling, pressing the edges firmly to seal. Trim off the excess pastry and press the edges firmly together. Use a fork to add a decorative edge to the pie. Make a small hole in the centre with the point of a knife., then brush with more beaten egg to glaze.

Bake the pie in the centre of the oven for 50–60 minutes until the pastry is golden brown. Remove from the oven and use a narrow knife to carefully loosen the pastry case away from the edge of the tin – this will help prevent the pastry from splitting. Leave the pie to stand for about 5 minutes before carefully removing the tin and sliding the pie onto a board or platter to serve.

While the pie is standing, make the gravy. Pour the reserved cooking liquor into a measuring jug and add enough cold water to make the quantity up to 400ml. Mix 2 tablespoons of the liquid with the cornflour in a small bowl. Pour the rest into a saucepan and place over a medium heat. Bring to the boil, then stir in the cornflour mixture, reduce the heat slightly and simmer for 2 minutes, while stirring. Adjust the seasoning to taste and strain into a warmed gravy jug. Serve with generous slices of the pie.

spinach & feta filo pie

Try saying feta-filo three times quickly after a few glasses of retsina! This is our version of the traditional Greek pie known as spanokopita.

Serves 6 as a main course, more as a starter or canapés

2 tbsp olive oil
2 medium onions, sliced and finely chopped
2 garlic cloves, crushed
450–475g young spinach leaves, or mature leaves trimmed and shredded
4 medium eggs
2 x 250g pots of ricotta cheese, drained
½ nutmeg
2 tsp roughly chopped fresh thyme leaves
2 x 200g packs of feta cheese, drained
2 tbsp plain flour
freshly ground black pepper

filo pastry

100g butter
10 filo pastry sheets (each about 32 x 38cm), thawed if frozen

You'll need a 20 x 30cm baking tin or ovenproof dish – a lasagne dish is fine

Heat the oil in a large saucepan. Gently fry the onions and garlic for 15 minutes until softened but not coloured, stirring from time to time. Add the shredded spinach and cook over a medium-high heat for 5–6 minutes. Tip the spinach mixture into a sieve over a bowl and press it down firmly with a ladle or wooden spoon to remove as much moisture as possible – this stops your pie being soggy. Leave the mixture to cool.

Beat the eggs in a large bowl, then stir in the ricotta. Grate in the nutmeg and add freshly ground black pepper – no need to add any salt as the feta cheese will make the pie salty enough. Add the thyme, then crumble little pieces of feta into the mixture. Add the flour and stir.

Preheat the oven to 200°C/Fan 180°C/Gas 6. Melt the butter in a saucepan over a low heat. Place a sheet of filo on a board and brush with butter. Top with a second sheet and brush with more butter. Repeat the layers 3 more times until you have a stack of 5 filo sheets. Brush your baking tin with a little butter and line with the pastry stack, leaving the excess pastry rising up the sides.

Mix the spinach with the cheese mixture, tip it into the tin and spread it evenly over the pastry. Fold over the excess filo and then cover with the remaining 5 sheets, buttering each one and placing butter-side down this time. Use a round-bladed knife to tuck the sheets down the sides and slightly underneath so the filling is neatly enclosed. Score the top into portion-sized squares, but only cut through 2–3 layers. Brush with melted butter and sprinkle with freshly ground black pepper.

Cook in the preheated oven for 45–50 minutes, until the pastry is crisp and golden and the filling has set. Cool for at least 15 minutes before serving.

proper cherry pie

The best cherry pies are made with fresh cherries instead of sticky canned fillings, so make this an annual treat when cherries are in season.

Serves 6

150g morello cherry jam
100ml cold water
2 tbsp ground arrowroot
900g fresh cherries, stoned

sweet shortcrust pastry
350g plain flour, plus extra for rolling
200g cold butter, cut into cubes
2 tbsp caster sugar
1 large egg, beaten with 1 tbsp cold water
beaten egg, to glaze
1 tbsp caster sugar, preferably golden

You'll need a 23cm round pie dish with a nice wide rim

To make the filling, put the cherry jam in a saucepan with 75ml of the water and place over a low heat. Cook for 3–4 minutes, stirring constantly until it softens and becomes quite saucey. Blend the remaining water with the arrowroot to form a smooth paste. Stir the cherries and the arrowroot mixture into the jam and cook for 2–3 minutes more, or until the sauce becomes thick and translucent, stirring constantly. Remove from the heat and leave to cool.

Preheat the oven to 200°C/Fan 180°C/Gas 6. Put a baking tray in the oven to heat.

To make the pastry, put the flour, butter and sugar in a food processor and blitz on the pulse setting until the mixture resembles breadcrumbs. With the motor running, add the beaten egg and water in a constant stream and process until the mixture is just beginning to come together. Remove, weigh the pastry and take off 280g. Roll it into a ball and set aside. Gather the rest of the pastry into a ball and flatten slightly.

Roll out the bigger ball of pastry on a lightly floured surface to the thickness of a £1 coin and a little larger than your pie dish. Lift the pastry into the pie dish and press it into place, making sure there are no air bubbles. It should overhang the dish by about 1cm.

Tip the cherry filling into the pie dish. Brush the edge of the pastry with beaten egg. Roll the reserved ball of pastry in the same way as the first. Cover the pie with the pastry, then seal the edges and trim. Make a small hole in the centre of the pie with the tip of a knife. Glaze the top of the pie with beaten egg, then decorate with pastry trimmings if you like (see page 370). Sprinkle the pie with sugar and bake in the centre of the oven for 35–40 minutes or until golden brown. If the crust starts to get too brown, cover with foil. Leave to cool in the dish for 10 minutes, then remove and leave for at least 15 minutes before serving.

Tip:
You can serve this pie straight from the oven, but it's easier to slice if served warm or even cold.

perfect apple pie

Nothing tastes better than an apple pie and this is a proper celebration of the great British Bramley.

Serves 6

150g caster sugar, preferably golden
½–1 tsp ground cinnamon
2 tbsp cornflour
600g Bramley cooking apples

sweet shortcrust pastry
400g plain flour, plus extra for rolling
2 tbsp caster sugar
finely grated zest 1 lemon
250g cold butter, cut into cubes
1 large egg, beaten with 2 tbsp cold water
beaten egg, to glaze
1 tbsp caster sugar, preferably golden

You'll need a 1.2-litre pie dish with a nice wide rim

To make the pastry, put the flour, sugar and lemon zest into a bowl and rub in the butter until the mixture resembles breadcrumbs. Add the beaten egg and stir with a round-bladed knife until the mixture forms a dough. Divide the dough into two-thirds for the base and one-third for the lid. Roll into balls and flatten slightly.

Roll out the larger ball of pastry on a lightly floured surface until it is about the thickness of a £1 coin and 5–7cm larger than the pie dish. The pastry should overhang the dish by 1–2cm. Lift the pastry over the rolling pin and drop it gently into the pie dish. Press the pastry firmly into the dish and up the sides, making sure there are no air bubbles. Put the dish in the fridge while you prepare the filling.

Mix the sugar, cinnamon and cornflour in a large bowl. Peel, quarter and core the apples, then slice them thinly and add them to the spiced sugar. Toss well together. Preheat the oven to 200°C/Fan 180°C/Gas 6. Put a baking tray into the oven to heat.

Tip the apple filling into the pie dish, making sure that it rises above the edge. Make sure you scrape all the sugary juices on top of the fruit too. Brush the rim of the dish with beaten egg.

Roll out the reserved ball of pastry in the same way as the first. Cover the pie with the pastry and press the edges together firmly to seal. Using a sharp knife, trim off the excess pastry, then gently crimp all around the edge. Make a few small holes in the centre of the pie with the tip of a knife. Glaze the top with beaten egg.

Lightly knead the pastry trimmings and re-roll. Cut into leaf shapes (see page 370). Place all around the edge of the pie, slightly overlapping each other, and glaze with more egg. Sprinkle the pie with sugar and bake in the centre of the oven for 45–55 minutes or until the pie is golden brown all over and the apples are tender. If the pie crust starts to get too brown, cover with foil for the remainder of the cooking time. Serve hot or cold.

Tip:
About 1 tsp of cinnamon in the filling does the trick for us, but add less if you prefer a milder cinnamon flavour.

baked ricotta pie

Perfect for elevenses with a good strong cup of coffee, this delicious pie is a variation on the cheesecake vibe. It also makes a fab dessert with a few lightly poached berries.

Serves 12

750g ricotta cheese
150g caster sugar
6 medium eggs
100ml double cream
finely grated zest of 1 orange
25g sultanas
25g cut mixed candied peel
sifted icing sugar, to decorate

shortcrust pastry
400g plain flour,
plus extra for rolling
250g cold butter, cut into cubes
2 tbsp caster sugar
1 large egg, beaten with
2 tbsp water
1 tbsp double cream or
beaten egg, to glaze

You'll need a 20cm square loose-based cake tin that's about 4cm deep

Drain the ricotta and put it into a mixing bowl with the sugar. Using electric beaters, whisk until well combined. Add the eggs one at a time, whisking well after each addition. Stir in the cream and orange zest. Preheat the oven to 180°C/Fan 160°C/Gas 4.

To make the pastry, put the flour, butter and sugar in a food processor and blitz on the pulse setting until the mixture resembles breadcrumbs. With the motor running, add the beaten egg and water in a constant stream and process until the mixture starts to form a ball. Remove, weigh the pastry and reserve 300g for the pastry lid.

Roll out the larger ball of pastry into a square, the thickness of a £1 coin and at least 5cm larger than the tin. Place the tin on a baking tray. Leave the excess pastry overhanging the edge and brush with a little cold water. Slowly pour in the filling until it almost reaches the top of the pastry. Gently sprinkle the sultanas and mixed peel over the top – they'll slowly slide through the mixture as it cooks.

Roll out the remainder of the pastry and carefully place over the mixture, leaving about 2cm overhanging the sides. Trim the edges by pressing the pastry gently with your thumb against the side of the tin. Brush lightly with cream or egg to glaze. Place the pie on its tray in the centre of the oven with great care – it will wobble!

Cook for 50–60 minutes until the pastry is pale golden brown and the filling is set. If you wiggle the tin you shouldn't see the filling ripple. You may find that the pastry rises as the pie cooks but this is quite normal and it will soon settle as it cools. If the pie begins to rise unevenly, turn the oven down a little and continue to bake.

Let the pie cool completely in the tin, then cover and pop in the fridge for several hours or overnight. Loosen the sides with a knife if necessary, then lift out of the tin and transfer to a board. Dust with sifted icing sugar and serve in squares or rectangles.

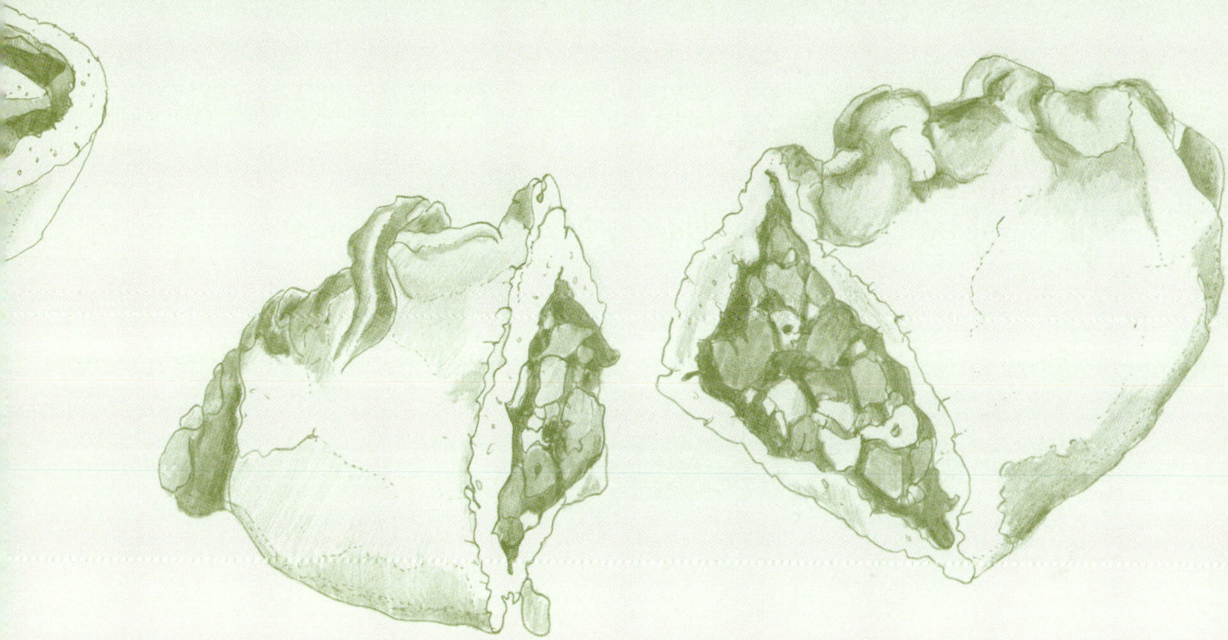

handheld pies

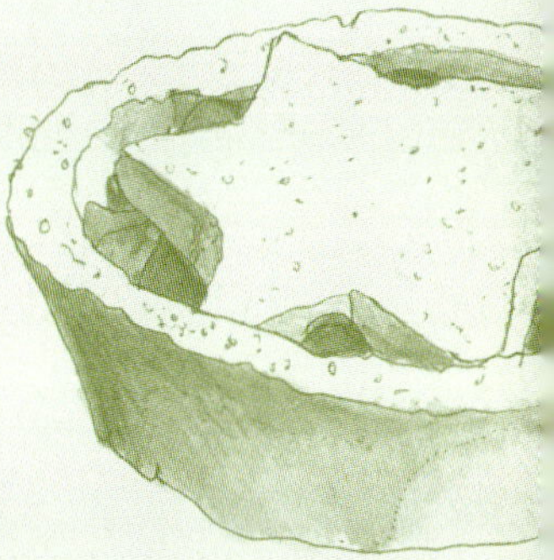

meat & vegetable pasties

These are the real deal and very simple to make. The meat and veg aren't cooked first and they steam inside the pastry cases, which gives a fantastic flavour.

Makes 6–7

2 medium potatoes (about 150g each), peeled and cut into rough 1cm cubes
125g swede, peeled and cut into rough 1cm cubes
1 medium onion, finely chopped
300g beef skirt, trimmed of any hard fat or gristle
2 tbsp plain flour
flaked sea salt
freshly ground black pepper

pasty pastry

450g plain flour, plus extra for rolling
2 tsp baking powder
½ tsp fine sea salt
175g cold butter
2 large egg yolks
125ml cold water
beaten egg, to glaze

To make the filling, put the potatoes, swede and onion in a bowl and season with a little salt and plenty of ground black pepper. Chop the beef as finely as you can and put it in a second bowl. Season with more salt and lots more pepper. Toss the beef with the flour until evenly coated.

For the pastry, pulse the flour, baking powder, sea salt, butter and egg yolks in a food processor until the mixture resembles breadcrumbs. Slowly pour in the water with the motor running, blending until the mixture just comes together to form a dough. (You may not need to use all of the water.) Roll the dough into a ball. Preheat the oven to 200°C/Fan 180°C/Gas 6.

Roll the pastry out on a lightly floured surface until it is about 5mm thick. Using a side plate or an upturned bowl of about 15cm in diameter, cut out 6 or 7 pastry rounds, re-rolling as necessary. Divide the vegetables between the pastry rounds, placing them across the centre. Top with the chopped meat. Brush the edges of a pastry round lightly with beaten egg, then bring 2 sides up around the filling and press the edges together to seal firmly. Crimp the edges neatly. Seal the rest of the pasties in the same way.

Transfer the pasties to a baking tray lined with baking parchment and brush with more egg to glaze. Bake for about 45 minutes or until the pastry is nicely browned and the filling is hot.

cheese & onion pasties

These yummy little packages always hit the spot, whether for a hangover cure or high tea. And they're a great way of using up those lumps of old cheese hiding in the fridge.

Makes 6–7

2 medium potatoes (about 150g each), peeled and cut into rough 3cm cubes
50g butter
2 medium onions, finely sliced
150g mature Cheddar cheese, coarsely grated
1 tsp English mustard
flaked sea salt
freshly ground black pepper

cheesy pasty pastry

450g plain flour, plus extra for rolling
2 tsp baking powder
½ tsp fine sea salt
125g cold butter, plus extra for greasing
2 large egg yolks
50g Parmesan cheese, finely grated
150ml water
beaten egg, to glaze

Tip:

If you don't have any Parmesan for the pastry, just use an extra 50g of butter instead.

Bring a saucepan of salted water to the boil and add the potato cubes. Bring the water back to the boil and cook the potatoes for 5 minutes, or until tender. Drain in a colander and set aside.

Melt the butter in a medium saucepan and gently fry the onions for 10 minutes or until softened but not coloured, stirring regularly. Remove them from the heat, put in a large bowl and leave to cool.

Scatter the potato cubes onto the cooled onions and add the grated cheese and mustard. Season with salt and pepper and stir to mix. Set aside while the pastry is made. Preheat the oven to 200°C/Fan 180°C/Gas 6.

For the pastry, pulse the flour, baking powder, salt, butter and egg yolks in a food processor until the mixture resembles breadcrumbs. Slowly pour in the water with the motor running, blending until the mixture just comes together to form a dough. (You may not need to use all of the water.) Roll the dough into a ball.

Roll the pastry out on a lightly floured surface until it is about 5mm thick. Using a side plate or an upturned bowl of about 15cm in diameter, cut out 6 or 7 pastry rounds, re-rolling as necessary. Divide the cooled filling between the pastry rounds, placing it across the centre. Brush the edges of a pastry round lightly with beaten egg, then bring 2 sides up around the filling and press the edges together to seal firmly. Crimp the edges neatly. Repeat to seal the rest of the pasties.

Transfer the pasties to a baking tray lined with baking parchment and brush with more egg to glaze. Bake for 25–30 minutes until the pastry is lightly browned and the filling is hot.

chicken curry pasties

Originally a Scottish idea, these spicy little chicken pasties are Glasgow meets the Gujerat. Give them a go – you'll be amazed at how good they taste.

Makes 6 7

2 medium potatoes (about 150g each), peeled and cut into rough 2cm cubes
2 tbsp sunflower oil
1 medium onion, finely sliced
3 garlic cloves, crushed
20g fresh root ginger, peeled and grated
1 long green chilli, halved, deseeded and finely sliced
2 boneless, skinless chicken breasts
1 tbsp garam masala
½ tsp hot chilli powder
¼ tsp ground turmeric
150ml water
3 tbsp finely chopped fresh coriander
2 tbsp plain flour
flaked sea salt
freshly ground black pepper

pasty pastry

450g plain flour, plus extra for rolling
2 tsp baking powder
½ tsp fine sea salt
175g cold butter
2 large egg yolks
125ml cold water
beaten egg, to glaze

To make the filling, bring a saucepan of salted water to the boil. Add the potato pieces, return to the boil and cook for 5 minutes, or until the potatoes are tender. Drain in a colander and set aside.

Heat the oil in a large non-stick frying pan and gently fry the onion, garlic, ginger and chilli for 5 minutes, stirring regularly. Cut the chicken breasts into rough 2cm pieces and add to the pan. Sprinkle in the spices and cook for 2 minutes, while stirring. Pour the water into the pan, add the potato pieces and coriander and simmer for 3–4 minutes until the water has almost all evaporated. Remove from the heat and leave to cool. Preheat the oven to 200°C/Fan 180°C/Gas 6.

For the pastry, pulse the flour, baking powder, salt, butter and egg yolks in a food processor until the mixture resembles breadcrumbs. Slowly pour in the water with the motor running, blending until the mixture just comes together to form a dough. (You may not need to use all of the water.) Roll the dough into a ball.

Roll the pastry out on a lightly floured surface until it is about 5mm thick. Using a side plate or upturned bowl of about 15cm in diameter, cut out 6 or 7 pastry rounds, re-rolling as necessary. Stir the flour into the chicken and divide the filling between the pastry rounds, placing it across the centre. Brush around the edges lightly with beaten egg, then bring 2 sides up around the filling and press the edges together to seal firmly. Crimp the edges neatly. Repeat to seal the rest of the pasties.

Transfer the pasties to a baking tray lined with baking parchment and brush with more egg to glaze. Bake for 25–30 minutes until the pastry is lightly browned and the filling is hot.

chilli beef pies

Any time, any place, anywhere, you'll love our chilli beef pies. They're tasty and spicy with a crumbly polenta crust.

Makes 8

2 tbsp sunflower oil
1 medium onion, finely chopped
2 garlic cloves, crushed
500g minced beef
1 heaped tsp smoked paprika
400g can chopped tomatoes
100ml red wine
300ml beef stock
(made with a stock cube)
50g green jalapeños (from a jar), drained and sliced
2 tbsp quick-cook polenta
3 tbsp roughly chopped fresh coriander
flaked sea salt
freshly ground black pepper
lime wedges, to serve (optional)

cornmeal shortcrust

100g plain flour, plus extra for rolling
200g quick-cook polenta
150g cold butter, cut into cubes
75ml just-boiled water
50g Parmesan cheese, finely grated
beaten egg, to glaze

Heat the oil in a large saucepan and gently fry the onion for about 5 minutes, adding the garlic for the final minute. Add the mince to the pan, breaking up the meat with a wooden spoon. Fry over a medium heat for 4–5 minutes, stirring regularly. Sprinkle the paprika over the mince and cook for 1 minute more.

Tip the tomatoes into the pan and add the red wine, stock and jalapeños to the pan. Season with salt and plenty of ground black pepper. Bring the mixture to a simmer and cook for 25 minutes, stirring occasionally. Stir in the 2 tablespoons of polenta and cook for a couple of minutes longer, stirring until the sauce thickens. Remove from the heat, stir in the coriander and leave to cool.

To make the pastry, put the flour and polenta in a large bowl and rub in the butter until the mixture resembles breadcrumbs. Make a well in the centre and pour in the just-boiled water. Stir well with a wooden spoon until the mixture comes together and forms a soft dough. Leave to cool, then wrap in clingfilm and chill for an hour or until firm enough to handle. Knead in the Parmesan until thoroughly combined.

Preheat the oven to 200°C/Fan 180°C/Gas 6. Divide the pastry into 8 and shape into balls, Roll out each ball on a lightly floured surface to make 16cm rounds. Divide the filling between the rounds. Brush the edge of a round lightly with beaten egg and bring up the sides to completely enclose the filling, pinching the edges to join and make a small parcel. Repeat to seal the rest of the pies.

Place the pies on a baking tray lined with baking parchment and brush with more beaten egg to glaze. Bake for 25 minutes until the pies are golden brown. Serve hot or cold with lime wedges for squeezing if you like.

spinach & goat's cheese burek

You'll find brik pastry in larger supermarkets and in North African or Mediterranean food stores. These go down well with a cold beer or some mint tea.

Makes 6

150–200ml olive oil
1 small onion, finely chopped
2 garlic cloves, crushed
1 tsp cumin seeds
2 pinches dried chilli flakes
500g spinach, rinsed well and tough stalks removed
125g soft rindless goat's cheese log, cut into 6 thick slices
flaked sea salt
freshly ground black pepper

pastry
120g ready-made brik pastry sheets, from the chiller cabinet (6 rounds, each 29cm in diameter)

Heat a tablespoon of the oil in a large non-stick frying pan and gently fry the onion and garlic for 5 minutes, stirring regularly until softened. Sprinkle the cumin seeds and chilli flakes into the pan, season generously and fry for another minute, while stirring.

Shred the spinach and add it to the pan. Cook for 5–6 minutes until well softened, stirring regularly. Remove from the heat and tip into a colander, then press to remove as much liquid as possible. Leave to cool. Preheat the oven to 200°C/Fan 180°C/Gas 6.

Unwrap 1 of the brik sheets, place it on a board and brush with a little oil. Imagine it is the face of a clock and spread one-sixth of the spinach mixture in a triangle between where 12 o'clock and 2 o'clock would be. Dot with a slice of goat's cheese, broken into small pieces.

Fold the pastry in half to enclose the filling and then fold the semi-circle of filled pastry over itself 3 more times, starting at the top. It should be a flat cone shape when you've finished. Place on a baking tray lined with baking parchment. Continue making the burek until all the pastry and filling are used up. Bake for 7–8 minutes until golden brown and serve warm.

seafood empanadas

These are a sort of Spanish tapas pie that have travelled the world over. We've baked our version, but you can also shallow fry empanadas in sunflower oil if you prefer.

Makes 6

2 tbsp olive oil
1 medium onion, finely diced
2 garlic cloves, crushed
1 small green pepper, halved, deseeded and cut into thin strips
1 small red pepper, halved, deseeded and cut into thin strips
85g chorizo sausage, skinned and cut into 1cm pieces
1 tsp smoked paprika
2 tbsp plain flour
200g mixed shellfish (thawed if frozen), patted dry
2 tsp lemon juice
3 tbsp chopped fresh parsley
fine sea salt
freshly ground black pepper

pastry

250g plain flour, plus extra for dusting and rolling
good pinch of fine sea salt
1 tsp baking powder
75g cold lard, cut into cubes, plus extra for greasing
1 medium egg, beaten
125ml water
beaten egg, to seal and glaze

To make the pastry, place the flour, salt and baking powder in a mixing bowl and rub in the lard until the mixture resembles breadcrumbs. Add the beaten egg, using a fork to gradually mix the flour into the liquid. Begin to add the water little by little until the mixture forms a slightly sticky (but not wet), elastic dough. (You may not need all the water.) Bring the dough together with your hands. Put the dough on a plate, then sprinkle with a little flour, cover with clingfilm and chill in the fridge while you make the filling.

Heat the oil in a large non-stick frying pan and gently fry the onion, garlic and peppers for 10 minutes until soft but not coloured, stirring regularly. Add the chorizo and paprika and cook for a further 3 minutes, while stirring. Take the pan off the heat and stir in the flour and plenty of seasoning. Leave to cool. Stir in the seafood, lemon juice and parsley.

Preheat the oven to 200°C/Fan 180°C/Gas 6. Weigh the pastry and divide it into 6 equal portions. Dust the work surface with flour and roll out each portion into a circle about 16cm in diameter. Keep turning the pastry as you roll in order to get a neat shape.

Spoon about a sixth of the filling onto one half of a pastry round, leaving a 2cm border. Brush the border lightly with beaten egg and fold over the other side to enclose the filling. Press the edges together well, then turn the edges together, pressing and crimping to seal them well. Repeat to make the rest of the empanadas.

Brush the empananadas with beaten egg and make a tiny slit in the top of each one to allow the steam to escape. Bake in the centre of the oven for 20 minutes or until the pastry is golden brown and the filling is hot. Serve warm or cold.

jamaican patties

Spice up your life with these little patties with a punch! We first saw these in chip shops down south, and couldn't wait to try making our own. Add extra chilli if you can take it.

Makes 8

500g lean minced beef or lamb
1 medium onion, finely chopped
2 garlic cloves, crushed
1 scotch bonnet chilli, finely chopped or ½ tsp dried chilli flakes
1 tsp dried thyme or 1 tbsp fresh thyme leaves, finely chopped
1 tbsp curry powder
1 tbsp tomato purée
300ml beef or lamb stock
50g fresh white breadcrumbs
flaked sea salt
freshly ground black pepper

flaky freezer pastry
400g plain flour, plus extra for rolling
2 tsp ground turmeric
½ tsp fine sea salt
250g butter, frozen for at least 1 hour
125ml cold water
beaten egg, to glaze

Put the mince, onion, garlic, chilli, thyme and curry powder in a large non-stick frying pan and cook over a medium heat for 5 minutes. Keep stirring the meat as it cooks, using 2 wooden spoons to break the meat up.

Stir the tomato purée, stock and plenty of seasoning into the pan and simmer gently for 30 minutes, stirring occasionally until the meat is tender. Add the breadcrumbs and leave to cool.

For the pastry, put the flour into a large bowl and stir in the turmeric and salt. Coarsely grate a third of the butter into the flour and toss lightly. Repeat twice more, tossing the butter through the flour mixture with a table knife, until all the butter strands are lightly dusted with the flour.

Slowly pour the water into the flour mixture, stirring constantly until it all comes together and makes a light dough. Shape into a ball and place on a floured surface. Preheat the oven to 200°C/Fan 180°C/Gas 6.

Roll the pastry out until slightly thicker than a £1 coin. Using a saucer or an upturned bowl of about 15cm in diameter, cut out as many pastry rounds as you can. Knead the trimmings together, re-roll and make a couple more. You should end up with 8 pastry rounds.

Spoon a couple of heaped tablespoons of the filling onto one half of each pastry round. Brush around the edges lightly with beaten egg. Bring the pastry over the filling to make a crescent shape and press the edges together. Press with a fork all the way around to seal.

Transfer to a baking tray lined with baking parchment, brush with more egg to glaze and bake for 25–30 minutes until the pastry is cooked and the filling is hot.

popular pizza pies

These are also called calzone – the pizza that thinks it's a pie. One fold and you're there. The trick is that the filling steams inside the crust, giving it a unique flavour.

Serves 6

2 tbsp olive oil
1 small onion, finely chopped
2 garlic cloves, crushed
400g can chopped tomatoes
½ tsp dried oregano
1 tsp caster sugar
25g butter
150g chestnut mushrooms, wiped and sliced
18 slices of medium salami
2 x 125g balls of mozzarella, drained and patted dry with kitchen roll
large handful of fresh basil leaves
flaked sea salt
freshly ground black pepper
olive oil and good quality balsamic vinegar, to serve

pizza dough
500g strong white flour, plus extra for kneading and rolling
7g sachet fast-action dried yeast
2 tsp flaked sea salt
2 tbsp olive oil, plus extra for oiling
325ml warm water

First make the pizza dough. Sift the flour into a large bowl and stir in the yeast and salt. Mix the olive oil with the water and stir into the flour. Stir with a wooden spoon until the dough comes together and forms a soft, spongy ball.

Put the dough on a lightly floured surface and give it a good kneading for 5 minutes until smooth. Place in a bowl and cover with lightly oiled clingfilm. Leave for about an hour in a warm place or until doubled in size.

Meanwhile, make the tomato sauce. Heat a tablespoon of the olive oil in a non-stick frying pan and fry the onion over a low heat for 5 minutes until softened and lightly browned. Stir regularly and add the garlic for the last minute of the cooking time.

Tip the tomatoes into the pan, add the oregano and caster sugar, then season with salt and pepper. Place over a fairly high heat and cook for 5–8 minutes until the sauce is very thick, stirring constantly. Remove from the heat and leave to cool. Melt the butter in a frying pan and fry the mushrooms for 3–4 minutes until golden. Season with plenty of black pepper.

Divide the dough into 6 balls. Roll out on a floured surface to make 6 x 20cm rounds – each about the size of a side plate. Spread some tomato sauce onto a round of dough, leaving a 2cm border around the edge. Arrange some salami and mushrooms on top, dot with mozzarella cheese and scatter some basil leaves on top.

Fold the dough over to enclose the filling. Press the edges together firmly, then roll the border inwards to make a rope-like seal. Repeat to make the other 5 pies. Place the pies on a large baking sheet lined with baking parchment and leave to prove for a further 30 minutes. Preheat the oven to 200°C/Fan 180°C/Gas 6. Brush the rest of the oil over the dough, season with a little more salt and pepper and bake for 25 minutes or until risen and golden brown.

tandoori chicken samosas

Samosas are a bit of a fiddle the first time you make them, but they're well worth the effort – a million miles away from shop-bought. Serve with some raita and your favourite chutney.

Makes 10–12

1 tbsp tandoori paste
1 tbsp yoghurt
2 chicken breasts
2 medium potatoes, peeled
2 tbsp sunflower oil
1 small onion, very finely diced
½ tsp ground turmeric
2 tsp garam masala
½ tsp black mustard seeds
½ tsp ground black pepper
1 tsp fine sea salt
4 garlic cloves, crushed
1 green chilli (or half if you don't like things too hot), deseeded and finely chopped
10 curry leaves
75g frozen peas
1 tsp lemon juice
1 handful of coriander leaves, chopped
more sunflower oil, for deep frying

samosa pastry

250g plain flour
1 tsp fine sea salt
2 tsp sunflower oil
1 medium egg, separated
9 tbsp warm water

Mix the tandoori paste with the yoghurt. Put the chicken breasts in a bowl, cover them with the yoghurt mixture and leave in the fridge to marinate for an hour.

Meanwhile, make the pastry. Put the flour in a bowl and stir in the salt. Work in the oil and egg yolk with your fingertips until the mixture has a crumb-like texture. (Keep the egg white for assembling the samosas.) Gradually mix in the water to form a stiff elastic dough, adding more or less water to get a workable texture. Knead for 3 minutes, then wrap in clingfilm and chill.

Preheat the oven to 190°C/Fan 170°C/Gas 5. Put the chicken in a baking dish and bake in the oven for about 20 minutes or until just cooked through. Leave to cool, then chop into tiny chunks. Boil the potatoes whole for about 15 minutes or until tender. Drain and set them aside to cool, then dice finely.

Heat the 2 tablespoons of oil in a frying pan and sweat the onion until soft but not brown. Add the turmeric, garam masala, mustard seeds, black pepper and salt and cook for a minute. Then add the garlic and chilli and sauté for another 2 minutes. Add the curry leaves to the pan and cook for a further minute. Add the diced potato and mix well, but gently, into the spices and cook over a low heat for another 5 minutes. Add the peas and cook gently for 2–3 minutes. Finally, fold in the chicken, add the lemon juice and coriander and check the seasoning. Set aside to cool.

Now it's time to assemble these little beauties. Roll out the pastry to the thickness of a £1 coin. Take a side plate and cut round it and then cut the circle in half. Take 1 half and make a cone. Make sure the edges of the cone overlap, then use your fingers to squash the edges gently together to seal them. Spoon the filling into the cone until it is about three-quarters full – do not overfill. Brush the top edge with egg white and pinch the top edge together to seal in the filling. Repeat until you have used up all the filling.

Heat the oil in a large saucepan to about 180°C. Deep fry the samosas for about 5 minutes until they are golden and crunchy. Use a deep-fat fryer if you have one and never leave hot oil unattended.

tasty japanese gyozas

Oh how we love these little Japanese pies – well, dumplings really. They are shaped like little Cornish pasties, and you fry them first, then add water and steam them until they are cooked. This gives these tasty little pies a fantastic texture.

Makes 30–40

pork or chicken filling

500g minced pork or chicken
1 head of pak choi, very finely shredded
2cm piece of fresh root ginger, grated
3 garlic cloves, grated
½ tsp salt
½ tsp ground black pepper
1 tbsp chopped spring onion (green part only)
½ tsp ground chilli flakes
1 tsp sesame oil
1 tbsp oyster sauce
a pinch of sugar

dipping sauce

soy sauce
lime juice
chilli oil

dumpling pastry

300g strong white flour, plus extra for rolling
½ tsp fine salt
200ml boiling water
1 tbsp vegetable oil, for frying
1 tbsp sesame oil, to finish

First make the pastry. Sift the flour and mix in the salt. Stir in the boiling water with chopsticks or a knife until a ball forms. If the dough seems too wet, add a bit more flour; if it's too dry, add more boiling water. Cover the dough and leave to stand and cool for about an hour. This gives you time to make the fillings.

Put all the ingredients for the filling you have chosen in a bowl and mix with your hands until a gloopy paste is formed. Fry a little of the mixture so you can check the seasoning before using.

Remove the dough, place it on a lightly floured surface and knead for 5 minutes until it's very elastic. Use a dough hook in a food processor for this if you like. The kneading releases the gluten in the flour, which enables the dough to be rolled out really thinly.

There are many suggestions about how to form the dumpling skins, but we find that this is the easiest. Take a third of the dough and roll it out very thinly on a floured surface, stretching and turning it as you go. Cut out circles with a 10cm round pastry cutter, stacking the discs with a dusting of flour between them to stop them sticking. Continue until all the dough is used up.

Now it's time to assemble the gyozas. Take a disc of pastry and lay it flat. Place a spoonful of filling in the middle, dip your finger in water and brush this around the edge. Fold the pastry over and seal the edges firmly to form a semi-circular pasty shape. In the middle, make a pleat and press it into place with your thumb and for finger. Make 2 other pleats on either side to make 5 in total. Now the gyoza will look like a cross between a pasty and a purse. Set aside on a floured plate while you make the rest.

Continued overleaf...

gyozas continued...

crab & prawn filling

1 dressed crab
(dark and white meat)
200g raw prawns,
shelled and chopped
½ tsp fine salt
½ tsp black pepper
1 tsp sesame oil
grated zest of ½ lemon
1 tbsp oyster sauce
1 tbsp chopped spring onion
(green part only)
2cm piece of fresh root ginger,
grated

Heat a tablespoon of vegetable oil in a large frying pan with a lid. Lay the gyozas into the pan leaving space between each one. Fry for about 3 minutes or until the bottoms are golden. Take care as they will burn quickly. Add about 100ml of water, put the lid on the pan and steam the dumplings for 2 minutes.

Give the pan a shake to release the gyozas from the bottom of the pan and cook for another 2 minutes with the lid off. Drizzle a spoonful of sesame oil around the side of the frying pan and shake. Serve with a dipping sauce made from soy sauce, lime juice and chilli oil to taste.

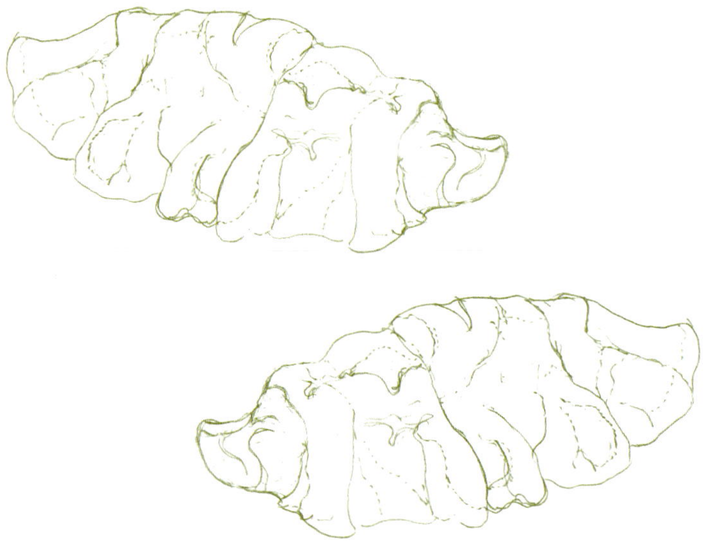

orange & cranberry mince pies

This mincemeat is perfect for making and using on the same day. We've added orange marmalade to make it more luscious with heaps of tangy citrus flavours. Any unused mincemeat can be covered and kept in the fridge for up to a week.

Mincemeat recipe makes enough for at least 36 pies

mincemeat
125g raisins
125g sultanas
125g currants
125g dried cranberries
75g cut mixed peel
50g soft light brown sugar
1 tsp ground mixed spice
½ tsp ground cinnamon
125ml brandy or cherry brandy
finely grated zest and juice of 1 orange
300g Bramley cooking apple
100g orange marmalade
100g shredded suet

sweet shortcrust pastry (for 12 pies)
200g plain flour, plus extra for rolling
125g cold butter, cut into cubes
finely grated zest ½ lemon
1 tbsp caster sugar
1 medium egg, beaten
beaten egg, to glaze
icing sugar, for dusting

You'll need 1 x 12-hole bun tin

To make the mincemeat, put the dried fruit, mixed peel, sugar, spices, brandy, orange zest and juice in a medium saucepan. Place over a low heat and bring the liquid to a simmer. Cook for 5 minutes, stirring occasionally. While the mixture is cooking, peel the Bramley and cut it into quarters, then remove the cores and coarsely grate the apple. Stir the apple into the pan and cook for 1 minute more. Remove from the heat, tip everything into a bowl and stir in the marmalade, then leave to cool. As soon as the mincemeat is cold, stir in the shredded suet and set aside.

To make the pastry, put the flour, butter, sugar and lemon zest in a food processor and blitz on the pulse setting until the mixture resembles breadcrumbs. With the motor running, slowly add the beaten egg and blend until the mixture forms a ball. Take off about a third of the pastry to make lids for the pies, then roll the rest into a ball and flatten slightly. Roll out on a lightly floured surface until about the thickness of a £1 coin. Cut out 10cm rounds with a biscuit cutter and use them to line a 12-hole bun tin, pressing well into the base and sides. Prick lightly and chill for 30 minutes.

Spoon a heaped teaspoon of the cooled mincemeat into each pastry case. Roll out the reserved pastry and cut out festive shapes or make pastry lids for the pies. Press the edges firmly to seal and fix any lids in place with a little beaten egg. Make a small hole in each pie. If using pastry shapes, you won't need to make any holes in the pastry. Brush the tops with beaten egg to glaze.

Preheat the oven to 200°C/Fan 180°C/Gas 6. Bake the mince pies for 20 minutes until the pastry is lightly browned and crisp. Remove from the oven and leave to cool for 15 minutes as the mincemeat will be hot. Dust with sifted icing sugar before serving.

Chocolate pastry (see page 343) makes delicious mince pies. We sometimes add a few small chunks of white and dark chocolate to the mincemeat too.

Fresh fruit
pies are the
best of all puds.
Use whatever
is in season.

fried apple pies

A fried pie sounds like our idea of a good time. This is based on a traditional American recipe but using fresh apples instead of dried. Junk food made good! Serve with cream or ice cream if you really want to go for broke.

Makes 8–10

650g Bramley cooking apples, peeled, quartered, cored and cut into small chunks
5 tbsp caster sugar
2 tbsp cold water
½ tsp ground cinnamon
2 tbsp cornflour, blended to a smooth paste with 2 tbsp cold water
sunflower oil, for frying (you'll need at least 250ml)
sifted icing sugar, to serve

scone pastry

375g self-raising flour, plus extra for rolling
pinch of fine sea salt
50g caster sugar
75g cold butter, cut into cubes
225ml whole milk,
sifted icing sugar, for dusting

To make the apple filling, put the apple chunks, sugar, water and cinnamon in a saucepan and place over a medium heat. Cook for about 5 minutes, stirring often, until the apples are almost all softened and pulpy but a few larger pieces remain. Stir in the cornflour paste and cook for 2–3 minutes more, stirring constantly. Leave to cool.

To make the pastry, put the flour, salt and sugar in a large bowl and rub in the butter with your fingers until the mixture resembles breadcrumbs. Add the milk, stirring constantly, until the mixture comes together and forms a soft, spongy dough.

Roll out half the dough on a lightly floured surface until it's about 5mm thick. Take a saucer or basin of about 15cm in diameter and cut round it to make 4 rounds of dough. Re-roll the trimmings and cut another round. Repeat with the remaining piece of dough.

Spoon some apple filling onto each dough round, dividing it evenly between them. Brush the edges of the dough with a little water. Fold over to encase the filling, pushing out any air, and press the edges firmly to seal. Use a fork to double seal the pastry, pressing firmly through both layers.

Pour the oil into a large non-stick frying pan – it should be about 1cm deep. Place over a medium heat and leave for a couple of minutes until the oil is hot enough to brown a cube of white bread in 15 seconds. Don't let it overheat and never leave hot oil unattended.

Using a spatula, put 4 or 5 of the pies into the hot oil and cook for 2–3 minutes on each side until lightly browned and slightly puffed up, turning once. Remove and drain on kitchen roll while you cook the rest. You may need to add a little more oil between batches. Serve warm, dusted with lots of sifted icing sugar.

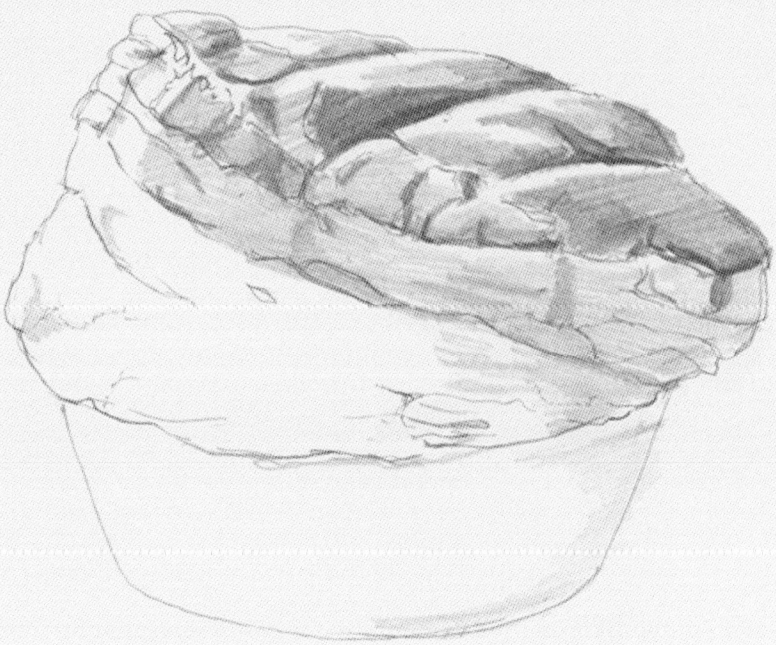

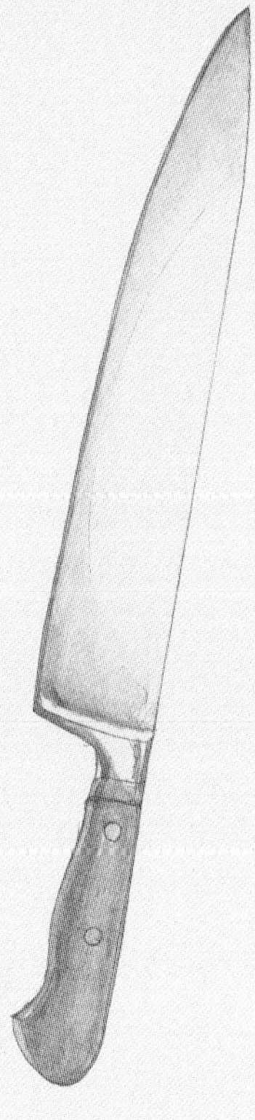

top-crust pies

Justine's chicken & tarragon pie

We got this recipe for a really speedy chicken pie with a fab crunchy filo topping from our lovely friend Justine. It's a cracker, we promise you, just like our Justine.

Serves 5–6

small knob of butter
1 tbsp sunflower oil
1 medium onion, finely chopped
2 garlic cloves, crushed
150ml white wine
1 chicken stock cube
1kg whole cooked chicken (you can buy a ready-roasted one from your butcher or use 550g cooked chicken meat instead)
400ml crème fraiche
2 tbsp fresh tarragon leaves, roughly chopped
2 tbsp plain flour
flaked sea salt
freshly ground black pepper

filo topping
40g butter, melted
4 filo pastry sheets (each about 32 x 38cm), thawed if frozen

You'll need a 1.5-litre pie dish

Melt the butter with the oil in a large frying pan over a low heat, then add the onion and the crushed garlic. Fry gently for 5–6 minutes until the onion is softened, but not coloured, stirring occasionally.

Pour in the white wine, then crumble the stock cube into the pan and stir well until it dissolves. Simmer over a high heat, stirring constantly, until the liquid has reduced by half and thickened. Remove from the heat.

Take the skin off the chicken, then strip the meat from the bones and tear it into bite-sized pieces. Place these in a large bowl. Add the onion and garlic mixture and spoon the crème fraiche on top. Scatter over the tarragon, sprinkle the flour on top and season with a good pinch of sea salt and plenty of freshly ground black pepper. Toss everything together until just combined, then spoon into your pie dish. Preheat the oven to 210°C/Fan 190°C/Gas 6½.

Now for the topping. Brush a sheet of filo pastry with melted butter and cut it into 6. Scrunch up each portion with your hands and place it on top of the filling. Repeat with the remaining sheets of filo until the filling is completely covered.

Bake the pie in the centre of the oven for 30 minutes or until the filo pastry topping is crisp and golden brown and the filling is bubbling beautifully.

chicken & wild mushroom pie

No wild mushrooms? No problem. Use chestnut or button mushrooms instead. If you want a bit of extra flavour, rehydrate some dried wild mushrooms, then drain them and chop roughly. Fry with the fresh mushrooms.

Serves 5 6

300g mixed fresh wild mushrooms, cleaned and trimmed
2 tbsp sunflower oil
25g butter
3 tbsp plain flour
2 tbsp finely chopped fresh parsley
2 long shallots, finely chopped
2 garlic cloves, crushed
4 boneless, skinless chicken breasts
2 tsp finely chopped fresh thyme leaves
100ml white wine
150ml chicken stock, fresh or made with ½ chicken stock cube
150ml double cream
flaked sea salt
freshly ground black pepper

pastry

1 quantity of rough puff pastry (see page 344) or 500g block of ready-made puff pastry
beaten egg, to glaze

You'll need a 1.25-litre pie dish, or a couple of smaller ones if you like, and a pie funnel

Cut the mushrooms in half, or slice if large. Melt half the butter with a tablespoon of the oil in a large non-stick frying pan. Fry the mushrooms for 2–3 minutes until they're golden but not too soft. Put them into a bowl and toss with the flour and parsley.

Return the pan to the heat and add the remaining butter and oil. Gently fry the shallots and garlic for 5 minutes until softened, stirring regularly. Cut each chicken breast into 6 evenly sized pieces and toss with the thyme and plenty of seasoning.

Turn up the heat a little and cook the seasoned chicken for just 2 minutes, turning occasionally until coloured on all sides. Add the wine and simmer for a few seconds, then stir in the stock and cream and leave to bubble for a minute more. Stir in the mushrooms, plus any excess flour in the bowl, and cook for about a minute, stirring until the sauce thickens. Adjust the seasoning, then tip the mixture into your pie dish and leave to cool.

Roll out the pastry on a lightly floured surface until it's about 5mm thick and at least 5cm larger than the top of the pie dish. Cut some strips, about 1cm wider than the rim of the dish, from around the edge. Brush the rim of the pie dish with beaten egg and fix the strips in place, overlapping a little where necessary, then brush with more egg (see page 361 for more detail on this). Nudge a pie funnel into the centre of the pie dish.

Before adding the pastry lid, cut a small cross in the centre. Lift the pastry onto the pie, gently fitting it over the pie funnel. Press the edges firmly to seal and press the pastry around the neck of the pie funnel. Trim the excess pastry with a sharp knife, then knock up the edges (see page 367).

Preheat the oven to 220°C/Fan 200°C/Gas 7. Brush the pie with beaten egg and place it on a baking tray. Bake for 30–40 minutes until the pastry is puffed up and golden and the filling is hot.

pheasant, chestnut & bacon pie

This is a proper celebration of autumn – pheasant has never tasted so good. Make life easier by using vacuum-packed chestnuts and some ready-rolled puff, then spoil yourself and have a night in with this pie and a nice glass of red wine.

Serves 4

150g unsmoked lardons or rindless streaky bacon rashers, cut into 1.5cm pieces
1 tbsp sunflower oil
1 medium onion, chopped
1 celery stick, stringed and sliced
4 skinless pheasant breasts (about 440g), each cut into 4 pieces
1 bay leaf
200g vacuum-packed cooked chestnuts
2 garlic cloves, crushed
100ml red or white wine
3 tbsp plain flour
200ml chicken stock (made with ½ chicken stock cube)
2 tbsp double cream
2 tbsp finely chopped parsley (optional)
flaked sea salt
freshly ground black pepper

pastry
375g ready-rolled puff pastry sheet
plain flour, for rolling
beaten egg, to glaze

You'll need a 1.1-litre pie dish

Place a large non-stick frying pan over a medium-high heat and fry the bacon for 3–4 minutes or until it's beginning to turn golden. Add the oil, onion and celery and fry for 4–5 minutes until softened and lightly browned, stirring regularly.

Add the pheasant and bay leaf to the pan and fry for 1½ minutes, turning the pheasant in the pan. Don't fry it for any longer than this because the pheasant will be cooked again in the oven and you don't want it to become dry. Season well with salt and pepper.

Working quickly, add the chestnuts, garlic and wine to the pan and allow them to bubble furiously for a few seconds. Sprinkle the flour into the pan and stir it through the pheasant and vegetables until they're lightly coated.

Take the pan off the heat and gradually stir in the chicken stock, scraping the bottom of the pan to lift the sediment and sticky juices. Stir in the cream and parsley if using. Spoon the mixture into the pie dish and leave to cool for about 30 minutes before adding the crust or the heat could cause the pastry to sink onto the filling.

Preheat the oven to 220°C/Fan 200°C/Gas 7. Unroll the puff pastry on a well-floured surface Cut some strips, about 1cm wider than the rim of the dish, from around the edge. Brush the rim of the pie dish with beaten egg and fix the strips in place, overlapping a little where necessary, then brush with more egg (see page 361 for more detail on this).

Lift the remaining pastry over a rolling pin and place it over the filling. Press the edges firmly to seal, then trim with a sharp knife and knock up the edges (see page 367). Brush with egg to glaze. Put the pie on a baking tray and bake for 20–25 minutes or until the pastry is well risen and golden brown and the filling is hot.

desperate biker cow pie

This is the big 'un – a sight for hungry eyes. This hearty pie is a meal in itself, although you could serve it with extra greens or chips. The filling can be made a day ahead if you like.

Serves 8

6–8 tbsp sunflower oil
3 medium onions, halved and sliced
4 garlic cloves, crushed
1kg well-marbled braising steak, trimmed of any hard fat or gristle
1 tsp flaked sea salt
200ml red wine or water
600ml hot beef stock (made with 2 beef stock cubes)
400g can chopped tomatoes
2 tbsp tomato purée
1 tbsp English mustard
1 tsp caster sugar
1 tsp dried mixed herbs
2 bay leaves
3 tbsp cornflour, blended with 3 tbsp cold water
750g potatoes (preferably Maris Pipers), peeled and cut in 5cm chunks
400g chantenay carrots, trimmed and peeled (optional)
freshly ground black pepper

pastry
2 x 500g blocks of ready-made puff pastry
plain flour, for rolling
beaten egg, to glaze

Heat 2 tablespoons of the oil in a large non-stick frying pan. Fry the onions and garlic for 5 minutes over a medium heat until golden, stirring regularly, then tip them into a large flameproof casserole dish. While the onions are cooking, cut the steak into rough 3.5cm cubes and toss them with a teaspoon of salt and plenty of freshly ground black pepper.

Return the pan to the heat and add another 2 tablespoons of the oil. Fry the meat in 3 batches until well browned all over. Add extra oil in between each batch so the pan doesn't become dry. Transfer the beef to the casserole dish as it is browned.

Preheat the oven to 180°C/Fan 160°C/Gas 4. Deglaze the pan with the wine or water, then bring it to the boil, stirring hard to lift all the sediment from the bottom of the pan. Pour this over the beef, add the stock, chopped tomatoes, tomato purée, mustard, sugar and herbs. Bring everything to the boil, then cover and cook in the oven for 1½ hours.

Remove the casserole dish from the oven and stir in the cornflour mixture and the potatoes and carrots. Cover and return to the oven for 1–1½ hours or until the beef is very tender and the sauce is thick. Check the seasoning, then leave the casserole to cool. (If making this filling a day ahead, cover and chill in the fridge once cooled. Stand at room temperature for an hour before cooking.)

Preheat the oven to 200°C/Fan 180°C/Gas 6. Spoon the beef and vegetable mixture into your pie dish or tin, piling it up in the centre to support the pastry.

Place one of the blocks of pastry on a well-floured surface, brush it very lightly between with water, then place the other one on top.

You'll need a casserole dish and a 2-litre pie dish or a roasting tin

Make 3 indentations down the pastry with a rolling pin and then roll out until it is at least 5cm larger than the dish. Cut some strips, about 1cm wider than the rim of the dish, from around the edge. Brush the rim of the pie dish with beaten egg and fix the strips in place, overlapping a little where necessary, then brush with more egg (see page 361 for more detail on this). Lift the rest of the pastry over your rolling pin and drop it gently on top of the pie. Press firmly to seal, leave the excess overhanging the sides and stand for 10 minutes.

Trim off the excess pastry with a sharp knife and knock up the edges (see page 367). Make a small hole in the centre, then brush the surface of the pie with beaten egg, avoiding the sides – if you drip beaten egg on them they won't puff up properly.

Bake in the centre of the oven for 45 minutes, then reduce the temperature to 180°C/Fan 160°C/Gas 4 and cook for a further 15–25 minutes or until the pastry is puffed up and golden brown.

To make the cow horns, make horn shapes out of crumpled foil and wrap them in leftover pastry, smoothing down any bumps or splits. You'll need to make them a bit smaller than you want them as they'll really puff up in the oven. Place on a baking sheet lined with foil. Brush with beaten egg. Bake in the oven for 15–20 minutes before you cook the pie, then cool.

When ready to serve the pie, make two incisions in the cooked pastry and poke the bottom 2–3cm of each horn into the holes. You may need to go deeper to make them stand up. Carry to the table with a flourish.

superb steak & ale pie

Beef and beer – a classic. No shandy drinkers in sight for this great pie, which is more British than Vera Lynn. Make sure you use steak that's well marbled with fat for flavour.

Serves 6

4–5 tbsp sunflower oil
200g smoked, rindless, streaky bacon rashers, cut into 2cm strips
2 medium onions, sliced
2 garlic cloves, finely chopped
850g well-marbled braising steak, trimmed of any hard fat or gristle
500ml bottle of real ale
500ml good beef stock
1 tbsp tomato purée
3–4 sprigs of fresh thyme, leaves stripped from the stalks
2 bay leaves
2 tbsp cornflour, blended with 2 tbsp cold water
250g small chestnut mushrooms, wiped and halved or quartered
flaked sea salt
freshly ground black pepper

pastry
1 quantity of rough puff pastry (see page 344)
or 500g block of ready-made puff pastry
beaten egg, to glaze

You'll need a casserole dish and a 1.2-litre pie dish

Heat 1 tablespoon of the oil in a frying pan. Fry the bacon strips with the onions until pale golden brown, stirring regularly. Add the garlic and fry for a minute or two until softened. Using a slotted spoon, transfer the onions, garlic and bacon to a flameproof casserole dish. Cut the steak into rough 2.5cm cubes and season with salt and pepper. Heat 2 tablespoons of the oil in the frying pan and fry the meat over a medium heat in 2 or 3 batches until well browned all over. Add extra oil if the pan seems dry. Transfer the beef to the casserole dish as it is browned.

Preheat the oven to 180°C/Fan 160°C/Gas 4. Deglaze the frying pan with half the ale. Bring it to the boil while stirring hard to lift all the sediment from the bottom of the pan. Pour this over the beef. Add the remaining ale, then the stock, tomato purée and herbs. Bring everything to the boil, then cover and cook in the oven for 1½–2 hours or until the meat is very tender. Remove the dish from the oven, stir in the cornflour paste, then put it back for 5 minutes or until the juices are thick. Adjust the seasoning to taste and leave to cool. Turn the oven up to 200°C/Fan 180°C/Gas 6. Heat the remaining oil in a frying pan and fry the mushrooms over a high heat for about 5 minutes until golden, then add them to the meat. Spoon everything into your pie dish.

Roll out the puff pastry on a well-floured surface until about 5mm thick and at least 5cm larger than your pie dish. Cut some strips, about 1cm wider than the rim of the dish, from around the edge. Brush the rim of the pie dish with beaten egg and fix the strips in place, overlapping a little where necessary, then brush with more egg (see page 361 for more detail on this).

Place the pastry lid carefully over the filling. Trim off the excess pastry with a sharp knife and knock up the edges (see page 367). Brush the top with beaten egg. Place the dish on a baking sheet and bake in the centre of the oven for 30–35 minutes until puffed up and golden brown.

mince & dumplings pie

This pie was a great favourite when we were kids – still is – and we love the way the fluffy dumplings swell to cover the top. It's important to give the pie that extra five minutes in the oven, uncovered, so the dumplings are brown and crispy.

Serves 6

2 tbsp sunflower oil
1 large onion, halved and chopped
2 garlic cloves, finely chopped
2 celery sticks, stringed and finely sliced
2 medium carrots, peeled and diced
500g lean minced beef
400g can chopped tomatoes
2 tbsp tomato purée
350ml beef stock (fresh or made with 1 stock cube)
150ml red wine or extra beef stock
pinch of caster sugar
1 bay leaf
flaked sea salt
freshly ground black pepper

dumplings
250g self-raising flour
125g shredded beef suet
½ tsp fine sea salt
2 tbsp finely chopped parsley
200ml cold water
butter, for greasing

You'll need a 1.2-litre pie dish

Heat the oil in a large saucepan. Cook the onion, garlic, celery and carrots for 15 minutes, stirring occasionally, until they are beginning to soften and colour lightly. Add the beef and cook with the vegetables for another 5 minutes until the mince is no longer pink. Stir regularly to break up the meat.

Add the tomatoes, tomato purée, beef stock, red wine, sugar and bay leaf. Add a good pinch of salt and plenty of black pepper. Bring to the boil, then reduce the heat and simmer gently for 20 minutes, stirring occasionally. Tip everything into your pie dish.

To make the dumplings, put the flour in a bowl and stir in the suet, salt and parsley. Make a well in the centre and add enough cold water – you'll need about 200ml – to mix to a soft, spongy dough. Lightly flour your hands and roll the dumpling mixture into 12 small balls.

Preheat the oven to 200°C/Fan 180°C/Gas 6. Drop the dumplings carefully on top of the mince and cover with buttered foil. Make sure the foil is tightly sealed around the edges but billows up above the pie to allow the dumplings to rise without sticking. Cook for 15 minutes until the dumpings are well risen, then remove the foil and put the pie back in the oven for another 5 minutes to brown the top.

gloucestershire squab pie

Once filled with young pigeons, or squab, this pie is now made with lamb and apples. A juicy, lip-smacking dish.

Serves 6

1kg lamb neck fillet
3 tbsp plain flour
½ tsp flaked sea salt, plus extra to taste
2–3 tbsp sunflower oil
2 medium onions, halved and sliced
½ tsp freshly grated nutmeg
¼ tsp ground allspice
1 sprig of fresh rosemary, leaves finely chopped
500ml chicken or lamb stock (made with 1 stock cube
300ml cold water
300g Bramley cooking apple
4–5 large fresh sage leaves, finely shredded
freshly ground black pepper

shortcrust pastry

75g cold lard, cut into cubes
75g cold butter, cut into cubes
300g plain flour, plus extra for rolling
good pinch salt
1 large egg, beaten with 1 tbsp cold water

First make the filling. Trim the meat of any excess fat and cut it into rough 3cm chunks. Tip the 3 tablespoons of flour into a large bowl and add the salt and a good grinding of black pepper. Add the lamb and toss well until all the chunks of meat are lightly coated with the seasoned flour.

Heat a large non-stick frying pan and add 2 tablespoons of the sunflower oil. Cook the lamb pieces in 2 batches, turning every now and then until they're golden brown on all sides. As the lamb browns, transfer it to a large, heavy-based saucepan or flameproof casserole dish with tongs or a slotted spoon.

Add the onions to the frying pan and cook them in the remaining fat until nicely browned, stirring regularly. Add a little extra oil if the pan seems too dry. Tip the onions into the casserole dish with the lamb and add the nutmeg, allspice and rosemary. Pour in the stock and add the 300ml of cold water. Bring the liquid to the boil, then reduce the heat and leave to simmer for 40 minutes or until the lamb is just tender and the liquid has reduced to a good gravy consistency. Season to taste, then remove the pan from the heat, cover and leave to cool for 30 minutes.

To make the pastry, rub the lard and butter into the flour and salt until the mixture resembles breadcrumbs. Reserve 2 tablespoons of the egg mixture for glazing the pastry and stir the rest into the bowl to form a dough. Knead very lightly on a floured surface and shape into a ball.

Once the pie filling has cooled to room temperature, preheat the oven to 200°C/Fan 180°C/Gas 6. Peel and core the apple, then slice and toss with the chopped sage and a little ground black pepper. Spoon half of the lamb mixture into the pie dish.

You'll need a casserole dish, a 2-litre pie dish and a pie funnel

Top with half the apple slices and cover with another layer of lamb. Finish with a final layer of apple, piling up above the edge of the pie. Nudge a pie funnel into the centre of the pie to help support the pastry and set aside.

Roll out the pastry on a floured surface until it is at least 5cm larger than your dish. Cut some pastry strips, at least 1cm wider than the rim of the dish. Brush the rim with beaten egg and place the strips on top, overlapping where necessary (see page 361 for more detail on this). Brush the pastry strips with more beaten egg.

Before adding the pastry lid, cut a small cross in the centre. Lift the pastry onto the pie, gently fitting it over the pie funnel. Press the edges firmly to seal and press the pastry around the neck of the pie funnel. Brush the top of the pie with egg and put the dish on a baking tray. Place in the centre of the oven and bake for 25 minutes or until the pastry is golden brown. Serve piping hot.

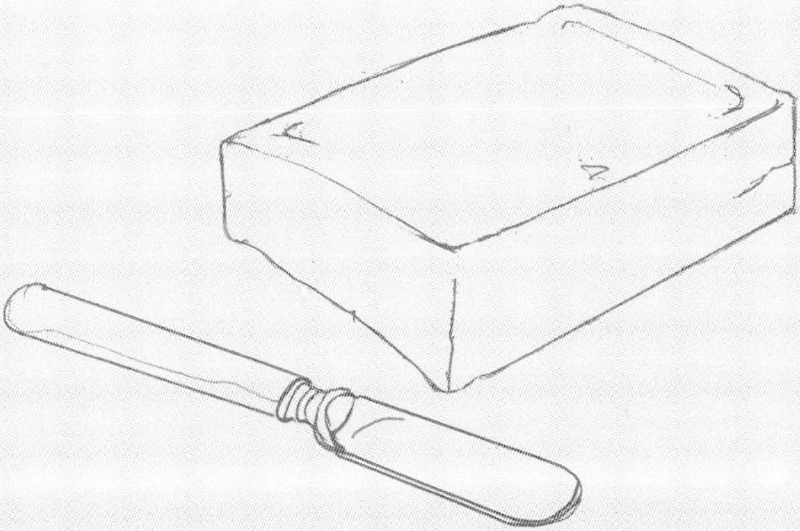

rich venison cobbler

We don't brown the meat first in this recipe because it stays more succulent if bubbled in the sauce from raw. Using a darker beer or stout will result in a deeper, richer cobbler but it is just as delicious with real ale.

Serves 6

2 tbsp sunflower oil
2 large onions, sliced
2 celery sticks, stringed and sliced
1 medium carrot, peeled and cut into rough 1.5cm cubes
2 tbsp plain flour
1 tsp English mustard powder
500ml real ale or stout
250ml water
1kg venison meat (ideally shoulder or leg), cut into 3cm chunks
2 heaped tbsp redcurrant jelly
1 tbsp fresh thyme leaves, roughly chopped
2 bay leaves
1–2 tbsp fresh lemon juice
flaked sea salt
freshly ground black pepper

cobbler topping
500g self-raising flour, plus extra for rolling
½ tsp fine sea salt
100g cold butter, cut into cubes
300ml whole milk, plus extra for brushing
beaten egg, to glaze (optional)

You'll need a casserole dish and a 2-litre pie dish

Preheat the oven to 180°C/Fan 160°C/Gas 4. Heat the oil in a medium, flameproof casserole dish and fry the onions, celery and carrot gently for 10 minutes until the onion is softened and lightly coloured, stirring occasionally. Add the flour and mustard and cook for a few seconds before slowly stirring in the ale and water.

Add the venison, redcurrant jelly, thyme leaves and bay leaves and stir. Season with a little salt and lots of coarsely ground black pepper. Bring to a gentle simmer, stirring occasionally, then cover with a lid. Carefully transfer the dish to the oven and cook for 1¾–2 hours or until the venison is very tender and the sauce is thick. Check the seasoning and adjust to taste, adding a little lemon juice to lift the richness. At this point you can cool the venison mixture and leave it in the fridge to finish off later or the next day if you like. The cobbler topping contains self-raising flour, so needs to be made not too long before it is baked.

When you're ready to cook your cobbler, spoon the venison mixture into an ovenproof pie dish. Preheat the oven to 200°C/Fan 180°C/Gas 6. To make the cobbler topping, put the flour and salt in a large bowl and rub in the butter with your fingertips until the mixture resembles breadcrumbs. Add the milk, stirring constantly, until the mixture comes together and forms a soft, spongy dough.

Turn the dough out onto a floured surface and roll out until it is about 2cm thick. Cut out 6cm rounds with a biscuit cutter, kneading and re-rolling the dough as necessary. Place the 'cobbles' over the surface of the pie so they nearly cover the filling and brush them with milk or beaten egg. Bake for 30 minutes or until the topping is golden brown and the filling is hot.

salmon & leek gratin pie

Use half a side of salmon for this recipe and cut it into three pieces, so that they fit in one layer in your largest pan. If you can't get a side of salmon, use ready-cut fillets but they might cost a bit more. Make one big pie or little ones for a starter.

Serves 6

750g salmon fillet, pin-boned but not skinned
300ml dry white wine
200ml water
2 small bay leaves
1 small onion, quartered
300ml whole or semi-skimmed milk
75g butter
3 medium leeks, trimmed and cut into 5mm slices
50g plain flour
150ml single cream
3 tbsp dry vermouth or white wine
1 tsp Dijon mustard
flaked sea salt
freshly ground black pepper

gratin topping

2 tbsp sunflower oil
4 slices of thick white bread, torn into small cubes
75g Cheddar cheese, finely grated
3 tbsp roughly chopped parsley

You'll need a 2-litre ovenproof dish

Place the salmon in a large saucepan. Pour over the wine, then add the water, bay leaves and onion. Bring to a gentle simmer, cover with a tight-fitting lid and simmer very gently for 5 minutes. Remove from the heat and leave to stand for another 5 minutes.

Remove the lid and strain the salmon through a colander into a wide jug. Discard the onion and bay leaves. Pour the liquid back into the saucepan and bring to the boil over a high heat, stirring occasionally, until the liquid is reduced to 200ml. (You'll need to pour the liquid back into the jug to measure it.)

Melt 25g of the butter in a large non-stick frying pan and gently fry the leeks for 5 minutes until softened. Set aside to cool. Melt the remaining butter in a large non-stick saucepan and stir in the flour. Cook for 1 minute, while stirring. Slowly add the reserved cooking liquor, then the milk, whisking constantly with a silicone whisk until the sauce is smooth and thick. Add the cream, vermouth and mustard and simmer gently for 5 minutes, stirring regularly. Season to taste.

To make the topping, heat the oil in a frying pan. Add the bread and fry over a medium heat until the cubes are lightly toasted, stirring regularly. Tip the bread into a bowl and leave to cool.

Preheat the oven to 200°C/Fan 180°C/Gas 6. Scatter a third of the leeks into the dish. Break the fish into large chunks and discard the skin. Arrange a third of the fish on top of the leeks. Pour over a third of the sauce. Repeat the layers twice more, ending with the sauce. Toss the toasted bread cubes with the cheese and parsley and scatter over the filling. Place the dish on a baking tray and bake for 25 minutes or until the top is golden brown and the filling is bubbling up around the edges.

A sprinkling
of caster sugar
on a sweet pie
gives a lovely
crunchy finish
and looks great.

peach & raspberry cobbler

Sweet or savoury, you can't go wrong with a cobbler. Peaches and raspberries are a dream combo but you can use any of your favourite fruits when they're in season.

Serves 6

6 firm, ripe peaches, halved and stoned
300g fresh raspberries
3 tbsp caster sugar

cobbler topping
375g self-raising flour, plus extra for rolling
75g caster sugar, plus extra for sprinkling
75g cold butter, cut into cubes
225ml whole milk, plus extra for glazing

You'll need a 1.5-litre ovenproof dish

To make the cobbler topping, put the flour and sugar in a large bowl and rub in the butter with your fingertips until the mixture resembles breadcrumbs. Add the milk, stirring constantly until the mixture comes together and forms a soft, spongy dough.

Preheat the oven to 200°C/Fan 180°C/Gas 6. Cut the peaches into thick slices and put them into an ovenproof dish. Add the raspberries and sugar and toss everything together gently.

Turn the dough out onto a floured surface and roll out until it is about 1.5cm thick. Cut out 6cm rounds with a biscuit cutter, kneading and rolling the dough again as necessary. Poke your finger into each round to make a deep dimple and place them on top of the fruit, overlapping slightly if necessary. Brush the 'cobbles' with milk, taking care to avoid the sides as it could prevent them from rising, and sprinkle with a little caster sugar.

Bake for 30–35 minutes or until the topping is risen and golden brown and the peaches are tender. The juice should be bubbling up at the sides, but exactly when this happens will depend on how ripe your peaches are and how deep your dish is. With very ripe peaches, this cobbler can take as little as 20 minutes – just enough time for the scone topping to cook and the raspberries to soften.

apricot & almond crumble

Fantastic with fresh apricots, this is almost as good made with a couple of cans of apricots instead. And you'll love our special crumble topping, with almonds and marzipan.

Serves 6

750g apricots, halved and stoned (16–20 apricots, depending on size)
3 tbsp caster sugar

crumble topping
125g plain flour
50g caster sugar
125g cold butter, cut into cubes
50g flaked almonds
175g ready-made golden marzipan

You'll need a 1.2-litre pie dish that's at least 4cm deep

Tip:
You can cook the crumble in individual dishes if you like. Quarter the apricots and cook the crumbles for about 30 minutes.

Preheat the oven to 180°C/Fan 160°C/Gas 4. Put the apricots and sugar in a shallow ovenproof dish and toss together.

Mix the flour and sugar in a large bowl. Add the butter and rub it into the dry ingredients with your fingertips until the mixture has the texture of coarse breadcrumbs. Stir in the flaked almonds, then coarsely grate the marzipan and add it to the crumble mix in 2 or 3 batches, tossing lightly.

Sprinkle the topping evenly over the apricot filling and bake for 40–45 minutes or until the crumble is golden and the filling is just beginning to bubble up from underneath the crust. If the topping begins to get too brown before the filling is ready, cover loosely with a piece of foil.

Serve hot with lashings of cream or crème fraiche.

spiced plum crumble

Crumbles have to be among our very favourite puds and there is an endless variety of toppings and fillings you can use. The oats in this crumble topping give it a fab chewy texture.

Serves 6–8

1kg fresh plums, stoned and quartered
50g golden caster or demerara sugar
1 tsp ground mixed spice
½ tsp cinnamon
juice and finely grated zest of 1 orange

crumble topping
200g plain flour
50g jumbo porridge oats
125g demerara sugar
125g cold butter, cubed

You'll need a 2-litre shallow ovenproof dish

Put the plums into your dish and sprinkle over the sugar, mixed spice and cinnamon. Add the zest and toss everything together until the plum quarters are lightly coated in the spices. Pour over the orange juice and set aside while the topping is prepared.

Preheat the oven to 200°C/Fan 180°C/Gas 6. Put the flour, oats and sugar in a large bowl and add the cubes of butter. Rub the butter into the dry ingredients with your fingertips until the mixture resembles coarse breadcrumbs.

Sprinkle the crumble mixture evenly over the plums and bake for about 45 minutes or until the plums are softened and the topping is golden brown. Poke a knife into the centre of the crumble to check that the plums are ready – they should be soft and juicy. Serve with cream, custard or ice cream.

toffee, banana & pineapple crumble

The luxury leg of the humble crumble, this goes down a treat with some good vanilla ice cream. Make in one smallish ovenproof dish if you don't have individual pie dishes.

Serves 4

3 large, firm bananas
425g can pineapple pieces or chunks, in juice or syrup, drained
25g butter
75g soft light brown sugar, preferably muscovado
2 tbsp rum (optional)
3 tbsp double cream

coconut crumble topping
125g plain flour
50g desiccated coconut
75g demerara sugar
75g cold butter, cut into cubes

You'll need 4 x 300ml ovenproof dishes or ramekins, or a 1.2-litre pie dish

Preheat the oven to 200°C/Fan 180°C/Gas 6. To make the topping, put the flour, coconut and sugar in a large bowl and add the butter. Rub the butter into the dry ingredients with your fingertips until the mixture resembles coarse breadcrumbs. Set aside while the filling is prepared.

Diagonally slice the bananas, and drain the pineapple in a sieve. Melt the butter in a large non-stick frying pan over a medium-high heat. Add the pineapple and sugar, then fry for 2 minutes, while stirring. Drop the banana slices into the pan and continue frying for a further minute or until the sugar is looking glossy and coats the fruit. Add the rum, if using, and bubble for a few seconds before stirring in the cream.

Remove the pan from the heat and divide the filling between 4 individual ovenproof dishes or large ramekins. Sprinkle the crumble mixture loosely over the top and place the dishes on a baking tray. Bake in the centre of the oven for 12–15 minutes or until the topping is golden brown and the filling is bubbling. Leave to stand for a few minutes before serving as the toffee filling will be very hot.

If you're making a large crumble, cook it for 15–18 minutes.

rhubarb & ginger crumble

The ginger adds a delicious twist to this crumble, but leave it out if you prefer. Try to choose sticks of rhubarb with similar widths so they cook evenly. The cornflour is a good tip – it soaks up some juice so the crumble doesn't get too soggy.

Serves 6

750g fresh rhubarb, trimmed, washed and cut into small lengths
4 balls of Chinese stem ginger, drained and cut into thin slivers
5 tbsp golden caster sugar
1 tbsp cornflour

crumble topping
175g plain flour
125g demerara sugar
50g jumbo porridge oats
125g cold butter, cut into cubes

You'll need a 1.2-litre ovenproof pie dish or tin that's about 4cm deep

Preheat the oven to 220°C/Fan 200°C/Gas 7. Put the rhubarb, ginger, sugar and cornflour into your pie dish and toss everything together well.

In a large bowl, mix the flour, sugar and oats. Add the butter and rub it into the dry ingredients with your fingertips until the mixture resembles coarse breadcrumbs.

Sprinkle the crumble evenly over the rhubarb filling and bake for 25–35 minutes or until the topping is golden and the filling is just beginning to bubble up from underneath the crust. Serve piping hot with lashings of custard or cream.

You can get everything ready in advance if you like and bung the pud in the oven about 30 minutes before you want to eat.

lovely gooseberry slump

A slump is a traditional American pudding made with fruit and a topping that's a cross between a cobbler and a dumpling. We love this made with juicy gooseberries.

Serves 6

750g fresh gooseberries, topped and tailed
100g golden caster sugar, plus an extra 1 tbsp
200ml crème fraiche

topping
115g cold butter, cut into cubes
175g self-raising flour
115g golden caster sugar
125ml milk
¼ tsp vanilla extract

You'll need a 1.2 litre ovenproof dish

Preheat the oven to 200°C/Fan 180°C/Gas 6. Put the gooseberries in the pie dish and toss with the 100g of sugar. Keep the rest for sprinkling on top. Spoon the crème fraiche roughly over the fruit.

Put the butter, flour and sugar in a food processor and blend on the pulse setting until the mixture resembles breadcrumbs. Mix the milk and vanilla extract together and pour into the food processor with the motor running. Blend until the mixture reaches a soft, dropping consistency.

Spoon this batter on top of the gooseberries and crème fraiche. Sprinkle with the remaining sugar and bake for 30–35 minutes or until the topping is risen and golden and the filling is bubbling. Cover with foil if the top starts to get to brown before the slump is cooked through. Serve with ice cream or cream or just as it is.

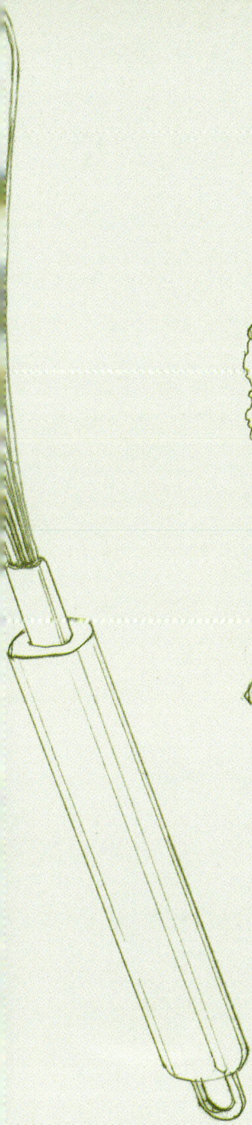
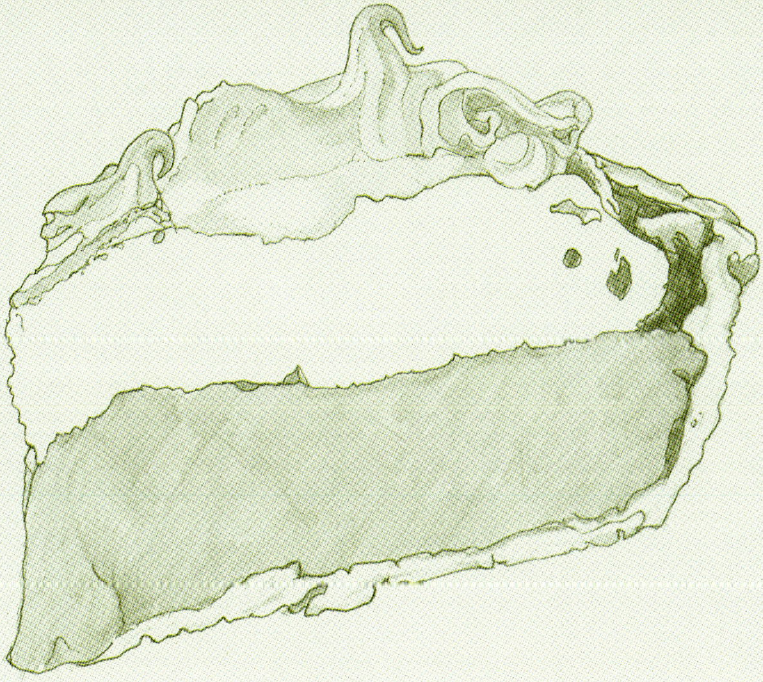
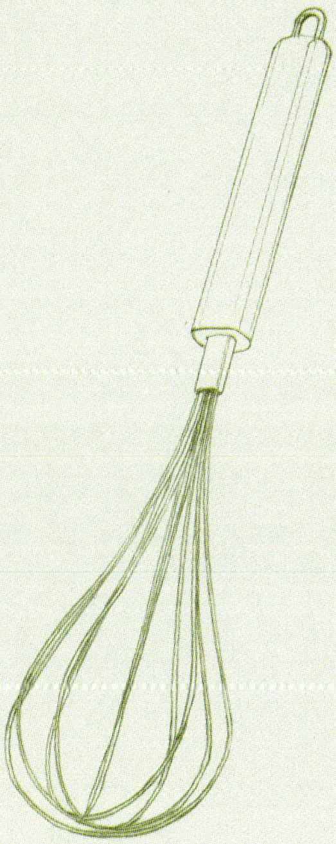

open-topped pies & tarts

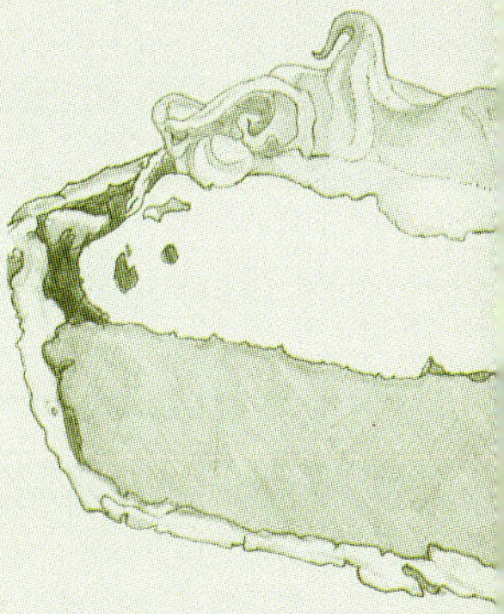

salmon, dill & new potato tart

A celebration of everything summery, this tart is delicious served with a salad and a glass of home-made lemonade. It's a good way of making a small amount of salmon and smoked salmon go a long way too.

Serves 6–8

2 x 150g fillets fresh salmon
200g new potatoes
200ml double cream
200ml crème fraiche
3 large eggs, beaten
100g smoked salmon, cut into strips 1.5cm wide
5 spring onions, sliced
1 small bunch of dill
flaked sea salt
freshly ground black pepper

shortcrust pastry
250g plain flour, plus extra for rolling
150g cold butter, cut into cubes
1 large egg, beaten

You'll need a 25cm loose-based tart tin

Preheat the oven to 200°C/Fan 180°C/Gas 6. Wrap the salmon fillets in foil, put them on a baking tray and cook for 15 minutes. Leave to cool.

To make the pastry, put the flour and butter in a food processor and blitz on the pulse setting until the mixture resembles breadcrumbs. With the motor running, add the beaten egg and process until the mixture is just beginning to come together into a ball. Remove and shape the dough into a slightly flattened ball. If you prefer to make your pastry by hand, see page 337.

Roll out the pastry on a lightly floured surface to the thickness of a £1 coin and use it to line your tart tin. Trim the edges neatly. Prick the base lightly with a fork and chill for 30 minutes. Preheat the oven to 200°C/Fan 180°C/Gas 6. Bake the pastry case blind (see page 358) for 25 minutes. Carefully remove the paper and beans, then return the pastry to the oven for a further 5–10 minutes.

Meanwhile, cook the potatoes in salted, boiling water for 15–18 minutes, until tender but not too soft. Leave to cool slightly, then them cut in half or into thick slices, depending on size. Turn the oven down to 170°C/Fan 150°C/Gas 3½. Beat the cream, crème fraiche and eggs in a bowl and season. Flake the cooked salmon into chunks and arrange in the pastry case with the smoked salmon, potatoes and spring onions. Pour in most of the cream and egg mixture, then snip the dill over the top.

Put the tart on a baking tray and place in the oven, with the oven shelf pulled just a little, then pour in the rest of the filling and carefully push the oven shelf in. Bake for 35–40 minutes, until the filling is just set and the top is beginning to brown. Cool in the tin for 15 minutes before removing and serving.

We cooked this in a vineyard in Alsace Lorraine, home of the quiche. It's simple and straightforward, with no extra ingredients – just how a really good quiche should be.

quiche lorraine

Serves 6–7

1 tbsp olive oil
1 medium onion, finely sliced
200g smoked bacon lardons or rindless smoked streaky bacon, cut into 2cm pieces
300ml double cream
200ml half-fat crème fraiche
3 large eggs, beaten
75g Gruyère cheese, coarsely grated
flaked sea salt
freshly ground black pepper

shortcrust pastry
250g plain flour, plus extra for rolling
150g cold butter, cut into cubes
1 large egg, beaten

You'll need a 23cm loose-based tart tin

To make the pastry, put the flour and butter in a food processor and blitz on the pulse setting until the mixture resembles breadcrumbs. With the motor running, add the beaten egg and process until the mixture is just beginning to come together in a ball. Remove and shape the dough into a slightly flattened ball. If you prefer to make your pastry by hand, see page 337.

Preheat the oven to 200°C/Fan 180°C/Gas 4. Roll out the pastry on a lightly floured surface to the thickness of a £1 coin. Using the rolling pin, lift the pastry and place it in the tart tin, pressing it well into the sides. Trim away any excess pastry and lightly prick the base of the tart. Chill for 30 minutes, then bake blind on a baking tray for 25 minutes (see page 358). Remove the beans and paper, then return the pastry to the oven for a further 5–10 minutes. Take it out of the oven, then turn the temperature down to 170°C/Fan 150°C/Gas 3½.

Heat the oil in a large non-stick frying pan and fry the onion and bacon together until lightly browned, stirring regularly. Remove from the heat, tip onto a plate and leave to cool. Put the cream, crème fraiche and eggs in a jug and beat with a wooden spoon until well combined. Season with a little salt and lots of pepper.

Spoon the onion and bacon into the pastry case and spread evenly. Scatter over the cheese. Slowly pour in nearly all the egg mix, then place the baking tray in the centre of the oven, with the oven shelf pulled out just a little, and pour in the rest. Carefully push the shelf back in. This will help make sure you have a good, deep filling without it sloshing everywhere.

Bake for 35–40 minutes until the filling is just beginning to brown and has lost its wobble. If you press the back of a teaspoon gently onto the centre of the quiche, no liquid should be visible. Take the quiche out of the oven and leave to cool in the tin for 15 minutes before removing. Serve warm or cold.

sliced potato, leek & ham tart

This is a complete meal in a tart and only needs something like a rustic celery, rocket and walnut salad to make a perfect supper. Good served warm or cold.

Serves 6

1kg floury potatoes (preferably Maris Pipers)
25g butter
1 medium leek, trimmed and sliced
150g hand-carved smoked ham, cut into 1.5cm cubes
300ml double cream
finely grated whole nutmeg
flaked sea salt
freshly ground black pepper

shortcrust pastry
250g plain flour, plus extra for rolling
150g cold butter, cut into cubes
1 large egg, beaten

You'll need a 25cm loose-based tart tin

First make the filling. Bring a pan of water to the boil. Peel the potatoes and cut into slices about 5mm thick, then add them to the hot water and return to the boil. Cook for 3 minutes, then drain and rinse under running water until cold. Leave to drain. Melt the butter in a non-stick frying pan. Fry the leek over a medium heat for 4–5 minutes until softened but not coloured, stirring regularly. Add the ham to the pan, toss with the leeks and remove from the heat. Leave to cool.

To make the pastry, put the flour and butter in a food processor and blitz on the pulse setting until the mixture resembles breadcrumbs. With the motor running, add the beaten egg and process until the mixture is just beginning to come together. Remove and shape the dough into a slightly flattened ball. If you prefer to make your pastry by hand, see page 337.

Roll the pastry out on a lightly floured surface to the thickness of a £1 coin and use it to line the tin, pressing well into the base and sides. Trim the edge by pinching it between your thumb and finger, leaving the pastry 3–4mm above the edge. Lightly prick the base and chill for 30 minutes.

Place a sturdy baking tray in the oven and preheat to 190°C/Fan 170°C/Gas 5. Season the cream with a good grating of nutmeg, salt and pepper. This pie can take a lot of seasoning. Arrange a layer of potatoes in the pastry case and top with a scattering of leeks and bacon and a slurp of the seasoned cream. Continue to make 3 more layers or until the pastry case is full. Slowly pour the remaining cream mixture into the pastry case, stopping every now and then to allow the cream to find its way between the layers.

Bake the pie on the preheated baking tray for 45–55 minutes until pale golden brown and cooked through. Test the pie by piercing the centre with a sharp knife – the potatoes should be soft and the cream firm. Remove and leave to stand for at least 10 minutes before serving. This will allow the cream to set a little more.

caramelised red onion & goat's cheese tarts

These tangy tartlets make a brilliant starter or light lunch. You can get everything ready in advance, then pop them in the oven just before you want to eat. They'll be ready in no time.

Serves 6

50g butter
4 medium red onions, halved and thinly sliced
50g light brown sugar
3 tbsp red wine vinegar
3 x 100g rounds of goat's cheese
2–3 tsp extra virgin olive oil
freshly ground black pepper
fresh oregano or parsley leaves, to garnish

pastry

375g ready-rolled puff pastry sheet
1–2 tbsp plain flour, for rolling
1 tbsp milk, to glaze

Melt the butter in a large non-stick saucepan and gently fry the onions for 30 minutes until well softened, stirring occasionally. Increase the heat and fry the onions for 3–4 minutes longer, stirring constantly until they are beginning to brown.

Stir the sugar and vinegar into the onions and simmer for 5 minutes, stirring until the liquid has almost all reduced. Remove from the heat and leave to cool. Preheat the oven to 220°C/Fan 200°C/Gas 7.

Unroll the puff pastry and put it on a board. Roll it out on a lightly floured surface until it is about 4cm longer. Trim the edges and then cut the pastry into 6 evenly sized rectangles. Place these on a baking sheet, prick with a fork and brush very lightly with milk. Bake for 10 minutes, then remove from the oven and flatten the pastry gently with a spatula.

Divide the onion mixture between the pastry rectangles. Cut the cheeses in half vertically, then horizontally, and place 2 pieces on top of each pastry rectangle. Season with black pepper.

Bake immediately or set aside until 10 minutes before serving. (If making more than 1 hour ahead, pop the tarts into the fridge.) Bake them in the centre of the oven for 6–8 minutes until the pastry is golden brown and the cheese has just begun to melt. Transfer the tarts to plates and drizzle with olive oil. Garnish with oregano or parsley leaves and serve warm.

quick mediterranean tuna tart

The taste of this tart is like a blast of Mediterranean sunshine – it's a salad niçoise in a pastry case. You'll probably have most of the ingredients in your store cupboard so it can be knocked up at a moment's notice.

Serves 5–6

125g fine green beans, trimmed
soft butter, for greasing
3 tbsp sun-dried tomato pesto
or tomato and olive stir-through sauce
280g jar char-grilled peppers, drained
200g can tuna steak in oil, drained
50g pitted black olives, drained
300ml crème fraiche
freshly ground black pepper

pastry
375g ready-rolled puff pastry sheet

You'll need a 23cm pie dish or ceramic quiche dish

Bring a small pan of water to the boil and add the trimmed green beans. Bring the water back to the boil, then immediately drain the beans and rinse them in a colander under running water until cold. This helps the beans keep their lovely bright green colour.

Preheat the oven to 220°C/Fan 200°C/Gas 7. Grease your pie dish with a little butter, then unroll the puff pastry and use it to line your dish. Trim away the overhanging pastry with a sharp knife to give a clean edge and use the trimmings to patch any areas where the pastry is not covering the base and sides of the dish – brush the patches with a little water to fix them in place.

Spread the base of the pastry case with the tomato and olive sauce or pesto. Flake the tuna into chunky pieces, then scatter the tuna, beans, peppers and olives over the sauce. Make sure the beans aren't sticking up too much or they might burn. Spoon the crème fraiche over the top and season with plenty of black pepper. Bake for 25–30 minutes or until the pastry is golden brown and the filling is hot.

tomato, mozzarella & pesto tarts

There are some super-punchy flavours in these tarts – roasting the tomatoes really intensifies their taste. Use fresh pesto from the chiller cabinets or make your own – you'll get a much better, fresher green colour. If you do have to use pesto from a jar though, just garnish with fresh basil.

Serves 6

12 ripe medium vine tomatoes
1 tbsp extra virgin olive oil
145g fresh pesto sauce (from a 200g tub)
2 x 125g balls of mozzarella, well drained
flaked sea salt
freshly ground black pepper

pastry
500g block of ready-made puff pastry
plain flour, for rolling
extra virgin olive oil, for brushing and drizzling

First, prepare the tomatoes. Preheat the oven to 150°C/Fan 130°C/Gas 2 and line a baking tray with baking parchment. Cut the tomatoes in half and place them, cut side up, on the tray. Drizzle with the oil and season generously with salt and pepper. Bake for 2 hours or until the tomatoes are lightly roasted and feel almost semi-dried. Remove from the oven and leave to cool.

Increase the oven temperature to 220°C/Fan 200°C/Gas 7. Place the pastry on a lightly floured surface with a short side facing you. Press the pastry 3 times down its length with a rolling pin to make light impressions in the dough. Roll into a long rectangle, a little wider than the original block and about 5mm thick. If the pastry gets too long for your work surface, cut it in half and roll each piece separately.

Using a saucer as a template or a biscuit cutter, cut out 6 circles of about 12.5cm in diameter and place them on a baking tray. Prick the surface of each one with a fork and brush lightly with olive oil. Bake for 12 minutes until the pastry is well risen and golden brown. Remove from the oven and gently push down the puffed pastry with a spatula to flatten slightly. Spoon a little pesto into the centre of each pastry base and spread roughly.

Pat the mozzarella balls with kitchen roll to absorb any excess moisture, then tear them into rough pieces. Arrange the mozzarella slices and tomatoes on top of the pesto and season with salt and pepper. Return the tarts to the oven for a further 6–8 minutes until the cheese has just begun to melt and the tomatoes are warm. Drizzle with a little more olive oil and serve hot with salad.

Tip:
You can prepare the tarts in advance up to the point at which they are returned to the oven. Cover the tray with a large piece of clingfilm and pop into the fridge for up to 8 hours. Bake for 8–10 minutes from cold.

roasted vegetable tart

The roasted vegetables in this tart give it a wonderful flavour and it's a fantastic dish for veggies and non-veggies alike. If you don't have any fresh herbs handy, sprinkle with a little dried thyme and rosemary instead.

Serves 6–8

2 medium red onions, cut into wedges
2 medium courgettes, cut into 1.5cm diagonal slices
1 small red pepper, halved, deseeded and cut into 4cm chunks
1 small yellow pepper, halved, deseeded and cut into 4cm chunks
2 tbsp olive oil
4–5 sprigs of thyme
1 sprig of rosemary
½ tsp flaked sea salt
200ml double cream
200ml crème fraiche
3 large eggs, beaten
75g Gruyère cheese, coarsely grated
freshly ground black pepper
basil leaves, to garnish (optional)

wholemeal shortcrust pastry
125g plain flour, plus extra for rolling
125g wholemeal flour
150g cold butter, cut into cubes
1 large egg, beaten

You'll need a 25cm loose-based tart tin

Preheat the oven to 220°C/Fan 200°C/Gas 7. Put the onion, courgettes and peppers in a large baking tray and pour over the oil. Strip the thyme and rosemary leaves from the stalks and scatter them over the vegetables. Season well. Roast the vegetables for 15 minutes, then remove from the oven and turn with a spatula. Put them back in the oven for 15 minutes or until tender and browned in places. Leave to cool.

To make the pastry, put the flour and butter in a food processor and blitz on the pulse setting until the mixture resembles breadcrumbs. With the motor running, add the beaten egg and process until the mixture is just beginning to come together. Remove and shape the dough into a slightly flattened ball and use immediately – this pastry doesn't like to wait around.

Roll out the pastry on a lightly floured surface to the thickness of a £1 coin and use it to line your tart tin, pressing it well into the sides. Trim neatly and lightly prick the base of the tart, then chill for 30 minutes. Preheat the oven to 200°C/Fan 180°C /Gas 6 and bake the pastry case blind on a baking tray for 25 minutes (see page 358). Remove the beans and paper, then return the pastry to the oven for a further 5–10 minutes. Take it out and turn the oven down to 170°C/Fan 150°C/Gas 3½.

To make the filling, put the cream, crème fraiche and eggs in a jug. Season, then beat with a wooden spoon until thoroughly combined. Don't use a whisk or the mixture could become too frothy. Scatter the roasted vegetables and cheese evenly over the pastry. Slowly pour over nearly all the egg mix, then place the baking tray in the centre of the oven, with the oven shelf pulled out just a little and pour over the rest.

Bake for 35–40 minutes until the filling is beginning to brown and has lost most of its wobble. If you press the back of a teaspoon gently onto the centre, no liquid should be visible. Take the tart out of the oven and leave to cool in the tin for 15 minutes before removing. Serve warm or cold.

pear, walnut & dolcelatte tarts

We love these flighty little tarts with their magic combination of salty tangy cheese, crunchy walnuts and sweet pears – a classic mix of flavours in crispy pastry cases. Use deep tart tins if you can, as they will hold more yummy filling.

Makes 8

knob of butter
1 tsp olive oil
2 medium conference pears, peeled, quartered and cored, then cut into thick slices
300ml crème fraiche
3 large eggs, beaten
3 sage leaves, finely shredded
150g Dolcelatte cheese, rind removed
25g walnuts, broken into small pieces
flaked sea salt
freshly ground black pepper

shortcrust pastry

300g plain flour, plus extra for rolling
175g cold butter, cut into cubes
1 large egg, beaten

You'll need 8 loose-based individual tart tins

Put the flour and butter in a food processor and blitz on the pulse setting until the mixture resembles breadcrumbs. With the motor running, add the beaten egg and process until the mixture is just beginning to come together in a rough ball. If you prefer to make your pastry by hand, see page 337.

Divide the pastry into 8 portions and roll into slightly flattened balls. Roll out on a lightly floured surface and use them to line the tart tins, pressing the pastry well into the base and sides of the tins. Neatly trim away any excess pastry and lightly prick the base of each tart. Chill for 30 minutes.

Preheat the oven to 200°C/Fan 180°C/Gas 6. Put the tart cases on a baking tray and line them with small squares of crumpled baking parchment. Half fill with baking beans and bake for 20 minutes. Remove the paper and beans and return the tart cases to the oven for 10 minutes until the pastry is pale golden brown. Take out of the oven and reduce the temperature to 170°C/Fan 150°C/Gas 3½.

To make the filling, melt the butter with the oil in a large non-stick frying pan. Fry the pear slices for 2–3 minutes over a medium heat until lightly browned on both sides, then drain on kitchen roll. Put the crème fraiche and eggs in a jug and beat with a wooden spoon until thoroughly combined, then add the sage. Don't use a whisk or the mixture could become too frothy. Season with a good pinch of salt and lots of black pepper.

Break the cheese into chunky pieces and divide it between the tarts. Add the pear slices and scatter the walnuts on top. Slowly add all the egg mixture, topping up each tart when the liquid has had a chance to settle. Bake for about 30 minutes or until the filling is just set. Take out of the oven and leave to stand in the tins for 15 minutes before carefully removing. Serve warm or cold.

broad bean, pea & mint tart

Light and delicious, this is a perfect tart for a summer lunch or a picnic and it's no trouble to put together. You can make this all year round using frozen peas and beans, and the salty feta gives a great texture and flavour.

Serves 6–8

1 tbsp sunflower oil
1 long shallot, finely chopped
1 garlic clove, crushed
200g baby broad beans
150g peas
200g feta cheese, drained and crumbled
200ml double cream
200ml crème fraiche
3 large eggs, beaten
2 tsp freeze-dried mint
freshly ground black pepper

shortcrust pastry
250g plain flour, plus extra for rolling
150g cold butter, cut into cubes
1 large egg, beaten

You'll need a 25cm loose-based tart tin

To make the pastry, put the flour and butter in a food processor and blitz on the pulse setting until the mixture resembles coarse breadcrumbs. With the motor running, add the beaten egg and process until the mixture is just beginning to come together. Remove and shape the dough into a slightly flattened ball. If you prefer to make your pastry by hand, see page 337.

Roll out the pastry on a floured surface and use it to line the tart tin. Trim the edges neatly. Prick the base lightly with a fork and chill for 30 minutes. Preheat the oven to 200°C/Fan 180°C/Gas 6 and bake the pastry case blind (see page 358) for 25 minutes. Carefully remove the paper and beans, then return pastry to the oven for 5–10 minutes.

Heat the oil in a non-stick frying pan and fry the shallot and garlic until softened, but not browned. Set aside to cool. Bring a pan of salted water to the boil, add the broad beans and cook for a couple of minutes. Rinse the beans under cold running water, drain, then remove their outer skins. This might seem like a chore but it really makes a difference to the finished dish. Bring another pan of salted water to the boil, add the peas and cook for a couple of minutes, then rinse under cold water.

Preheat the oven to 170°C/Fan 150°C/Gas 3½. Spread the softened shallot and garlic over the bottom of the tart case, then add the peas and beans. Sprinkle over the feta cheese. Put the cream, crème fraiche and eggs in a jug and beat with a wooden spoon until thoroughly combined. Add the mint and season with pepper.

Pour half the egg mixture into the dish, then place the baking tray in the centre of the oven, with the oven shelf pulled out just a little, and pour in the rest. Carefully push the oven shelf back in. Bake the tart for 35–40 minutes until set but with a friendly little wobble in the middle.

PYREX

Pies and tarts are like a gastronomic cuddle.

fresh lemon tart with berries

This is a feast for your eyes as well as your tummy. You can use a block of ready-made sweet shortcrust pastry if you like. See page 358 for some tips on mending any cracks in your shortcrust to make it completely watertight.

Serves 8

6 medium eggs
225g caster sugar
finely grated zest of 2 lemons
175ml fresh lemon juice (about 4 lemons)
250ml single cream

sweet shortcrust pastry
250g plain flour, plus extra for rolling
25g icing sugar
175g cold unsalted butter, cut into cubes
1 medium egg, beaten

to decorate
mixed fresh berries
sifted icing sugar

You'll need a 25cm loose-based tart tin

To make the pastry, put the flour, sugar and butter in a food processor and blitz on the pulse setting until the mixture resembles breadcrumbs. With the motor running, add the beaten egg and process until the mixture is just beginning to come together in a ball. Remove and shape the dough into a slightly flattened ball. If you prefer to make your pastry by hand, see page 337.

Transfer the pastry to a large sheet of baking parchment lightly dusted with sifted flour and roll into a circle about the thickness of a £1 coin. Carefully lift the pastry into the tart tin, leaving any excess hanging over the edge. Prick the base lightly with a fork and chill for 30 minutes. Preheat the oven to 200°C/Fan 180°C/Gas 6.

Bake blind (see page 358) for 25 minutes. Remove the paper and beans and return to the oven for a further 4–5 minutes until the surface of the pastry is dry and lightly browned. Carefully trim away any excess pastry. Turn the oven down to 150°C/Fan 130°C/Gas 2.

To make the filling, put the eggs in a jug and whisk until smooth. Add the sugar, lemon zest and lemon juice and stir with a wooden spoon until well combined. Don't use a whisk or you'll end up with a bubbly tart. Pour the cream into the lemon mixture, stirring well.

Return the tart on its baking tray to the oven. Pull the oven shelf out about halfway so you can fill the tart to the top without moving it and sloshing the contents. Pour the lemon mixture slowly into the tart case and carefully slide the shelf back into the oven. Bake for 30–35 minutes or until the filling is just set. It should still wobble a little in the middle. Cool completely in the tin.

Remove the tart from the tin just before serving and slide onto a serving plate or cake stand. Arrange the berries in the middle of the tart and dust with sifted icing sugar to serve.

toffee & chocolate ice cream pie

Our friend Justine introduced us to this devilish pie, which has become very popular in both our households. Using biscuits such as bourbons, which are sandwiched with chocolate icing, keeps the frozen base softer and makes it easier to slice.

Serves 6

500ml tub of good-quality chocolate ice cream
6 tbsp ready-made toffee sauce
500ml tub of good-quality vanilla or caramel ice cream
2 x 37g packs of Maltesers
3 x 25g chocolate flake bars

biscuit base
300g chocolate bourbon biscuits
75g butter

You'll need a 23cm pie dish – we used one with sloping sides – or a ceramic quiche dish

To make the biscuit base, break the biscuits into chunky pieces and blitz them to crumbs in a food processor. Melt the butter in a small saucepan. With the motor running, pour the butter onto the biscuits and blitz until evenly combined. Alternatively, crush the biscuits in a strong plastic food bag by bashing with a rolling pin. Tip the crumbs into a bowl and stir in the melted butter.

Line the pie dish with clingfilm, leaving it hanging over the edges – this will help you remove the pie later. Press the biscuit mixture over the base and sides of a 23cm tart tin dish, making sure it is spread evenly. Cover with clingfilm and freeze for an hour.

Take both ice creams out of the freezer and leave them to stand for 5 minutes. Take the biscuit base out of the freezer and scoop half the chocolate ice cream over the base. Spoon 2 tablespoons of toffee sauce over the ice cream. Then scoop half the vanilla or caramel ice cream over the pie and add 2 more tablespoons of toffee sauce. Freeze for 30 minutes.

For the final layer, add alternating scoops of chocolate and vanilla ice cream, dotting them with Maltesers and chunks of flaked chocolate as you go. Return to the freezer for at least an hour until solid, covering the pie with clingfilm after the first 30 minutes.

When ready to serve, set the dish on the work surface. Take hold of the clingfilm lining the dish and gently lift the frozen pie out of the dish and onto a serving plate. Slide the clingfilm out from underneath. Drizzle the pie with the remaining toffee sauce and leave to stand for a few minutes to allow the ice cream to melt a little before serving.

Tips:
Once this tart is solid, you can wrap it in foil and freeze for up to a week.

To make it easier to spoon out the toffee sauce, dip your spoon into just-boiled water between each spoonful.

yummy treacle tart

Thick sliced white bread makes great crumbs for this best of all trad tarts. It's always called treacle tart, but you use syrup, not treacle. Funny really, but there you are. Delicious on its own or served with custard, fresh cream or ice cream.

Serves 6–8

2 large eggs, beaten
454g can of golden syrup
about 1 tsp finely grated lemon zest
140g white breadcrumbs, made from a day-old loaf

shortcrust pastry
250g plain flour, plus extra for rolling
150g cold butter, cut into cubes
1 large egg, beaten

You'll need a 23cm tart tin or shallow pie dish

To make the filling, beat the eggs in a large bowl and stir in the syrup. Add the lemon zest, then the breadcrumbs and mix really well with a wooden spoon. Set the mixture aside while you make the pastry. This will give the breadcrumbs time to soften and soak up the syrup.

To make the pastry, put the flour and butter in a food processor and blitz on the pulse setting until the mixture resembles breadcrumbs. Reserve a tablespoon of the beaten egg to use for glazing the pastry. With the motor running, add the rest of the egg and process until the mixture is just beginning to come together in a ball. Remove and shape the dough into a slightly flattened ball. If you prefer to make your pastry by hand, see page 337.

Weigh the dough and set aside 150g of the dough for the lattice top. Form the rest into a flattish ball. Place on a lightly floured surface and roll it out into a circle about the thickness of a £1 coin, turning the pastry and flouring the surface and rolling pin regularly. Use the pastry to line the tin, then trim the edges neatly with a sharp knife. Prick the base lightly with a fork and chill for 30 minutes.

Preheat the oven to 200°C/Fan 180°C/Gas 6. Stir the syrup mixture, then pour it into the pastry case and smooth the surface. Brush the pastry edge with the reserved egg. Roll out the remainder of the pastry into a rectangle and cut it into long strips, about 1.5cm wide. Twist each strip 3 or 4 times to create a spiral effect. Place the strips evenly across the top of the pie to form a criss-cross lattice pattern. Press them firmly onto the pastry edge, but try not to stretch the pastry.

Brush the top with more egg to glaze and bake for about 30 minutes until the pastry is golden brown and the filling has set. Cool for at least 30 minutes before serving – this is great hot or cold.

chocolate tart

If you like chocolate – and we do – you have to make this. It has real wow factor and is very rich, so serve in thin slices with coffee, or with fresh berries and cream as a pudding.

Serves 12

white chocolate filling
200g white chocolate, broken into squares
100ml double cream

dark chocolate filling
200g dark chocolate, broken into squares
150ml double cream

topping
50g white chocolate, broken into squares

sweet shortcrust pastry
175g plain flour, plus extra for rolling
115g cold unsalted butter, cut into cubes
2 tbsp caster sugar
1 medium egg, beaten

You'll need a 10.5 x 34cm rectangular, loose-based tart tin

Place your tart tin on a baking sheet. To make the pastry, put the flour, butter and sugar in a food processor and pulse until the mixture resembles breadcrumbs. With the motor running, add the beaten egg and blend until the mixture begins to form a ball. Transfer to a large sheet of baking parchment dusted with flour and roll with the palms of your hands into a long, fat sausage shape, about 2cm shorter than the tin. Turn the pastry on the sheet and roll with a floured rolling pin until it is about 4cm larger than the tin.

Lift the pastry with the paper and gently turn it over and lower into the tin. Carefully peel off the paper and press the pastry gently into the base and sides of the tin, leaving the excess overhanging the edge. Press any tears in the pastry together. Prick the base lightly with a fork and chill for 1 hour.

Preheat the oven to 200°C/Fan 180°C/Gas 6. Bake the pastry case blind for 20 minutes (see page 358), then take it out of the oven and remove the paper and beans. Return to the oven for a further 5–10 minutes until the pastry is cooked and very lightly browned. Carefully trim away the excess pastry with a sharp knife.

To make the white chocolate filling, melt the white chocolate with 50ml of the cream in a heatproof bowl over a pan of gently simmering water. Remove from the heat while there are still some lumps remaining and stir until smooth. Stir in the rest of the cream and pour onto the pastry base. Smooth the surface and chill for 1 hour until set. Make the dark chocolate filling in the same way and pour it onto the white chocolate filling. Smooth the surface and chill for 1 hour until set.

Very carefully remove the tart from the tin and slide it onto a serving platter. To make the topping, melt the white chocolate in a heatproof bowl as before and, while it is still warm, drizzle all over the tart with a teaspoon. Leave to set before serving.

proper custard tart

This tart is a real crowd pleaser and children love it. Make in a good, deep Victoria sandwich tin for the best results. Bake the pastry blind until it is properly cooked and then the custard can be cooked in a nice low oven with no risk of curdling.

Serves 8

3 large eggs
2 large egg yolks
100g caster sugar
300ml double cream
300ml whole milk
½ tsp pure vanilla extract
½ whole nutmeg

shortcrust pastry
150g plain flour, plus extra for rolling
100g cold butter, cut into cubes
1 medium egg, beaten

You'll need a 20cm loose-based Victoria sandwich tin

To make the pastry, put the flour and butter in a food processor and blitz on the pulse setting until the mixture resembles breadcrumbs. With the motor running, add the beaten egg and process until the mixture is just beginning to come together in a ball. Remove and shape the dough into a slightly flattened ball. If you prefer to make your pastry by hand, see page 337.

Roll out the pastry on a floured surface to the thickness of a £1 coin. Use it to line the tin, pressing it firmly into the base and sides. Leave the excess pastry overhanging the sides. Don't worry if there are couple of tiny cracks – either pinch them together or patch with a little of the excess pastry. Keep a small ball of pastry handy in case more cracks appear when the pastry is baked. Prick the base very lightly with a fork, taking care not to go all the way through to the tin. Chill for 30 minutes.

Preheat the oven to 200°C/Fan 180°C/Gas 6. Bake the pastry case blind for 35 minutes (see page 358), then remove the paper and beans and return to the oven for 5 minutes more. Take the pastry case out of the oven and turn the temperature down to 160°C/Fan 140°C/Gas 3. Trim away the excess pastry with a sharp knife, ensuring that as few pastry crumbs as possible fall into the tart case.

To make the custard, mix the eggs, egg yolks and sugar in a heatproof bowl with a wooden spoon until smooth. Pour the cream and milk into a medium saucepan, then add the vanilla extract and finely grate in half the nutmeg. Heat until the mixture is hot but not boiling, stirring occasionally. Slowly pour the milk mixture onto the eggs, stirring well. Pour the custard slowly into the pastry case and grate the rest of the nutmeg over the top.

Bake in the oven for 30–45 minutes or until just set, then remove from the oven and leave to cool – the custard should still be fairly wobbly in the middle, as it will continue to set as it cools. – then chill for 2–3 hours. Run a knife around the edge of the custard and slowly release from the tin. Serve with a little extra cream.

very simple raspberry tarts

These little raspberry treasures are a doddle to make and have a light chocolate biscuit base, topped with a white chocolate mousse and lots of fresh raspberries. You can knock them up in no time and you'll relish every mouthful, we promise you.

Makes 8

150g white chocolate, broken into squares
300ml double cream
350g fresh raspberries
1½ tsp icing sugar, sifted

biscuit crust

sunflower oil, for greasing
300g chocolate digestive biscuits
75g butter

You'll need 8 x 8cm loose-based tartlet tins or you could use large ramekin dishes instead

Grease the tartlet tins very lightly with sunflower oil. To make the biscuit base, break the biscuits into chunky pieces and blitz to crumbs in a food processor. Melt the butter in a small saucepan and pour onto the crumbs with the motor running and blitz until evenly combined. Alternatively, crush the biscuits in a strong plastic food bag by bashing with a rolling pin. Tip the crumbs into a bowl and stir in the melted butter.

Divide this mixture between the tins, spreading it over the base and up the sides of each one and pressing down lightly. Make sure you press the crumbs well into the curved sides and into the corners so the crumbs are as evenly distributed as possible. If any areas are too thin, the cases could crack. Put the tins on a baking tray and leave to set in the fridge for 30 minutes.

Melt the white chocolate with 100ml of the cream in a heatproof bowl over a pan of very gently simmering water. Remove from the heat while there are still some lumps remaining and stir until smooth. Watch your fingers as the bowl will be hot. Leave to cool for 30 minutes, but do not allow it to set.

Whip the rest of the cream in a medium-sized bowl until soft peaks form. Do not over-whip or the filling will be too stiff. Pour the melted chocolate slowly into the whipped cream and fold it in gently with a large metal spoon. Divide the chocolate cream between the biscuit cases and put them back in the fridge for an hour or until set.

Take the tarts out of the fridge and very gently remove them from the tins by pushing up the loose bases and sliding onto individual serving plates or a large platter. Top with the fresh raspberries and sprinkle with sifted icing sugar before serving.

Tip:

You can make these tarts up to a day in advance. Once they're filled, cover them with clingfilm and keep them in the fridge. Add the fruit when you're ready to eat.

lemon meringue pie

Is there anyone who doesn't like lemon meringue pie? We don't think so. With the tangy lemony filling, sweet pastry and melting meringue topping, this is as close to heaven as a pudding gets. Use a deep fluted tin for best results.

Serves 8–10

75g cornflour
500ml cold water
300g caster sugar
finely grated zest of 4 large lemons
freshly squeezed juice of 4 large lemons (you'll need 250ml)
8 large egg yolks

meringue topping
5 large egg whites
250g caster sugar, plus 1 tsp
2 tsp cornflour
½ tsp vanilla extract

sweet shortcrust pastry
250g plain flour,
plus extra for rolling
1 tbsp caster sugar
150g cold butter, cut into cubes
1 large egg, beaten

You'll need 23cm loose-based tart tin – must be about 4cm deep to contain the filling

To make the pastry, put the flour, sugar and butter in a food processor and blitz on the pulse setting until the mixture resembles breadcrumbs. With the motor running, add the egg and process until the mixture is beginning to come together. Remove and shape the dough into a flattened ball. Preheat the oven to 200°C/Fan 180°C/Gas 6. Roll out the pastry on a lightly floured surface and use it to line the tin. Trim neatly, lightly prick the base, and chill for 30 minutes. Bake the pastry case blind on a baking tray for 25 minutes (see page 358), then remove the paper and beans and bake for 8–10 minutes more until the pastry is lightly browned.

Put the cornflour in a bowl and mix with enough of the cold water to make a thin paste. Pour the rest of the water into a saucepan and add the sugar, zest and juice. Heat gently until the sugar dissolves, then bring to the boil. Reduce the heat slightly, then stir in the cornflour and the mixture should start to thicken. Stir over a low heat for 3 minutes until the mixture is thick and glossy. Remove from the heat and cool for 5 minutes. Whisk the egg yolks until smooth, then stir into the lemon mixture. Return the pan to the hob and cook over a low heat for 3 minutes, stirring constantly. Pour the lemon mixture into the pastry case and leave to cool.

Preheat the oven to 170°C/Fan 150°/Gas 3½. To make the meringue, whisk the egg whites in a large, clean bowl with an electric whisk until stiff but not dry. Mix the sugar and cornflour and whisk into the egg whites, a tablespoon at a time, until all is incorporated and the meringue looks thick and glossy. Whisk in the vanilla extract. Spoon the meringue into a piping bag and pipe swirls over the lemon filling, or spoon the meringue onto the pie. Sprinkle with the teaspoon of sugar and place in the centre of the oven. Turn the oven down to 150°C/Fan 130°C/Gas 2 and bake the pie for 20–25 minutes, until the meringue is set and beginning to brown very lightly. Remove and cool, before carefully lifting the pie out of the tin to serve.

Tip:
Whisk the egg whites for the meringue until you can hold the bowl upside down without the egg whites sliding out. Don't over whisk or they won't hold the sugar.

raspberry bakewell pudding

Is it tart? Is it a pie? Is it a pudding? This dessert is a bit of all three and whatever you want to call it, we think you'll agree that it tastes fantastic!

Serves 8–10

- 200g softened butter
- 250g ground almonds
- 200g caster sugar
- 65g self-raising flour
- 4 medium eggs
- 150g raspberry jam
- 125g fresh raspberries
- 15g flaked almonds

pastry

- 500g block of ready-made puff pastry
- plain flour, for rolling

You'll need a 25cm ceramic dish or loose-based, fluted tart tin

Preheat the oven to 200°C/Fan 180°C/Gas 6. Put the butter, ground almonds, sugar, flour and eggs in a food processor and blend until smooth and fluffy. Alternatively, put everything into a mixing bowl and beat like hell with a wooden spoon

Roll out the puff pastry on a lightly floured surface until it is about 5cm larger than your dish. Lift it carefully with the rolling pin and drop it gently into the tin. Press firmly into the corners and sides, then prick the base lightly with a fork. Trim the edges with a sharp, horizontally held knife.

Spoon the jam onto the uncooked base and use the back of a spoon to spread it gently and evenly right up to the edges. Spoon the almond mixture on top of the jam, working it around the outside before working towards the middle of the pastry case. Smooth the surface. Dot the raspberries over the tart, pressing them gently into the filling. Bake in the preheated oven for 20 minutes.

Carefully pull the oven shelf with the tart a little way out and scatter over the flaked almonds. Push the shelf back and bake the tart for another 15 minutes. Turn the oven down to 180°C/Fan 160°C/Gas 4 and cook for a final 10 minutes until the filling is nicely risen and golden brown. It should also feel firm to the touch. If the tart starts to look too brown towards the end of the cooking time, loosely cover with foil. Serve warm or cold with cream.

fresh strawberry tart

Don't wait until Wimbledon for this one. Make it as soon as the strawberries appear in the shops for a real summer treat that tastes as good as it looks. You can make the pastry case up to two days ahead of time, then fill just before serving.

Serves 8–10

250ml good-quality ready-made vanilla custard (from the chiller cabinet)
300ml double cream
600g strawberries, hulled and cut into halves or quarters
4 tbsp redcurrant jelly
2 tbsp water

sweet shortcrust pastry
250g plain flour, plus extra for rolling
175g cold unsalted butter, cut into cubes
25g icing sugar
1 medium egg, beaten

You'll need a 23cm loose-based, fluted tart tin

Place the tart tin on a baking sheet. To make the pastry, put the flour, butter and icing sugar in a food processor and pulse until the mixture resembles breadcrumbs. With the motor running, add the beaten egg and blend until the mixture starts to come together in a ball. Shape into a slightly flattened ball. If you prefer to make your pastry by hand, see page 337.

Transfer the pastry to a sheet of baking parchment lightly dusted with sifted flour and roll into a circle about the thickness of a £1 coin. Lift the pastry gently into the tart tin, then push it into the base and sides of the tin and leave the excess overhanging the edge. Cut off a small amount of the overhanging pastry to keep for patching the cooked tart if necessary. Prick the base lightly with a fork and chill for 30 minutes.

Preheat the oven to 200°C/Fan 180°C/Gas 6. Bake the pastry case blind for 25 minutes (see page 358), then remove the paper and beans and return to the oven for a further 5–10 minutes. Trim off any excess pastry with a sharp knife. If the pastry has any holes, simply patch with the reserved pastry and pop the pastry case back in the oven for a few minutes. Leave to cool before filling.

To make the filling, put the custard and cream in a large bowl and beat with an electric whisk for 3–4 minutes or until the mixture thickens and holds in stiff peaks. Spoon the custard mixture into the tart case. Scatter the strawberries over the creamy filling. Melt the redcurrant jelly with the water in a small saucepan over a medium heat, stirring constantly. Brush the melted jelly over the strawberries to glaze. Leave the tart in the tin until just before serving – chill in the fridge if leaving for longer than 30 minutes.

To serve, place the tin on an upturned saucepan or bowl that is slightly smaller than the loose base and gently lower the sides. Loosen the pastry base with a palette knife and slide the tart onto a serving dish – take great care as the pastry is very delicate. Serve immediately.

perfect pecan pie

My, my, pecan pie. This is one of our favourite American imports and one you don't have to declare at customs. We're nuts for it!

Serves 6

4 large eggs, beaten
100ml maple syrup
50g butter, melted
75g light muscovado sugar
2 tbsp plain flour
½ tsp vanilla extract
300g pecan nut halves

shortcrust pastry
250g plain flour, plus extra for rolling
150g cold butter, cut into cubes
1 large egg, beaten

You'll need a 23cm loose-based, fluted tart tin

To make the pastry, put the flour and butter in a food processor and blitz on the pulse setting until the mixture resembles breadcrumbs. With the motor running, add the beaten egg and process until the mixture is just beginning to come together. Remove and shape the dough into a slightly flattened ball. If you prefer to make your pastry by hand, see page 337.

Roll out the pastry on a floured surface and use it to line the tart tin. Trim the edges neatly. Prick the base lightly with a fork and chill for 30 minutes.

Preheat the oven to 200°C/Fan 180°C/Gas 6. Bake pastry case blind for 20 minutes (see page 358). Carefully remove the paper and beans, then return pastry to the oven for a further 5 minutes.

To make the filling, whisk the eggs together in a large bowl with the syrup, butter, sugar, flour and vanilla extract until smooth. Stir in the nuts. Pour the mixture gently into the pastry case. Using your fingers, quickly turn some of the nuts, so the tops rather than the bottoms are showing. This will help give a more eye-catching appearance to the pie but you don't have to do it – the pie will still taste just as good.

Reduce the oven temperature to 190°C/Fan 170°C/Gas 5. Bake for 25–30 minutes or until the filling is golden brown and set. Leave the tart in the tin for 15 minutes before carefully removing. Serve warm or cold with whipped cream or ice cream.

best-ever banoffee pie

When it comes to banoffee pie you just have to forget the calorie counting – bananas, cream, chocolate, what's not to like? Use a deep tin so there's plenty of room for the filling.

Serves 12

toffee filling

115g butter

115g soft dark brown sugar

397g can sweetened condensed milk

topping

5 ripe but firm medium bananas

450ml double cream

1 tsp fresh lemon juice

25g plain dark chocolate, coarsely grated, or chocolate curls

biscuit base

75g butter

300g chocolate oaty biscuits, such as Hobnobs

You'll need 23cm loose-based tart tin – must be about 4cm deep to contain the filling

Tip:

Make the chocolate curls by melting dark chocolate and pouring onto a flat surface. Leave until set, then scrape the chocolate carefully with a long, sharp knife held at a slight angle, until it curls up towards you. Alternatively, run a swivel-peeler down the back of a bar of cooking chocolate.

To make the base, melt the butter in a small pan. Break the biscuits into chunky pieces and blitz them to crumbs in a food processor. With the motor running, add the melted butter and blend until thoroughly mixed. Alternatively, put the biscuits in a strong plastic food bag and bash with a rolling pin. Tip the crumbs into a bowl and stir in the melted butter.

Tip the biscuit mixture into the centre of your tart tin and press it firmly into the base and sides. Make sure the mixture is evenly distributed, especially where the base meets the sides. Chill for 30 minutes until set.

To make the toffee filling, melt the butter in a non-stick saucepan and stir in the sugar. Cook over a low heat, stirring constantly, until the sugar has dissolved and the butter and sugar look smooth with no oil floating to the surface. Add the condensed milk and bring to a gentle simmer, stirring constantly. Cook for 3 minutes, stirring, until the mixture turns a deep, creamy caramel brown. Pour the toffee gently onto the biscuit base and quickly smooth over the surface. Leave to chill for at least 1 hour and up to 8 hours before topping.

Just before serving, lightly whip the cream. It should stand in very soft peaks – any thicker and it will look over-whipped when mixed with the bananas. Diagonally slice 4 of the bananas and scatter half of them over the toffee. Fold the rest lightly into the cream and spoon gently on top.

Slice the remaining banana and put it in a bowl with the lemon juice. Toss very gently – this will stop the banana turning brown. Decorate the top with the lemony banana slices, poking them into the cream randomly, then sprinkle the pie with grated chocolate or decorate with chocolate curls. Serve the pie in fairly thin slices, as it is very rich.

individual zesty lime tarts

Key lime pie is another popular American import and we love the way the zingy hit of citrus cuts through the rich creamy texture. Try making our mini versions.

Makes 8

300g sweetened condensed milk
200ml double cream
finely grated zest and juice of 4 limes (you need 100ml of juice)

lime syrup topping
1 lime
100ml water
50g caster sugar

biscuit base
100g butter
200g chocolate digestive biscuits
200g dark chocolate sandwich biscuits, such as Oreos

You'll need 8 x 7.5cm deep fluted tartlet tins

To make the base, melt the butter in a small pan. Break the biscuits into chunks and put them in a food processor. Blitz into crumbs then add the butter and with the motor running, blend until thoroughly mixed. Alternatively, put the biscuits in a strong plastic food bag and bash with a rolling pin. Tip into a bowl and stir in the melted butter.

Divide the mixture between the tins and press firmly into the base and sides. Make sure the biscuit base is evenly distributed, especially where the base meets the sides and in between the flutes. Put the tins on a baking tray and chill for 30 minutes.

To make the filling, put the condensed milk and cream in a large bowl and whisk with electric beaters for about 3 minutes until light and soft peaks form. Whisk in the lime zest and fresh lime juice until the mixture thickens. Spoon into the biscuit cases and return to the fridge for 2–3 hours until set. Cover loosely with foil if leaving for longer.

To make the lime syrup for the topping, use a vegetable peeler to peel very fine strips of zest from half the lime. Cut the strips into 1mm matchsticks with a sharp knife. Squeeze the juice of the lime and put into a small saucepan with the water and any lime juice left over from the filling. Add the lime zest and bring to a simmer.

Cook for 5 minutes, stirring occasionally, until the lime zest is tender. Stir in the sugar, return to the boil and cook for a further 2–3 minutes until the sauce is syrupy, stirring every now and then. It will thicken a little as it cools too, so don't reduce too much. Remove from the heat and leave to cool. Spoon a little of the lime syrup onto each tart. If the syrup has cooled and thickened too much, add a little water and warm it for a few seconds on the hob. Serve with single cream.

Tip:
When you're ready to serve the tarts, lift them out of the tins very gently and slide them onto plates. You may need to use a palette knife to help you remove the tarts from the bases.

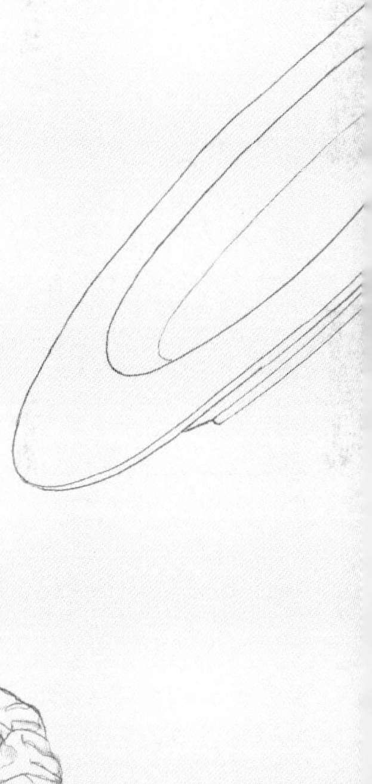

plate pies

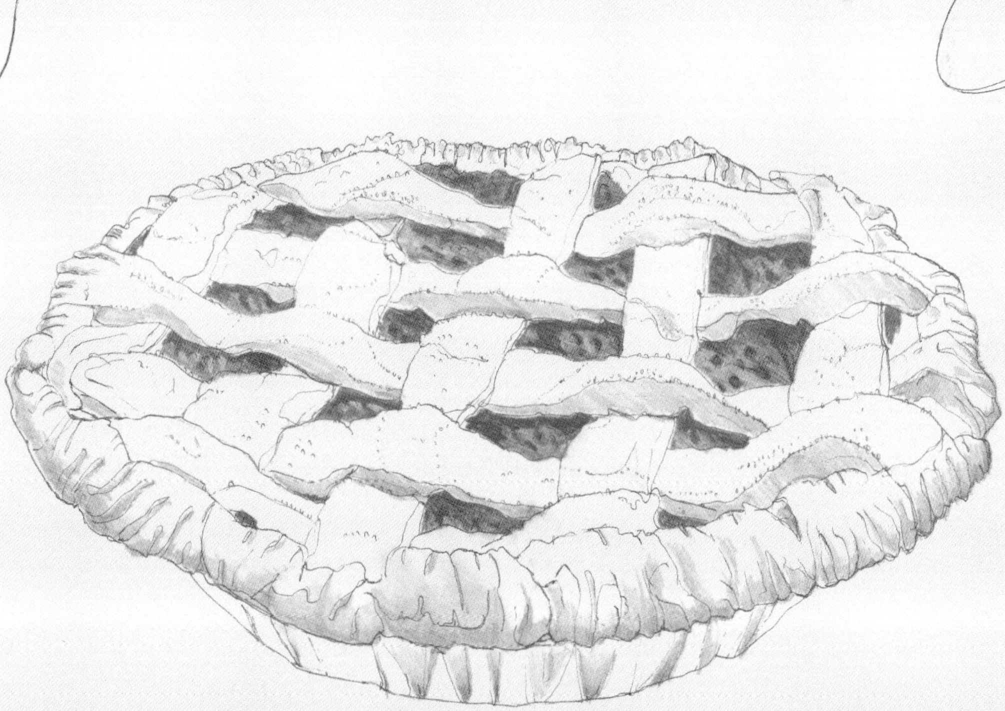

tuna & sweetcorn plate pie

This is like a tuna and sweetcorn sarnie in a pie and it tastes great hot or cold – brilliant for packed lunches and picnics. You'll probably have most of the ingredients in your store cupboard so it's a good standby supper.

Serves 6

2 x 185g cans tuna steak in sunflower oil, drained
198g can sweetcorn
75g mature Cheddar cheese, coarsely grated
6 spring onions, trimmed and finely sliced
5 heaped tbsp mayonnaise
freshly ground black pepper

shortcrust pastry
300g plain flour, plus extra for rolling
175g cold butter, cut into cubes
1 large egg, beaten with 1 tbsp cold water
beaten egg, to glaze

You'll need a 23–25cm pie plate

For the filling, tip the tuna and sweetcorn into a bowl and add the cheese, spring onions and mayonnaise. Season with lots of ground black pepper and mix well. Set aside until the pastry is made.

To make the pastry, put the flour and butter in a food processor and blitz on the pulse setting until the mixture resembles breadcrumbs. With the motor running, add the egg and water and process until the mixture is just beginning to come together in a ball. Remove and divide the dough into 2 slightly flattened balls. If you prefer to make your pastry by hand, see page 337.

Preheat the oven to 190°C/Fan 170°C/Gas 5. Roll out 1 ball of pastry on a lightly floured surface until slightly thicker than a £1 coin. Use it to line the pie plate, leaving the excess pastry hanging over the edge. If you find the pastry cracks or breaks as you line the plate, don't worry – just patch any gaps with the leftovers and press firmly to seal. Spoon the filling over the pastry base, leaving it nicely heaped up in the centre.

Roll out the remaining ball of pastry as before to make a lid for the pie. Brush the edge of the pastry case with beaten egg and gently lift the pastry lid over the filling. Press the edges firmly to seal, then trim and brush with beaten egg. Press a fork around the edge to seal. Use any pastry trimmings to decorate the pie if you fancy (see page 371). Brush the top of the pastry with beaten egg and place the pie on a baking tray. Bake for 30–35 minutes or until the pastry is golden brown and the filling is hot. Serve hot or cold with salad or vegetables.

When making pastry, keep lifting the mixture up out of the bowl to get as much air in the dough as possible.

corned beef & onion pie

When we were kids, every household had a old chipped plate, a bit brown around the edges, that was used for making plate pies. This recipe brings back childhood memories and we've even added the ketchup for you.

Serves 6

knob of butter
1 tbsp sunflower oil
1 large onion, sliced or chopped
2 celery sticks, trimmed, stringed and sliced
2 medium carrots, cut into rough 1cm dice
300g potatoes, preferably Maris Pipers, peeled and cut into rough 1cm dice
good squirt of tomato ketchup (1–2 tbsp)
340g can corned beef
freshly ground black pepper

shortcrust pastry
300g plain flour, plus extra for rolling
175g cold butter, cut into cubes
1 large egg, beaten with 1 tbsp cold water
beaten egg, to glaze

You'll need a 23–25cm pie plate

For the filling, melt the butter with the oil in a large non-stick frying pan. Add the onion, celery, carrots and potatoes. Cook over a low heat for about 15 minutes until the vegetables are softened and beginning to colour, stirring regularly. The carrots should retain a little 'bite'.

Add the ketchup and stir into the vegetables for a few seconds before adding the corned beef. Break the beef into chunky pieces with a wooden spoon and mix with the vegetables. Season with pepper – you shouldn't need salt as the corned beef is fairly salty anyway – and remove from the heat. Leave to cool for about 20 minutes. Preheat the oven to 190°C/Fan 170°C/Gas 5.

To make the pastry, put the flour and butter in a food processor and blitz on the pulse setting until the mixture resembles breadcrumbs. With the motor running, add the egg and water and process until the mixture is just beginning to come together in a ball. Remove and divide the dough into 2 slightly flattened balls. If you prefer to make your pastry by hand, see page 337.

Roll out 1 ball of pastry on a lightly floured surface until slightly thicker than a £1 coin. Use it to line the pie plate, leaving the excess pastry hanging over the edge.

Spoon the filling into the pastry base and spread it out to the sides. Roll out the remaining ball of pastry as before to make a lid for the pie. Brush the edge of the pastry case with beaten egg and gently lift the pastry lid over the filling. Press the edges firmly to seal, then trim and brush with beaten egg. Press a fork around the edge to seal. Brush the top of the pastry with egg, cut a cross in the centre and place on a baking tray. Bake for about 40 minutes or until the pastry is golden brown and the filling piping hot.

egg & bacon pie

This butch quiche needs plenty of salt and pepper so don't skimp on the seasoning. Serve warm or at room temperature to taste it at its best.

Serves 4

1 tbsp sunflower oil
8–10 smoked, rindless streaky bacon rashers
9 large eggs
4 tbsp whole milk
flaked sea salt
freshly ground black pepper

shortcrust pastry
300g plain flour, plus extra for rolling
175g cold butter, cut into cubes
1 large egg, beaten with 1 tbsp cold water
beaten egg, to glaze

You'll need a 23–25cm pie plate

To make the pastry, put the flour and butter in a food processor and blitz on the pulse setting until the mixture resembles breadcrumbs. With the motor running, add the beaten egg and water and process until the dough is just beginning to come together. Remove and divide into 2 slightly flattened balls. If you prefer to make your pastry by hand, see page 337.

Now start the filling. Heat the oil in a large non-stick frying pan. Cut the bacon rashers in half through the middle and add them to the pan. Fry for 4–5 minutes until the fat is golden and crisp, turning them once. Remove the bacon from the pan and leave to cool. Place a sturdy baking tray in the oven and preheat to 190°C/170°C/Gas 5.

Roll out 1 ball of the pastry on a lightly floured surface until slightly thicker than a £1 coin. Use it to line your pie plate, leaving any excess pastry overhanging the edge. Scatter the bacon loosely over the pastry. Gently break 6 of the eggs into the pastry case, spacing them evenly between the bacon rashers. Beat the remaining eggs with the milk and plenty of salt and pepper.

Slowly pour the beaten eggs into the pastry case, stopping every now and then to allow the egg mixture to find its way between the whole eggs and the bacon.

Roll out the remaining ball of pastry as before to make a lid for the pie. Brush the edge of the pastry case with beaten egg and gently lift the pastry lid over the filling. Press the edges firmly to seal, then trim and brush with beaten egg.

Bake the pie on the preheated baking tray for 45–55 minutes until pale golden brown and cooked through. Test by piercing the centre with a sharp knife – the filling should be just set. If it's still runny, put the pie back in the oven for a few minutes. Leave to stand for at least 15 minutes before serving.

broccoli & cauliflower cheese pie

A brassica bonanza – this is cauliflower cheese in a pie and makes a brilliant warming supper. You need about 200g (prepared weight) each of broccoli and of cauliflower.

Serves 6

1 medium sweet potato, peeled and cut into 1.5cm cubes
½ small cauliflower, trimmed and cut into small florets
1 small head broccoli, trimmed and cut into small florets
25g butter
25g plain flour
1 tsp English mustard powder
300ml milk
75g mature Cheddar cheese or Gruyère, coarsely grated
25g Parmesan cheese, finely grated
flaked sea salt
freshly ground black pepper

cheese shortcrust pastry
350g plain flour, plus extra for rolling
25g Parmesan cheese, finely grated, plus 2 tsp
200g cold butter, cut into cubes
1 large egg, beaten with 2 tbsp cold water
beaten egg, to glaze

You'll need a 23–25cm pie plate

Bring a large pan of water to the boil and add the sweet potato and cauliflower. Return to the boil and cook for 4 minutes. Add the broccoli, bring the water back to the boil and cook for 1 minute more. Drain in a colander under running water until completely cold. Drain well and return to the pan.

Melt the butter in a medium non-stick pan. Mix the flour and mustard powder in a bowl, then stir into the melted butter. Cook for about 30 seconds, then gradually add the milk, stirring constantly until the sauce is smooth and thick and all the milk is used. Add the cheeses and bubble gently for 2–3 minutes, while stirring. Season to taste, then remove from the heat and pour the white sauce over the vegetables. Toss gently, taking care not to break them up too much. Set the filling aside while you make the pastry.

Preheat the oven to 200°C/Fan 180°C/Gas 6. To make the pastry, put the flour, 25g of the Parmesan and the butter in a food processor and blitz on the pulse setting until the mixture resembles breadcrumbs. With the motor running, add the egg and water and process until the mixture begins to form a ball.

Divide the pastry in half and shape into 2 slightly flattened balls. Roll out 1 ball of the pastry on a lightly floured surface until it is slightly thicker than a £1 coin. Use it to line the pie plate, leaving any excess pastry overhanging the edge. Spoon the filling over the pastry base, heaping it up a little in the centre.

Roll out the remaining ball of pastry as before to make a lid for the pie. Brush the edge of the pastry case with beaten egg and gently lift the pastry lid over the filling. Press the edges firmly to seal, then trim and brush with beaten egg. Place on a baking tray and bake for 30 minutes. Sprinkle with the 2 teaspoons of Parmesan and return to the oven for a further 10 minutes or until the pastry is golden brown.

mince & onion plate pie

A simple but delicious pie that you just can't stop eating. Dave remembers that his mum used to make a pie to last a couple of days, but once everyone had sneaked just one more sliver it never stayed around that long.

Serves 6

750g good-quality minced beef
2 onions, chopped
1 beef stock cube
400ml boiling water
flaked sea salt
freshly ground black pepper
butter, for greasing the plate

pastry
60g butter, cut into cubes
60g lard, cut into cubes
450g plain flour, plus extra for rolling
2 tsp baking powder
½ tsp salt
1 large egg yolk
up to 125ml cold water
beaten egg, to glaze

You'll need a casserole dish and a 23–25cm pie plate

To make the pastry, rub the butter and lard into the flour, baking powder and salt until the mixture resembles breadcrumbs. Stir in the egg and as much of the water as you need to form a dough and knead very lightly. Divide the dough into 2 balls and flatten slightly.

Meanwhile, make the filling. This is Si's mam's method and it worked for several decades, so give it a go. Preheat the oven to 180°C/Fan 160°C/Gas 4. Mix the mince with the onions in a casserole dish. Dissolve the beef stock cube in the water and pour this over the meat. Season well, going heavy on the pepper. Put the lid on the casserole dish and cook in the preheated oven for 30 minutes.

Then, take the lid off and leave the meat to cook until most of the liquid has evaporated and the flavour has developed. This will take about another 30 minutes. Remove from the oven and leave to cool.

Preheat the oven to 180°C/Fan 160°C/Gas 4. Grease the pie plate with a splodge of butter. Roll out half the pastry on a lightly floured surface until slightly thicker than a £1 coin. Use it to line the pie plate, then add the meat filling, leaving a good rim of pastry. Brush the edges of the pastry with the beaten egg.

Roll out the rest of the pastry as before to make the lid and place it over the filling, sealing the edges together well. Cut a couple of slashes in the pastry lid to let out the steam, brush with beaten egg and bake for about 30 minutes until the pastry is golden.

scotch egg pie

A deconstructed Scotch egg in a pie – how good can it get? Use good bangers and nice fresh eggs and all the family will lap it up. If this doesn't scream brown sauce, nothing does.

Serves 6

6 medium eggs (fridge cold)
450g pack of good-quality pork sausages, any kind you fancy
75g fresh white breadcrumbs
freshly ground black pepper

shortcrust pastry
300g plain flour,
plus extra for rolling
100g cold butter, cut into cubes
75g cold lard, cut into cubes
1 large egg, beaten
with 1 tbsp cold water
beaten egg, to glaze

You'll need a 23–25cm pie plate

Bring a pan of water to the boil, add the eggs and boil for 9 minutes. Drain, then cool the eggs under cold running water.

Separate the sausages and untwist the skins. Squeeze the sausage meat into a bowl and add the breadcrumbs. Season with lots of black pepper and squish everything together with clean hands until well mixed.

Preheat the oven to 200°C/Fan 180°C/Gas 6. To make the pastry, blitz the flour, butter and lard in a food processor on the pulse setting until the mixture resembles breadcrumbs. With the motor running, add the egg and water and process until the mixture begins to form a ball.

Divide the pastry in half and shape into 2 flattened balls. Roll out 1 ball of pastry on a lightly floured surface until it is slightly thicker than a £1 coin. Use it to line your pie plate, leaving the excess pastry overhanging the edge. Spoon half of the sausage filling into the pastry base and spread to the sides.

Make 6 hollows in the filling with the back of a spoon, spacing them evenly around the dish. Peel the eggs and place one in each indentation, with the pointy end facing the centre of the pie. Cover with the remaining sausage meat.

Roll out the remaining pastry as before to make a lid for the pie. Brush the edge of the pastry case with beaten egg and gently lift the pastry lid over the filling. Press the edges firmly together, then trim and seal neatly. Brush the top of the pie with beaten egg, make a small hole in the centre and place on a baking tray. Bake for 45–55 minutes or until the pastry is golden brown and the filling is cooked right through to the centre. Serve hot or cold.

mincemeat lattice pie

There's more mincemeat than crust here and this pie is a brilliant way of using up your jars of Christmas mincemeat. Serve with a jug of good home-made custard (see page 310) and brighten up the grey days after the festive season.

Serves 8–10

2 x 410g jars of luxury mincemeat, such as cranberry and port (or see our home-made mincemeat on page 60)
granulated sugar or golden caster, to sprinkle

citrus shortcrust pastry
250g plain flour, plus extra for rolling
150g cold butter, cut into cubes
finely grated zest of ½ orange (optional)
1 large egg, beaten with 1 tbsp water

You'll need a 25cm pie plate

Preheat the oven to 200°C/Fan 180°C/Gas 6. Put a baking tray in the oven to warm up. To make the pastry, put the flour and butter into a food processor, add the orange zest, if using, and pulse until the mixture resembles breadcrumbs. Take a tablespoon of the beaten egg mixture and set it aside in a small dish to use for glazing. With the motor running, slowly add the remaining egg and blend until the mixture forms a ball.

Weigh the pastry and reserve 150g of the dough for the lattice top. Roll the rest of the pastry into a ball and flatten slightly. Place it on a lightly floured surface and roll it out until slightly thicker than a £1 coin. Use the pastry to line your pie plate, pressing it well into the base and trimming the excess with a sharp knife to leave a neat edge.

Spread the mincemeat over the pastry, trying to keep it as even as possible. Brush the pastry edge with beaten egg. Roll out the remainder of the pastry as before, and cut into 1cm-wide strips. Place the strips across the top of the pie in 2 directions to form a criss-cross lattice pattern, spacing them evenly. Brush the pastry strips with more egg and sprinkle with a little sugar.

Place the pie on the hot baking tray and cook for 30–35 minutes or until the pastry is golden brown. Leave the tart to cool for about 5 minutes before serving.

fresh blackcurrant & mint tart

Fresher than a dewy meadow in the morning sunlight, this simple blackcurrant tart is summer on a plate. Delicious served hot or cold.

Serves 6

350g fresh blackcurrants
2 tsp cornflour
100g caster sugar
200ml crème fraiche
12 small mint leaves (optional)

sweet shortcrust pastry
200g plain flour,
plus extra for rolling
1 tbsp caster sugar
125g cold butter, cut into cubes
1 medium egg

You'll need a 25cm pie plate

To make the pastry, put the flour, sugar and butter in a food processor and blitz on the pulse setting until the mixture resembles breadcrumbs. With the motor running, add the egg and process until the mixture is just beginning to come together in a ball. Remove and shape into a slightly flattened ball. If you prefer to make your pastry by hand, see page 337.

Preheat the oven to 200°C/Fan 180°C/Gas 6. Roll out the pastry on a lightly floured surface until it is about 25cm in diameter and slightly thicker than a £1 coin. Use the pastry to line your pie plate. Crimp the edges decoratively and chill for 30 minutes.

Toss three-quarters of the blackcurrants with the cornflour and all but a tablespoon of the sugar. Scatter over the centre of the pastry, then top with the remaining blackcurrants. Sprinkle both the pastry and the blackcurrants with the remaining sugar. Bake for 25–30 minutes or until the blackcurrants are softened and the pastry is cooked and lightly browned.

Remove the tart from the oven and leave to stand for 10 minutes. Top with spoonfuls of the crème fraiche and serve immediately, decorated with fresh mint leaves. Alternatively, leave until the tart cools and the crème fraiche sets, then scatter mint leaves on top and serve cold.

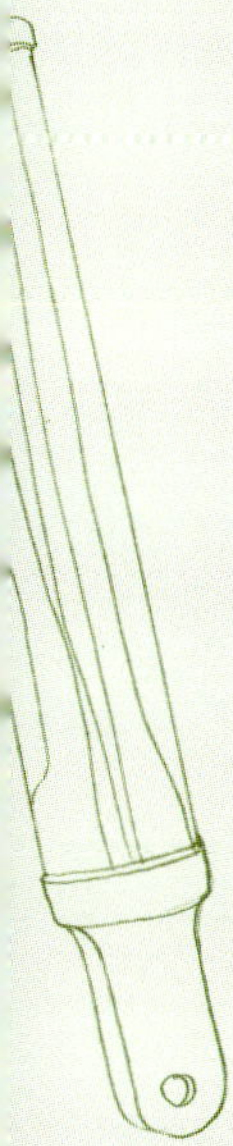

potato-topped pies

a truly fabulous fish pie

This is a decadent fish pie that's packed with flavour and uses three different types of fish in a rich-tasting dill sauce. It does take a while to put together, but there's nothing difficult – a good pie to make on a rainy Saturday afternoon.

Serves 6

600ml whole milk
1 medium onion, cut into sixths keeping the root end intact
2 bay leaves
500g thick white fish fillets, such as cod, haddock or pollock
500g smoked haddock fillet (undyed, if possible)
500g thick salmon fillet
6 medium eggs (optional)
75g butter
75g plain flour
3 tbsp white wine
100ml double cream
small bunch of fresh dill (about 15g)
flaked sea salt
freshly ground black pepper

cheesy mash topping
1.25kg medium potatoes, peeled and cut into even-sized pieces
75g butter, cut into cubes
75ml double cream
150g mature Cheddar cheese, coarsely grated
flaked sea salt
freshly ground pepper

You'll need a 2–2.5-litre ovenproof dish

To make the filling, pour the milk into a large pan and add the onion wedges and bay leaves. Season with salt and pepper. Add the fish fillets to the pan and bring to a very gentle simmer. Cover with a lid and cook for 2 minutes. Remove the pan from the heat and leave to stand and infuse for 5 minutes until the fish is almost cooked. Drain the fish through a colander into a bowl, then pour the milk into a jug.

Next, make the cheesy mash. Put the potatoes in a large saucepan and cover with cold water. Bring to the boil, then reduce the heat and simmer for 15 minutes or until the potatoes are soft. Drain, then return them to the pan and mash with the butter, cream and three-quarters of the grated cheese. Season to taste and set aside.

Preheat the oven to 200°C/Fan 180°C/Gas 6. To cook the eggs, if using, fill a medium saucepan a third full with water and bring to the boil. Gently add the eggs to the water and cook for 9 minutes. Drain in a colander under running water for a couple of minutes, then transfer to a bowl of very cold water and set aside. Cooling the eggs quickly like this helps to prevent a ring from forming around the cooked yolk.

Now finish the filling. Melt the butter in a medium saucepan and stir in the flour. Cook for a few seconds, then gradually add the infused milk and the wine and cream. Stir over a medium heat for 5 minutes until the sauce is smooth and thick. Season with salt and black pepper. Remove the pan from the heat and snip the dill fronds into the sauce with sharp scissors – or place the dill on a board and roughly chop before stirring into the sauce. Discard the stalks. Peel the eggs and cut them in half.

Continued overleaf...

a truly fabulous fish pie continued...

Spoon a third of the sauce into the base of the ovenproof dish. Scatter half the fish fillets over the sauce, breaking them into good chunky pieces as you go and discarding the skin, onion and bay leaves. Place half the eggs, if using, on top and pour over another third of the sauce. Continue with the layers, finishing with sauce.

Spoon the potato over the fish mixture, starting at the edges before making your way into the centre. Fluff up the potato with a fork and sprinkle with the remaining cheese. Place the dish on a baking tray and bake in the centre of the oven for about 45 minutes or until the top is golden and the filling is bubbling.

everyday fish pie

Everyone loves a good fish pie. This recipe is a lot quicker to make than our fabulous version and is almost as delicious – a great midweek supper.

Serves 4–5

400ml whole milk
1 small onion, thickly sliced
2 bay leaves
500g skinned thick white fish fillets, such as cod, haddock or pollock
40g butter
40g plain flour
150g frozen peas
200g large peeled prawns, thawed if frozen
flaked sea salt
freshly ground black pepper

mash topping

800g medium potatoes, peeled and cut into even-sized pieces
50g butter, cubed
3–5 tbsp milk
flaked sea salt
freshly ground pepper

You'll need a 1.5-litre ovenproof dish

To make the filling, pour the milk into a large pan and add the sliced onion and the bay leaves. Season with salt and pepper. Place the fish fillets in the pan and bring to a very gentle simmer, then cover and cook for 2 minutes. Remove from the heat and leave to stand and infuse for 20 minutes. Drain the fish through a colander into a bowl, then pour the milk into a jug.

Meanwhile, make the mash. Half fill a large saucepan with cold water. Add the potatoes and bring to the boil, then reduce the heat and simmer for 15 minutes or until the potatoes are soft. Drain the potatoes and return them to the pan, then mash with the butter and milk. Season to taste. Preheat the oven to 200°C/Fan 180°C/ Gas 6.

Now finish the filling. Melt the butter in a medium saucepan and stir in the flour. Cook for a few seconds, then gradually add the infused milk, stirring over a medium heat for 3–4 minutes until the sauce is smooth and thick. Stir in the peas and season with salt and black pepper.

Spread a third of the sauce into the base of the ovenproof dish. Scatter half the fish fillets over the sauce, breaking them into chunky pieces as you go and discarding the onion and bay leaves. Drop half the prawns on top and pour over another third of the sauce. Continue with the layers and finish with the final third of sauce.

Spoon the potato over the fish mixture and rough up the surface with a fork. Place the dish on a baking tray and bake in the centre of the oven for about 25 minutes or until the top is golden and the filling is bubbling.

We grew up eating pies and we love every one of them.

sausage & bean breakfast pie

Now this is something we wish our mums had made when we were kids – a real family all-day breakfast of a pie. We love it. Get some of your favourite sausages, open a tin of beans and you're almost there. Enjoy!

Serves 4

850g medium potatoes (preferably Maris Pipers)
3 tbsp sunflower oil
8 good-quality pork sausages
1 medium onion, finely sliced
415g can baked beans

You'll need a 1-litre ovenproof dish

Put the potatoes in a large saucepan and cover with cold water. Bring to the boil, then reduce the heat slightly and simmer for 15 minutes or until only just tender – they need to be firm enough to cut into chunks. If your potatoes are large, you'll need to cut them into similar-sized pieces so they cook evenly. Preheat the oven to 200°C/Fan 180°C/Gas 6.

While the potatoes are cooking, heat a tablespoon of the oil in a large non-stick frying pan. Fry the sausages gently for 10 minutes until nice and brown, turning every so often. Add the sliced onion and cook for 2–3 minutes more until golden, while stirring. Tip the sausages and onion into a shallow, flameproof dish and pour over the beans. Drain the potatoes and put them on a chopping board.

Return the frying pan to the hob and add the remaining oil. Cut the potatoes into chunky pieces and fry them in the oil for 2–3 minutes, turning regularly until golden. Scatter the potatoes over the sausages and beans. Bake for 15–20 minutes until the potatoes are crisp and brown and the beans are hot.

cottage pie with cheesy mash

Who doesn't like cottage pie? We don't see any hands coming up. This is one of our very favourite pies and a dish loved by families up and down the land. Simple to make and fab to eat any day of the week. Don't forget the ketchup!

Serves 4–5

1 tbsp sunflower oil
1 large onion, chopped
2 celery sticks, stringed and chopped
2 medium-large carrots, peeled and cut into 1cm chunks
2 garlic cloves, finely chopped
500g lean minced beef
150ml red wine
2 tbsp plain flour
250ml beef stock (fresh or made with stock cube)
250ml cold water
2 tbsp tomato purée
½ tsp mixed dried herbs
1 bay leaf
splash of Worcestershire sauce
flaked sea salt
freshly ground black pepper

cheesy mash topping

800g medium potatoes, peeled and cut into even-sized pieces
40g butter, cubed
3 tbsp milk
100g Cheddar cheese, grated
flaked sea salt
freshly ground pepper

You'll need a 1.2-litre ovenproof dish

Heat the sunflower oil in a large deep sauté pan or saucepan and gently fry the onion, celery and carrots for 8 minutes or until the onion has softened and is lightly coloured. Add the garlic and cook for 2 minutes more. Stir all the vegetables occasionally to prevent them from becoming too brown.

Tip the mince into the pan and cook with the vegetables for about 5 minutes or until no pinkness remains, stirring regularly to break up the meat. Pour the wine into the pan and cook until the liquid has reduced by about a half, then sprinkle in the flour and stir well for a couple of minutes.

Gradually stir the beef stock into the pan. Add 250ml of cold water, the tomato purée, herbs and bay leaf. Bring to a gentle simmer, cover and cook over a low heat for 25–30 minutes, stirring occasionally, until the mince is tender and the sauce has thickened. If it starts to look too dry, add some more stock or water. Season with Worcestershire sauce and salt and pepper to taste.

Remove from the heat and spoon the mince mixture into your ovenproof dish. Leave to stand while you get the mash ready. Half fill a large saucepan with cold water. Add the potatoes and bring to the boil, then reduce the heat and simmer for 15 minutes or until the potatoes are soft. Drain the potatoes, return them to the pan, then mash with the butter and milk until smooth and creamy and season to taste. Preheat the oven to 200°C/Fan 180°/Gas 6.

Spoon the potato over the mince mixture, working around the edge before heading towards the middle. When all the mince is covered, rough up the surface with a fork and place the dish on a baking tray. Bake for about 25 minutes or until the potatoes are golden brown and the filling is bubbling.

spiced smashed potato pie

Packed full of great flavours and with a touch of Middle Eastern promise, this is a veggie version of cottage pie. It tastes so good you won't even notice there's no meat.

Serves 6

6–8 tbsp mild olive oil
1 large aubergine, trimmed and cut into 1cm slices
1 red onion, finely chopped
1 medium sweet potato, peeled and cut into rough 1cm chunks
1 red pepper, deseeded and cut into rough 2cm chunks
2 garlic cloves, crushed
1 tbsp rose harissa paste
6 tomatoes, skinned and chopped
200ml red wine
2 bay leaves
1 tbsp cornflour, mixed to a paste with 1 tbsp cold water
flaked sea salt
freshly ground black pepper

potato topping
1kg medium potatoes (preferably Maris Pipers)
4 tbsp mild olive oil
1 tsp cumin seeds
flaked sea salt
freshly ground black pepper

You'll need a 2-litre shallow ovenproof dish – a lasagne dish is ideal

Peel the potatoes for the topping and cut them in half or into quarters if large – the pieces should be roughly the same size. Put them in a saucepan, cover with cold water and bring to the boil. Cook for 15 minutes. When the potatoes are done, drain and leave until they are cool enough to handle.

Meanwhile, start making the filling. Heat 2 tablespoons of the oil in a large non-stick frying pan and fry the aubergine slices until golden brown on both sides, turning once. Drain the slices on kitchen roll. Fry the aubergine in 2 batches, adding more oil when the pan begins to look dry.

Add another tablespoon of oil to the pan and fry the onion, sweet potato and pepper for 10 minutes, stirring regularly until softened. Add the garlic and harissa paste and cook for 2 minutes more, while stirring. Tip the chopped tomatoes into the pan, add the wine and bay leaves and season with salt and pepper. Bring the mixture to a simmer and cook for 8–10 minutes longer, or until the tomatoes are softened. Stir in the cornflour paste and cook for another minute until thickened. Remove from the heat and transfer half the mixture to your dish. Arrange a layer of aubergines over the tomato mixture and top with the rest of the mixture.

Preheat the oven to 200°C/Fan 180°C/Gas 6. Tip the potatoes into a bowl and pour over the olive oil. Season with salt and lots of ground black pepper. Roughly crush the potatoes with a fork and spoon them on top of the filling. Sprinkle with cumin seeds. Bake for 25–30 minutes or until the potato topping is golden brown and the filling is bubbling.

bikers' lamb hot pot

A hot pot that thinks it's a pie – this is our variation on a Lancashire classic that's guaranteed to make you clog dance with joy. We love these great traditional flavours and the golden crunchy potato topping.

Serves 4–6

800g lamb neck fillets
2–3 tbsp sunflower oil
2 medium onions, sliced
4 medium carrots, peeled and thickly sliced
3 tbsp plain flour
500ml lamb stock (made with 1 stock cube)
1 tbsp fresh thyme leaves or ½ tsp dried thyme
1 sprig of rosemary or ½ tsp dried rosemary
2 tbsp Worcestershire sauce
flaked sea salt
freshly ground black pepper

potato topping
4 medium potatoes (about 800g)
flaked sea salt
freshly ground black pepper

You'll need a medium casserole dish, with a lid, that holds at least 2.4 litres

Cut the lamb into rough 4cm chunks, trimming away any really hard fat or gristle. You need to leave quite a bit of fat to keep the meat succulent. Season the meat generously with salt and pepper.

Heat 2 tablespoons of the oil in a large non-stick frying pan and fry the lamb in 2 batches over a medium-high heat until nicely browned on all sides. Transfer the meat to your casserole dish.

Return the pan to the heat and cook the onions and carrots for 4–5 minutes or until the onions are lightly browned. Keep stirring and add a little extra oil if the pan begins to look dry. Tip the veg into the dish with the lamb, sprinkle with the flour and toss everything together well.

Pour over the stock and add the thyme leaves, rosemary and Worcestershire sauce. Stir together. Preheat the oven to 170°C/Fan 150°C/Gas 3½. Peel the potatoes and cut them into 5mm slices. Arrange them on top of the lamb, overlapping and layering where necessary. Season with salt and pepper and cover with the lid.

Bake for 1 hour, then remove the lid and bake for a further 45–60 minutes or until the potatoes are nicely browned and the lamb is tender. Check the meat with the point of a knife – it should slide in easily. Serve with freshly cooked greens.

spicy bean hot pot

Big flavours for a big pie, this hot pot pie has a topping of sliced potatoes over a scrumptious array of vegetables, beans and spices; a feast for all – vegetarian or not.

Serves 6

2 sweet potatoes (about 450g)
2 medium courgettes
2 tbsp sunflower or olive oil
2 medium onions, halved and sliced
2 garlic cloves, crushed
1 tsp hot chilli powder
1 tsp ground cumin
½ tsp smoked paprika
400g can chopped tomatoes
2 tbsp tomato purée
2 bay leaves
400g can red kidney beans, drained and rinsed
400g can cannellini beans, drained and rinsed
1 tbsp cornflour, mixed to a paste with 1 tbsp cold water
flaked sea salt
freshly ground black pepper

potato topping

600g potatoes (preferably Maris Pipers)
50g butter, melted
flaked sea salt
freshly ground black pepper

You'll need a 2.5-litre shallow ovenproof dish – a lasagne dish is ideal

Peel the sweet potatoes and cut them into rough 2.5cm chunks. Trim the courgettes and cut into 1cm slices.

Heat the oil in a large non-stick saucepan or deep frying pan. Gently fry the onions for 5 minutes, stirring often, until softened and lightly browned. Add the garlic, chilli powder, cumin and paprika. Cook for 1 minute, stirring.

Tip the tomatoes into the pan, refill the can with water and add this to the pan. Stir in the tomato purée, bay leaves and sweet potatoes. Bring to the boil and cook for 15 minutes. Stir in the beans and courgettes and bring the mixture back to a simmer. Cook for a further 3 minutes, stirring. Add the cornflour paste and stir until the sauce has thickened. Season to taste with salt and pepper.

Preheat the oven to 220°C/Fan 200°C/Gas 7. Peel and thinly slice the potatoes. Spoon the vegetable mixture into your ovenproof dish and top with overlapping slices of potato. Brush the potatoes with melted butter and season with salt and pepper. Bake for about 35 minutes until the potatoes are tender and lightly browned and the filling is bubbling.

super simple mini-quiches

We bake our yummy little quichelets in mini-muffin tins as the small but deep holes mean that the proportion of pastry to filling is well balanced. If the cases are too shallow, you end up with a mouthful of pastry and not much else.

Makes 24

basic egg filling
Makes enough for 24
2 large eggs
200ml crème fraiche
1 tbsp finely chopped parsley
flaked sea salt
freshly ground black pepper

crispy bacon and Gruyère
Enough for 12 mini-quiches
1 tbsp sunflower oil
½ small onion, finely chopped
100g smoked bacon lardons, diced
25g Gruyère or mature Cheddar cheese, finely grated

garlic and mushroom
Enough for 12 mini-quiches
knob of butter
2 tsp sunflower oil
100g chestnut mushrooms, chopped
2 spring onions, very finely sliced
1 garlic clove, crushed

pastry
250g plain flour, plus extra for rolling
150g cold butter, cut into cubes
25g Parmesan cheese, finely grated
1 large egg, beaten

You'll need 2 x 12-hole mini-muffin tins

To make the pastry, put the flour, butter and Parmesan in a food processor and blitz on the pulse setting until the mixture resembles breadcrumbs. With the motor running, add the beaten egg and blend until the mixture starts to come together. Gather the pastry into a ball and flatten slightly. Roll out on a floured surface and cut into 6.5cm rounds using a biscuit cutter. Use to line the mini-muffin tins and chill for 30 minutes.

To make the basic egg filling, whisk the eggs in a bowl until just combined – don't over whisk or you'll get too much air into the mixture. Stir in the crème fraiche and parsley, then add a good pinch of salt and plenty of pepper. Set aside. Preheat the oven to 200°C/Fan 180°C/Gas 6.

To make the crispy bacon and Gruyère filling, heat the oil in a non-stick frying pan and fry the bacon until it's starting to crisp. Add the onion and cook for a couple of minutes longer until softened, stirring regularly. Leave to cool. Divide the bacon and onion between 12 of the pastry cases. Cover with basic egg filling, using about half of the mixture, and sprinkle with the cheese. Bake for 18–20 minutes or until the pastry is nicely browned and the filling is set. Serve warm or cold.

To make the garlic and mushroom filling, melt the butter with the oil in a non-stick frying pan and stir-fry the mushrooms over a high heat for 2–3 minutes until golden. Add the spring onions and garlic and cook for 30 seconds more. Leave to cool. Divide the mushrooms between the rest of the pastry cases, then cover with the rest of the basic egg filling. Bake for 18–20 minutes or until the pastry is browned and the filling is set. Serve warm or cold.

These little tarts freeze beautifully so can be made a month ahead and reheated from frozen. Remove from the tins while warm.

the best party vol-au-vents

Our special square-shaped vol-au-vents are much easier to cut and fill than the round sort, and these are a couple of our favourite fillings. You can get the little beauties ready in advance, then pop them in the oven when your guests arrive.

Makes 30

chicken and tarragon (fills 30 vol-au-vents)
2 roasted boneless chicken breasts, skin removed
1 tbsp fresh tarragon leaves
1 tbsp white wine

smoked haddock and prawn (fills 30 vol-au-vents)
225g smoked haddock fillet
100g peeled, cooked prawns, thawed and drained
2 tbsp finely sliced chives

basic sauce
300ml whole milk
½ small onion, cut into quarters
2 bay leaves
3 sprigs of fresh thyme
25g butter
25g plain flour
5 tbsp crème fraiche
flaked sea salt
freshly ground black pepper

pastry
500g block of ready-made puff pastry
plain flour, for rolling

Preheat the oven to 200°C/Fan 180°C/Gas 6. Roll out the puff pastry on a lightly floured surface to make a rectangle about 32 x 32cm and 5mm thick. Trim the edges to make a 30cm square. Using a sharp knife, cut the square into 30 squares, each 6 x 6cm. Then score a smaller square inside each one, 75mm away from the edges, taking care not to cut all of the way through. This will allow you to remove the centre to make room for the filling. Place the squares on a large baking tray lined with baking parchment and bake for 18–20 minutes or until puffed up and golden brown. Remove from the oven, allow to cool, then carefully remove the central square of pastry.

To make the chicken and tarragon filling, cut the chicken into small pieces. Make the basic sauce, allow it to cool, then stir the chicken, tarragon and wine into the cooled sauce.

To make the smoked haddock and prawn filling, put the haddock in a pan with the 300ml of milk you'll use to make the basic sauce, bring to a simmer and leave to infuse. Remove the skin from the haddock and leave to cool, then use the cooking milk to make the basic sauce. Flake the fish into the cooled sauce, removing any missed bones, and stir in the prawns and chives.

To make the basic sauce, pour the milk into a saucepan and add the onion and herbs. Bring to a gentle simmer, then take off the heat and leave to infuse for 10 minutes. Pass the milk through a sieve into a jug and discard the onion and herbs. Melt the butter in a non-stick saucepan over a low heat. Add the flour and cook for a few seconds, stirring constantly. Slowly add the infused milk, stirring well. Cook for 1–2 minutes, stirring, until the sauce is smooth and thick. Season well, remove from the heat and stir in the crème fraiche. Cover with clingfilm and leave to cool.

Divide your chosen filling between the cases. Cover and chill for up to 24 hours before cooking. Bake on a baking tray in a preheated oven at 200°C/Fan 180°C/Gas 6 for 8–10 minutes until bubbling.

prawn & water chestnut rolls

These spicy little mouthfuls are quite easy to make once you get the hang of it and they look very fancy – one of our favourite party snacks.

Makes 10

200g raw shelled king prawns
50g canned water chestnuts, drained and sliced
1 tbsp finely grated fresh root ginger
4 spring onions, trimmed and finely sliced
2 small garlic cloves, crushed
2 tbsp finely chopped fresh coriander
2 pinches dried chilli flakes
2 tbsp cornflour
10 small rice flour pancakes (about 16cm in diameter) or spring roll wrappers
flaked sea salt
freshly ground black pepper
sunflower oil, for frying
sweet chilli dipping sauce and lime wedges, to serve

Cut down the back of each prawn with a small, sharp knife and open it out slightly. Remove the black vein with the point of your knife and chuck it away.

Chop the prawns fairly finely and put them in a bowl with the water chestnuts, ginger, spring onions, garlic, coriander and chilli flakes. Sprinkle over the cornflour, season and mix together well.

Soak 2 rice flour pancakes or spring roll wrappers in a large bowl of cold water for 1–2 minutes until soft, or as instructed on the packet. Drain and transfer them to a clean, damp tea towel. Do not soak for too long or they might tear when you come to roll them.

Place 2 heaped tablespoons of the mixture about 2cm up from the bottom of a disc. Spread it in a line from one side to the other, leaving a 2cm gap at each end. Fold the sides over the edges of the filling and then roll up from the bottom to enclose the filling completely. Transfer to a plate dampened with a little water to stop the rolls sticking. They should feel a little tacky but not wet. Repeat with the other disc, then set these rolls aside while you prepare the rest.

Pour oil into a large wok to a depth of about 1.5cm and heat until the oil reaches 180°C – when the oil is at the right temperature, a cube of white bread will brown in 15 seconds. Fry half the rolls for 4–5 minutes, turning frequently, until the wrappers are pale golden brown and the prawns are fully cooked and pink throughout. Do not allow the oil to overheat and never leave hot oil unattended. If you prefer, you can fry the rolls in an electric deep-fat fryer.

Remove the rolls from the pan with a slotted spoon and drain them on kitchen roll. Keep the first batch warm on a baking tray in a low oven while you fry the rest. Serve with sweet chilli dipping sauce and lime wedges.

spiced vegetable samosas

You can prepare these up two days in advance. After frying, allow the samosas to cool completely then cover and keep them in the fridge for up to 48 hours. Reheat on a baking tray in a preheated oven at 200°C/Fan 180°C/Gas 6 for 8–10 minutes.

Makes 28

2 tbsp sunflower oil, plus extra for frying
1 small onion, finely chopped
2 garlic cloves, finely chopped
1 medium potato, peeled and diced
2 tsp garam masala
½ tsp ground turmeric
½ tsp black mustard seeds
1 medium sweet potato, peeled and diced
200ml vegetable stock (made with ½ vegetable stock cube)
25g frozen peas
flaked sea salt
freshly ground black pepper

samosa pastry

250g plain flour, plus extra for rolling
1 tsp fine sea salt
1 tbsp sunflower oil
1 large egg, separated
1 heaped tbsp finely chopped fresh coriander
9 tbsp warm water

To make the filling, heat the 2 tablespoons of oil in a non-stick frying pan. Add the onion, garlic and potato and cook for 5 minutes until the onion is soft but not coloured. Sprinkle over the spices and fry for a minute more, while stirring.

Tip the sweet potato pieces into the pan and add the stock. Bring to a gentle simmer and cook for about 10 minutes, or until the liquid has evaporated, stirring occasionally. Gently stir in the peas, being careful not to break up the potato. Remove from the heat, season well and leave to cool.

To make the pastry, mix the flour and the salt in a large bowl. Pour in the oil, add the egg yolk and mix with clean fingertips until you have a crumb-like consistency. Stir in the coriander and mix well. Add the water until the mixture has combined to form a ball and knead briefly with clean hands.

Roll out onto a well-floured surface to the thickness of a £1 coin. Cut 14 x 10cm circles using a biscuit cutter, re-rolling as necessary, then cut each circle in half. Place a heaped teaspoon of the mixture in the centre of a semi-circle. Paint around the mixture with the egg white. Bring one straight edge over to meet the other and tuck under where they join to create a cone shape, pressing the edges together as you go. Pinch the curved edge together to seal the filling inside. Repeat until you have made 28 samosas.

Pour oil into a deep frying pan or wok to a depth of about 1.5cm and place over a medium-high heat for a couple of minutes. Never leave hot oil unattended. Using a slotted spoon, lower 7 or 8 of the samosas into the hot oil, where they should immediately begin to sizzle. Cook for 3–4 minutes, turning every minute or so until the pastry is golden and lightly puffed. Remove with a slotted spoon and drain on kitchen roll. Continue until all the samosas are cooked. Alternatively, you can cook the samosas in an electric deep-fat fryer set at 180°C.

Mini-tarts
are the ideal
no-fork food for
parties. Fill with
whatever takes
your fancy.

our cracking canapés

Home-made canapés are so much nicer than the shop-bought ones and here are some of our favourite filling ideas. You can make the pastry cases ahead of time and fill on the day so these couldn't be easier – especially if you raid your local deli.

Makes 12 small pastry cases and each recipe fills 12

ploughman's
1 crisp eating apple
2 tsp fresh lemon juice
60g Cheddar cheese
4 tbsp mayonnaise
1 celery stick
3 spring onions
6 cherry tomatoes, halved
4 tbsp pickle or chutney

smoked salmon
100g smoked salmon slices
5 tbsp crème fraiche
fresh dill sprigs

prawn cocktail
baby gem lettuce leaves
200g fresh prawn cocktail (from the chiller cabinet)
fresh chives, chopped

bacon and egg
2 tsp sunflower oil
4 thin rashers rindless streaky bacon
2 large eggs, hard-boiled
4 tbsp mayonnaise
6 quails' eggs, hard-boiled
fresh rocket leaves
sea salt and black pepper

shortcrust pastry
150g plain flour
100g cold butter, cut into cubes
1 medium egg, beaten

You'll need a 12-hole shallow bun tin

To make the pastry, put the flour and butter in a food processor and blitz on the pulse setting until the mixture resembles breadcrumbs. With the motor running, add the beaten egg and blend until the mixture starts to come together in a ball. Shape the dough into a ball and flatten slightly. Roll out on a floured surface and cut into 7cm rounds, using a biscuit cutter. Use to line a 12-hole shallow bun tin, then prick the pastry and freeze for 1 hour.

Preheat the oven to 200°C/Fan 180°C/Gas 6. Bake the pastry cases for 15–18 minutes until lightly browned and cooked through. Remove from the oven and leave to cool – once cool, they can be stored in an airtight tin for up 3 days.

To make the ploughman's filling, quarter, core and thinly slice the apple, then toss lightly in lemon juice to stop it turning brown. Cut the cheese into small wedges and trim and slice the celery and spring onions. Spoon a little mayonnaise into each pastry case and arrange small pieces of cheese, sliced celery, apple, spring onion and tomatoes on top. Add a half a teaspoon of pickle or chutney and garnish with celery leaves.

To make the smoked salmon filling, finely chop 65g of the smoked salmon and mix with the crème fraiche and a tablespoon of finely snipped dill. Divide between the pastry cases. Cut the rest of the smoked salmon into strips and curl on top of the crème fraiche mixture. Garnish with sprigs of dill.

To make the prawn cocktail filling, tear the lettuce leaves into small pieces and put some in each pastry case. Top with spoonfuls of the prawn cocktail, then garnish with chives.

To make the bacon and egg filling, heat the oil in a small non-stick frying pan. Cut the bacon into 5cm lengths and fry over a medium heat for 1–2 minutes on each side until crisp. Drain on kitchen roll. Peel the hard-boiled eggs. Mash the hens' eggs with mayonnaise and seasoning to taste, then spoon into the pastry cases. Cut the quails' eggs in half and place on top. Add a strip of bacon to each one and garnish with rocket leaves.

little lemon meringue tartlets

We'll take any chance to eat lemon meringue pie and we think these individual versions are a belter of an idea. We suggest you hide a couple away in the kitchen to eat while you're doing the washing up later – your guests won't leave any for you.

Makes 12

125g good-quality lemon curd
1 large egg white
50g caster sugar
½ tsp cornflour
a few drops of vanilla extract
1 tsp caster sugar, preferably golden

sweet shortcrust pastry
150g plain flour, plus extra for rolling
100g cold butter, cut into cubes
1 tbsp caster sugar
finely grated zest of ½ lemon
1 medium egg, beaten
beaten egg, to glaze

You'll need a 12-hole deep bun tin

To make the pastry, put the flour, butter, sugar and lemon zest in a food processor and blitz on the pulse setting until the mixture resembles breadcrumbs. With the motor running, slowly add the beaten egg and blend until the mixture is starting to come together in a ball. Shape the dough into a ball and flatten slightly.

Roll out the dough on a floured surface until it is about the thickness of a £1 coin. Using a biscuit cutter, cut out 8cm rounds and use them to line a 12-hole bun tin. Prick the pastry very lightly and freeze for 1 hour.

Preheat the oven to 200°C/Fan 180°C/Gas 6. Bake the pastry cases for 15–18 minutes until lightly browned and cooked through. Remove from the oven and leave to cool for 10 minutes. Spoon the lemon curd into the pastry cases.

Whisk the egg white in a clean bowl until stiff peaks form. Gradually add the sugar and cornflour, whisking constantly until smooth and glossy. Whisk in the vanilla extract. Using 2 teaspoons, spoon the meringue on top of the lemon filling and sprinkle the teaspoon of caster sugar on top.

Bake in the oven for 5 minutes or until the meringue is set and very lightly browned. Leave to cool before serving.

chocolate & hazelnut filo rolls

We had some leftover filo one day and came up with this brilliant way of using it up. Served with a bowl of vanilla cream, these crunchy little rolls filled with Nutella make a fab sweet treat to hand round at a party.

Makes 12

chocolate filling
250g chocolate and hazelnut spread, such as Nutella
sifted icing sugar, for dusting

vanilla cream dip
100ml double cream
1 tbsp caster sugar
½ tsp vanilla extract

pastry
25g butter
3 filo pastry sheets (each about 32 x 38cm), thawed if frozen

Preheat the oven to 200°C/Fan 180°C/Gas 6. Melt the butter in a small saucepan, then remove from the heat.

Take a sheet of filo pastry and cut it into 4 evenly sized rectangles, each measuring about 16 x 19cm. Take a rectangle and brush it lightly with melted butter.

With a long side facing you, spoon a level tablespoon of the chocolate spread across the filo rectangle, 2cm up from the bottom of the rectangle and about 2cm in from both sides. Try to keep it as even as possible.

Fold in the 2 short sides of the pastry over the filling to seal the chocolate spread into the parcel. Roll up from the long side closest to you, fully enclosing the filling. The chocolate filling will be encased in 3 layers of pastry by the time you've finished. Place the roll on a baking tray lined with baking parchment.

Continue to make 11 more rolls in exactly the same way. Brush the rolls with a little more melted butter, then bake for about 10 minutes until the pastry is light golden brown. Transfer the rolls to a rack and leave to cool. At this point, the rolls can be put in an airtight tin lined with kitchen roll and stored for up to 2 days.

To make the vanilla cream dip, whip the cream very lightly with the sugar and vanilla extract. Spoon into a small bowl. Arrange the chocolate filo rolls on a serving plate with the vanilla cream dip placed alongside them. Sprinkle with a little sifted icing sugar before serving.

fresh fruit tartlets

These look very glam and your friends will be well impressed. In fact, they're a cinch to make and you can even put them together with scraps of leftover pastry. Add the creamy filling and jewel-like berries and there'll be oohs and aahs all round.

Serves 6

200ml double cream
1 tbsp caster sugar
1 tbsp orange liqueur, such as Cointreau (or orange juice)
250–300g fresh mixed berries, such as strawberries, raspberries, blueberries and red currants
2 tbsp redcurrant jelly
1 tbsp cold water

sweet shortcrust pastry
150g plain flour, plus extra for rolling
100g cold butter, cut into cubes
1 tbsp caster sugar
finely grated zest of ½ lemon
1 medium egg, beaten

You'll need a 12-hole deep bun tin

Tip:
Once cold, the tartlet cases can be stored in an airtight tin for up to 3 days before filling. Warm through in a hot oven and leave to cool before adding the cream.

To make the pastry, put the flour, butter, sugar and lemon zest in a food processor and blitz on the pulse setting until the mixture resembles breadcrumbs. With the motor running, slowly add the beaten egg and blend until the mixture starts to come together in a ball. Roll into a ball and flatten slightly.

Roll the pastry out on a floured surface until it's about the thickness of a £1 coin. Using a biscuit cutter, cut out 8cm rounds and use to line a 12-hole bun tin. Prick the pastry very lightly and freeze for 1 hour.

Preheat the oven to 200°C/Fan 180°C/Gas 6. Bake the pastry cases for 15–18 minutes or until lightly browned and cooked through. Remove them from the oven and leave to cool.

Using a metal whisk, whip the cream with the sugar and liqueur, or orange juice, until it forms very soft peaks, but take care not to over whip. Spoon the mixture into the pastry cases using 2 teaspoons. Hull the strawberries and cut them in half, or quarters if large. Toss the fruit together very lightly in a large bowl.

Melt the redcurrant jelly with the water in a small saucepan. Bring to the boil and cook for 1 minute, stirring constantly until smooth and syrupy. Remove from the heat and leave to cool for a few minutes but do not allow the mixture to set.

Arrange the fruit on top of the cream. Brush with the redcurrant jelly to glaze. Serve immediately or chill for up to 6 hours. The pastry will begin to soften as time goes by, but the tarts will still taste smashing.

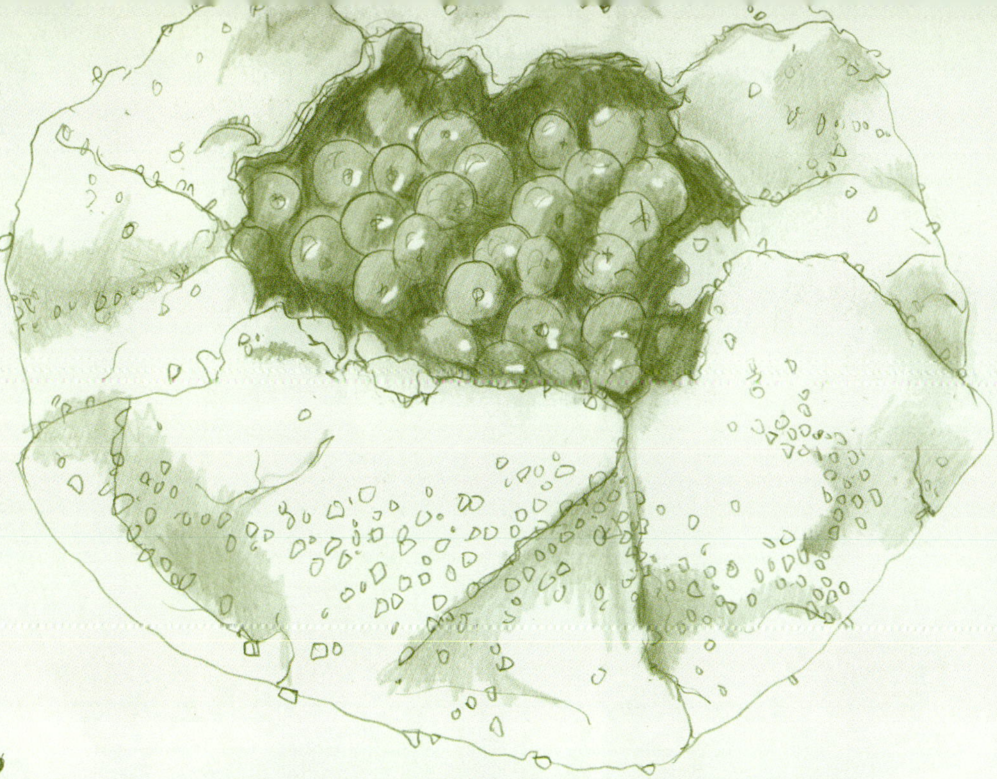

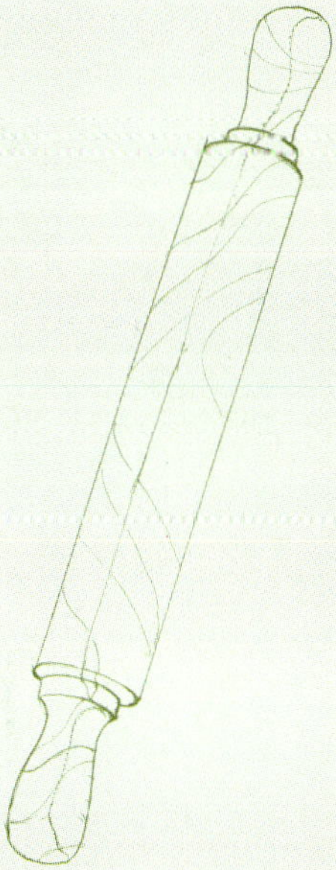

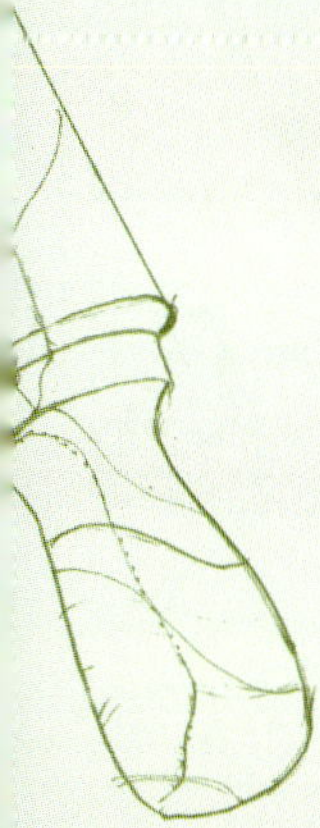

raised & free-form pies

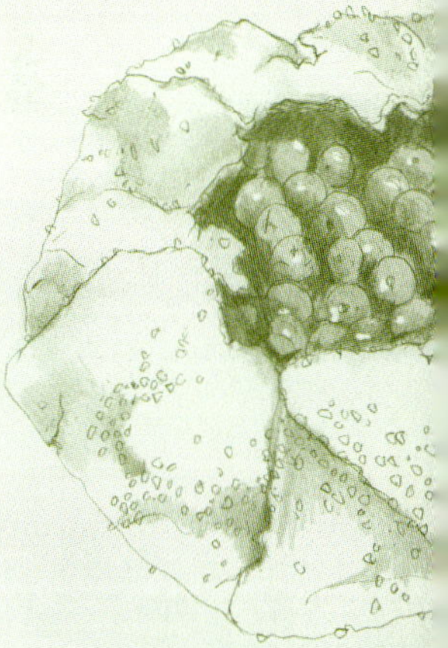

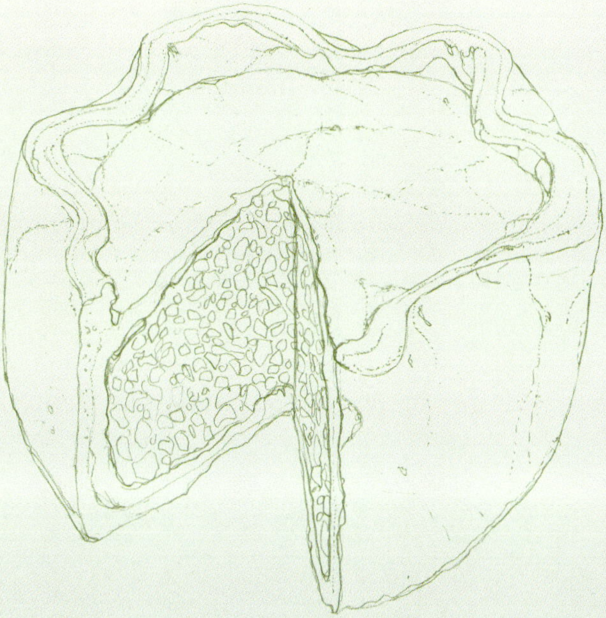

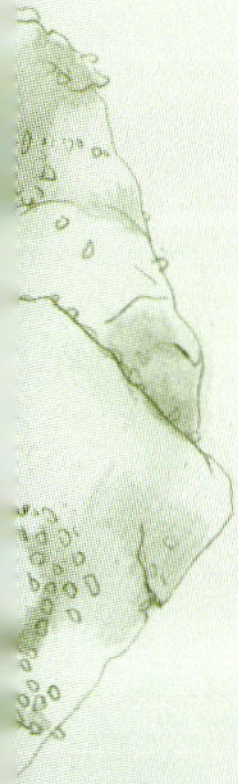

chicken, ham & apricot pie

We both love the combination of meat and fruit and there's nothing better than this densely packed raised pie. Raised pies aren't nearly as difficult to make as they look, so follow our instructions and you can't go wrong. Satisfaction guaranteed.

Serves 6

450g boneless, skinless chicken breasts (about 3 breasts)
200g thickly sliced hand-carved ham, cut into 2cm chunks
2 slender leeks, trimmed and cut into roughly 1.5cm slices
125g ready-to-eat dried apricots, halved
1 tsp ground ginger
1 tsp ground mace or ½ tsp finely grated nutmeg
2 tsp flaked sea salt
freshly ground black pepper
butter for greasing the tin
3 sheets of leaf gelatine (available in supermarkets)
300ml good fresh chicken stock

hot-water crust pastry
450g plain flour, plus extra for rolling
½ tsp ground black pepper
50g cold butter, cut into cubes
150g cold lard, cut into cubes
125ml water
2 tsp flaked sea salt
beaten egg, to glaze

You'll need an 18cm springclip cake tin

Cut each chicken breast into 5 large chunks and put them in a bowl with the ham, leeks, apricots, spices and salt. Season with lots of freshly ground black pepper and toss together until well combined. Grease the inside of your cake tin with butter.

To make the pastry, sift the flour into a large bowl and stir in the pepper. Rub in the butter and 50g of the lard until the mixture resembles coarse breadcrumbs. Make a well in the centre.

Put the remaining lard and the water and salt in a small saucepan. Bring to a simmer, then stir into the flour mixture with a wooden spoon. Mix with your fingers to make a smooth, pliable dough. Cover the dough with clingfilm and set aside for 30 minutes until it has cooled enough to work with. Do not put the dough in the fridge or it will go rock hard and crumbly.

Set aside just under a third of the dough to make a lid and form the rest into a ball. Roll out on a floured surface until it is about 5mm thick and use it to line the cake tin. Press the dough well into the base and sides to prevent air bubbles and leave the excess overhanging the edge. If it tears a little, just dampen the hole with a little cold water and smooth some extra dough on top. Make sure any gaps are sealed completely or the jelly could flow out later on. Spoon the chicken mixture into the tin and press down firmly.

Roll out the reserved pastry until it is large enough to cover the pie. Brush the overhanging edges of the pie with water and place the pastry lid on top. Press the edges together firmly to seal.

Continued overleaf...

chicken, ham & apricot pie continued...

Trim away most of the excess pastry using scissors, leaving just enough to pinch upwards into a neat crimped edge. Keep a ball of the trimmings to use for patching the pie if necessary. Make a small pea-sized hole in the centre of the pastry lid. This is where the jelly will be poured in, so make sure the hole is large enough for your funnel. Chill for 30 minutes. Preheat the oven to 180°C/Fan 160°C/Gas 4.

Place the pie on a baking tray and bake in the centre of the oven for 1 hour. Take it out of the oven and very carefully release the sides of the tin. You can do this by placing the tin on an upturned bowl and then dropping the sides of the tin down gently as the spring is released. Loosen any sticky edges with a knife if necessary. Leave the pie on the tin base and return it to the baking tray.

Have a good look over the pie. If there are any areas that look cracked, patch with a little of the reserved pastry, smoothing it into place with beaten egg or water. Brush the pie all over with beaten egg to glaze. Bake for a further 15 minutes, then remove from the oven and glaze again. Return to the oven for a final 15 minutes until the pastry is golden. Leave the pie to cool for 2–3 hours, putting it in the fridge after the first hour.

To make the jellied stock, soak the gelatine sheets in a bowl of cold water for 5 minutes until softened. Bring the chicken stock to the boil in a small saucepan and simmer for 1 minute, then take off the heat. Squeeze out the gelatine over the bowl, getting rid of the excess water, then drop it into the warm stock. Stir until completely dissolved, then transfer to a jug and leave to cool for 1 hour. Do not allow the mixture to set.

Using a narrow funnel, pour the stock slowly into the pie through the hole in the lid, stopping every so often to allow the liquid to trickle down between the chunks of filling. Stop when the stock reaches the top of the pie. Chill the pie for several hours or overnight until the stock sets into jelly. Serve in wedges.

Be creative with pie fillings. Leeks are a brilliant partner for chicken and ham.

our classic pork pies

This is a proper traditional raised pork pie. Everyone has eaten shop-bought pork pies and they can be good, but if you've never made your own you're missing out. Try this and we think you'll agree with us.

Makes 4 small pies – each pie serves 2

400g boneless pork shoulder, finely chopped
150g pork belly, finely minced
100g lean back bacon, finely chopped
1 tsp flaked sea salt
½ tsp ground allspice
½ tsp freshly grated nutmeg
freshly ground black pepper
1 medium egg, beaten

hot-water crust pastry

475g plain flour, plus extra for rolling
½ tsp freshly ground black pepper
50g cold butter, cut into cubes, plus extra for greasing the terrine
150g cold lard, cut into cubes
125ml water
2 tsp flaked sea salt
beaten egg, to glaze

jelly stock

900g pork bones
1 pig's trotter
2 large carrots, halved
2 celery sticks, halved
1 onion, quartered
2 bay leaves
3–4 sprigs of thyme
½ tbsp black peppercorns

You'll need 4 fairly squat jam jars

To make the jelly stock, put the pork bones and pig's trotter in a saucepan with the carrots, celery, onion, bay leaves, thyme and peppercorns. Add just enough water to cover and bring to a low simmer. Skim off any scum, then simmer gently for 3 hours, skimming occasionally. Drain in a colander over a bowl, reserving all the stock and discarding the bones, vegetables, bay leaves and peppercorns. Strain the stock through a fine sieve into a clean pan and bring to the boil. Boil hard until the liquid has reduced to about 600ml. Leave to cool, then cover and chill.

For the pastry, grease the outside of 4 jam jars with butter and set them upside down on a baking tray lined with baking parchment. To make the pastry, sift the flour into a large bowl and stir in the pepper. Rub in the butter and 50g of the lard until the mixture resembles breadcrumbs. Make a well in the centre. Put the remaining lard, water and salt in a small saucepan. Bring to a simmer, then stir into the flour with a wooden spoon and then your fingers to make a smooth, pliable dough. Cover with clingfilm and set aside for 30 minutes until the pastry is cool enough to handle.

Divide the pastry into 4 evenly sized pieces. Take 1 portion and remove just over a quarter of the dough to make a lid. Roll the larger piece into a ball, flatten slightly, then roll it out on a floured surface until it is about 7mm thick. Place it over the base and sides of a jam jar and smooth, so that the pastry covers the outside of the jar thickly and evenly. Put this on the baking tray and repeat with the rest of the dough and jars. Put them in the fridge for 45–60 minutes until the pastry is hard. Wrap the reserved pastry for the lids in clingfilm and leave at room temperature.

Just before the pastry has finished chilling, put the chopped pork shoulder, pork mince, bacon, flaked sea salt, allspice, nutmeg and plenty of freshly ground black pepper in a large bowl and add the egg. Mix thoroughly with clean hands.

Continued overleaf...

our classic pork pies continued...

Take the pastry out of the fridge and turn the jam jars the right way up. One at a time, pour about 3cm of water from a just-boiled kettle into a jar and ease the jar gently away from the pastry – the hot water will melt the fat and help the pastry come away from the mould without tearing. Don't leave the hot jar in contact with the pastry for too long. You should now have 4 pastry cases in which to put the filling. If the pastry tears, just smooth some extra dough on top.

Divide the filling between the pastry cases, taking care not to pack them too tightly. Brush the pastry rims with beaten egg. Roll the reserved pastry into 4 balls, and roll each one to about 1.5cm larger than the diameter of the jars. Place over the filling to form fairly thick lids and pinch the edges firmly together to seal. Trim away most of the excess using scissors, leaving just enough to pinch upwards into a neat crimped edge. Make a pea-sized hole in each pastry lid with the tip of a knife. This is where the jelly will be poured, so make sure the hole is large enough for your funnel. Chill for 30 minutes. Preheat the oven to 180°C/Fan 160°C/Gas 4.

Brush the pies with beaten egg and bake for 30 minutes. Remove from the oven and brush with more egg. Return to the oven for 15 minutes. Remove and brush with egg once more until the pies have cooked for 1 hour and are deep golden brown. Once baked, leave the pies to cool for 2–3 hours – put them in the fridge after the first hour. Scrape the fat off the top of the stock, which should have jellified, and bring the stock to the boil. Boil for 2 minutes, then remove from the heat and leave to cool for an hour. Do not allow it to set again.

Using a narrow funnel, pour the jelly stock slowly through the holes in the pies, stopping every so often to allow the liquid to trickle down inside. Stop when the stock reaches the top of each pie. You'll need about 300ml of the stock. If the filling hasn't shrunk away from where it meets the pastry, you may need to twiddle the funnel under the pastry a bit to lift the pastry and give the stock time to flow down. Chill the pies for several hours or overnight until the stock sets to jelly. Serve with salad and pickles.

Tips:

Keep a ball of the trimmings to use for patching the pies if necessary. If at any time the pies develop any splits or tears, simply remove from the oven, brush with a little beaten egg and smooth over the crack with some of the reserved pastry. Brush with more egg and return to the oven to continue cooking.

You need the pastry cases to be completely watertight so that they hold the jelly. If you see liquid escaping from the holes in the top of the pies, make small foil 'chimneys', about 4cm tall, and poke them into the pie. The liquid will travel up the tubes without drenching the pastry.

ham & egg pie

When we were kids we always used to wonder how you got the egg in the middle? It's a bit like a ship in a bottle. Now we know the secret and all is explained here.

Serves 6

1kg unsmoked ham hock
1 medium carrot, halved
1 medium onion, quartered
2 bay leaves
1 tsp black peppercorns
1.5 litres water
12 quails' eggs
300g pork shoulder, cut into 1cm pieces
150g pork belly, finely minced
½ tsp ground ginger
1 tsp freshly grated nutmeg
1 tsp flaked sea salt
freshly ground black pepper
butter, for greasing the terrine

hot-water crust pastry

475g plain flour, plus extra for rolling
½ tsp freshly ground black pepper
50g cold butter, cut into cubes
150g cold lard, cut into cubes
125ml water
2 tsp flaked sea salt
beaten egg, to glaze

You'll need a terrine measuring 6cm deep, 7cm wide and 24cm long

To make the filling, put the ham hock in a large saucepan with the carrot, onion, bay leaves and peppercorns. Pour over the water, making sure there is just enough to cover, and bring to a simmer, then skim off any scum. Continue to simmer, uncovered, for a further 2¼ hours until tender, turning the ham every 30 minutes. Top up the pan with just-boiled water if the level drops more than 3cm below the top of the pork. Drain in a colander over a saucepan, reserving the stock and ham hock and discarding the vegetables, bay leaves and peppercorns. Leave to cool. When the stock is cool, cover and chill.

Bring a pan of water to the boil and cook the eggs for 4 minutes. Drain in a sieve under running water until cold and peel off the shells. Remove the skin from the ham hock and take off all the meat. Weigh out 200g of the ham and cut it into 2cm chunks. Put these in a large bowl and add the pork shoulder, pork belly, spices, salt and lots of ground black pepper. Mix until well combined.

Grease the inside the terrine with butter and line with a double thickness of foil, leaving at least 5cm overhanging the sides. Rub with more butter.

To make the pastry, sift the flour into a large bowl and stir in the pepper. Rub in the butter and 50g of the lard until the mixture resembles fine breadcrumbs. Make a well in the centre. Put the remaining lard, water and salt in a small saucepan. Bring to a simmer and stir into the flour with a wooden spoon and then your fingers to make a smooth, pliable dough. Cover with clingfilm and set aside for 30 minutes until the pastry is cool enough to handle.

Reserve a third of the pastry to make a lid and form the rest into a fat sausage shape. Roll out on a floured surface until it is about 5mm thick and 5cm longer and twice as wide as the terrine. Use it to line the terrine, pressing well into the base and sides and leaving the excess overhanging the edge. If the pastry tears a little, simply dampen the hole with a little cold water and smooth some extra dough on top.

Spoon a third of the pork mixture into the terrine and press down. Top with half the eggs. Cover with another third of pork, then the rest of the eggs. Finish with the remaining pork, making sure all the eggs are completely covered.

Roll out the reserved pastry until it is large enough to cover the pie. Brush the overhanging edges of the pie with water and place the pastry lid on top. Press the edges together firmly to seal, then trim off most of the excess with scissors, leaving just enough to pinch upwards into a neat crimped edge. Keep a ball of the trimmings to use for patching the pie if necessary. Make a pea-sized hole in the pastry lid with a skewer or the tip of a knife. This is where the stock will be poured in, so make sure the hole is large enough for your funnel. Chill for 30 minutes. Preheat the oven to 180°C/Fan 160°C/Gas 4.

Place the pie on a baking tray and bake in the centre of the oven for 1 hour. Take out of the oven and very carefully lift the pie on the foil out of the terrine, taking great care not to tear the pastry. Return to the baking tray and gently peel the foil down to the base of the pie but do not remove it. Brush the pie all over with beaten egg to glaze. Bake for a further 15 minutes, then remove from the oven and glaze again. Return to the oven for a final 15 minutes until the pastry is golden. Leave to cool for 2–3 hours, putting the pie in the fridge after the first hour.

Scrape the fat off the top of the stock, which should have set, and bring the stock to the boil. Boil until reduced to about 600ml. Remove from the heat and leave to cool for an hour, but don't let it set again. Using a narrow funnel, pour the stock slowly through the hole in the top of the pie, stopping every so often to allow the liquid to trickle down inside. Stop when the stock reaches the top of the pie – you'll need about half the stock. Chill the pie for several hours or overnight until the stock sets to jelly. Serve in thick slices with salad and pickles.

smoked haddock & spinach pots

Smoked haddock and spinach are a marriage made in heaven. These are perfect for a light lunch or you could make smaller ones to serve as a starter. And if you want to be really fancy, how about tiny ones as canapés – how flash is that?

Serves 4

25g butter, plus extra for greasing
1 tbsp sunflower oil
1 small onion, finely chopped
200g baby spinach leaves
300g smoked haddock fillet (preferably undyed), skinned
150ml double cream
good pinch of freshly grated nutmeg
freshly ground black pepper

pastry

375g ready-rolled shortcrust pastry
beaten egg, to glaze

You'll need 4 x 150ml ramekin dishes

Heat the butter and the oil in a large non-stick saucepan. Add the onion and cook over a medium heat for 3–4 minutes, stirring, until soft but not coloured. Add the spinach and cook for 2–3 minutes more, tossing the leaves with two wooden spoons until they are well wilted. Tip everything into a colander and use the wooden spoons or a ladle to squeeze out as much of the water out of the spinach as possible. Preheat the oven to 200°C/Fan 180°C/Gas 6.

To make the pastry cases, unroll the pastry and place an upturned ramekin towards one corner. Cut out a circle that's about 2cm larger all round than the ramekin, then cut 3 more in the same way. These are the bases for your pies.

Butter the outsides of the ramekins and place them upside down on a baking tray. Place a pastry circle over the base of each ramekin, pressing gently down the sides to make small cup shapes. Brush with beaten egg and bake for 15 minutes. Take them out of the oven, turn them over and return to the oven for 5 minutes more. Cool for 4–5 minutes, then using an oven cloth, very gently ease the pastry cases off the ramekins.

Cut the haddock into 2cm chunks. Divide the haddock pieces and the spinach and onion between the pastry cases. Pour the cream over and season with a good pinch of nutmeg and lots of ground black pepper. Bake for 15–20 minutes or until the filling is bubbling and the haddock is just cooked. Transfer to small plates and serve with crusty bread and a green salad.

open chicken & pepper pie

This is a fantastically fast chicken pie that all the family will love. You can use a ready-made tomato pasta sauce to speed up the filling – we like the tomato and chilli sauce you find in the chiller cabinet of the supermarket, but use your favourite.

Serves 6

3 boneless, skinless chicken breasts
1 small red pepper, deseeded and cut into rough 3cm chunks
1 small yellow pepper, deseeded and cut into rough 3cm chunks
1 medium courgette, trimmed, quartered lengthways and cut into 1.5cm slices
½ x 350g tub of fresh tomato and chilli pasta sauce (from the chiller cabinet)
125g ball of mozzarella, well drained
freshly ground black pepper

pastry
500g block of ready-made puff pastry
plain flour for rolling
beaten egg, to glaze

Tip:
Instead of buying sauce, you can use the tomato sauce from the pizza pie recipe on page 53. Just add a pinch of chilli flakes.

Preheat the oven to 220°C/Fan 200°C/Gas 7. Line a large baking tray with baking parchment.

Cut each chicken breast into 5 or 6 chunks and place them in a large bowl. Add the peppers, courgette and pasta sauce. Season with black pepper and toss everything together.

Shape your block of pastry into a rough circle by pushing in the corners. Roll out on a lightly floured surface until you have a circle of about 30cm across, a bit bigger than a dinner plate. Pile the chicken mixture into the centre of the pastry. Tear the mozzarella into chunks and dot it over the filling. Brush the edge of the pastry with beaten egg and bring it up around the filling to create a loose bowl shape, pinching the sides to set the pastry in place. Brush the outside of the pastry with more egg.

Bake the pie in the preheated oven for about 35 minutes or until the pastry is puffed up and golden brown and the chicken is cooked. Take the pie out of the oven and leave it to stand for about 5 minutes. If the chicken has released lots of liquid you may need to absorb some of it by dabbing it with kitchen roll. Serve hot with a green salad.

creamy garlic mushroom pies

These are a doddle to put together, using a pack of garlic and herb soft cheese, and they make a great starter or light lunch. Quick as owt and lip-smackingly delicious to eat.

Serves 4

4 large portobello mushrooms, wiped
1 ½ tbsp sunflower oil
150g garlic and herb soft cheese (such as Boursin)
freshly ground black pepper
beaten egg or milk, to glaze

pastry
375g ready-rolled puff pastry sheet
plain flour, for dusting work surface

Trim the stems of the mushrooms so that they sit flat. Heat the oil in a non-stick frying pan. Fry the mushrooms over a medium-high heat for 3 minutes on each side, or until tender and lightly browned. As the mushrooms cook, they will give off quite a lot of water, so you'll need to drain them well on plenty of kitchen roll afterwards.

Preheat the oven to 220°C/Fan 200°C/Gas 7. Carefully unroll the pastry and put it on a lightly floured surface. Cut 4 large squares from the pastry, each about 4cm larger than the mushrooms. Place the squares on a baking sheet lined with baking parchment.

Cut the cheese into 4 thick slices and place a slice in the centre of each pastry square. Top with a mushroom, dark side up. Season with lots of freshly ground black pepper.

Bring the sides of the pastry up around the cheese and mushrooms, pinching lightly so it holds its shape, then brush with egg or milk to glaze. Bake for about 15 minutes or until the pastry is puffed up and golden brown.

nectarine & blueberry galettes

People will think you spent ages making these, or bought them from the best patisserie in town. In fact, they're a real cheat, dead quick to make and taste brilliant.

Makes 6

6 firm but ripe nectarines
3 tbsp apricot jam
1 tbsp water
65g fresh blueberries

pastry
375g ready-rolled puff pastry sheet
plain flour, for rolling
beaten egg, to glaze

Carefully unroll the pastry and put it on a lightly floured surface. Dust a rolling pin with flour and roll the pastry until it is about 3cm larger on all sides. Line a baking tray with baking parchment.

Upturn a saucer or cereal bowl measuring about 15cm onto a corner of the pastry and cut around it with a sharp knife. Place the pastry circle on the baking tray, then cut out 5 more circles in exactly the same way. Prick the circles with a fork and brush them lightly with beaten egg.

Holding a nectarine in the palm of your hand, use a small knife to cut very carefully from top to bottom, in towards the stone. Move the knife along a centimetre or so and do the same thing, but this time bring the knife forward over the stone to loosen the slice of fruit. Do the same thing all the way around the nectarine to make about 16 slices. Arrange in a concentric circle over 1 of the pastry circles. Repeat with the other nectarines and pastry.

Warm the jam with a tablespoon of water in a small pan, stirring until softened. Brush generously over the fruit to glaze. Place the baking tray in the centre of the oven and bake for 15 minutes.

Remove the tray from the oven and sprinkle a few blueberries on top of each galette. Return to the oven for 3 minutes more until the blueberries are softened and beginning to burst. Serve hot or cold. The individual tarts look great, but if you prefer, make 1 large one and cook it for an extra 10–15 minutes.

autumn plum & apple pie

If it grows in the autumn it's in this pie – a scrumper's special. What a way to get your five a day! We love these freeform pies and if you're a pastry virgin, they're a great way to start your pie-making career.

Serves 8–10

350g Bramley cooking apples
1 tsp fresh lemon juice
150g fresh blackberries
4 large ripe plums, halved, stoned and cut into thick slices
3 tbsp caster sugar, preferably golden
2 tbsp cornflour

shortcrust pastry
325g plain flour, plus extra for rolling
175g cold butter, cut into cubes
1 large egg, beaten
beaten egg, to glaze
2 tbsp caster sugar, preferably golden

To make the pastry, put the flour and butter in a food processor and blitz on the pulse setting until the mixture resembles breadcrumbs. With the motor running, add the beaten egg and blend until the mixture forms a ball. If you prefer to make your pastry by hand, see page 337.

Roll out the pastry on a lightly floured surface into a rough circle about 3mm thick. Transfer to a large baking tray. Preheat the oven to 220°C/Fan 200°C/Gas 7. Peel, quarter and core the apples, then slice them fairly thinly. Put the slices into a bowl, toss them with the lemon juice, then add the blackberries and plums. Mix the caster sugar and cornflour in a small bowl. Sprinkle this over the fruit and toss well together, using your hands so you don't bruise or damage the fruit. Tip the mixed fruit into the middle of the pastry, leaving a border of about 7cm all the way around it.

Fold the pastry up and over the fruit, but do not completely cover it; you should still be able to see the fruit in the centre of the pie. Pinch any cracks or splits in the pastry together to seal. Brush the pastry with beaten egg and sprinkle with sugar.

Bake in the centre of the preheated oven for 20 minutes. Reduce the temperature to 200°C/Fan 180°C/Gas 6 and cook for a further 30 minutes or until the pastry is crisp and golden and the fruit is tender. To check if the fruit is ready, poke a couple of slices of apple with the point of a sharp knife – it should slide in easily. If not, pop the pie back into the oven for a little longer. Serve the pie from the baking tray, or slide it onto a large platter or board.

pear & chocolate puff pie

Isn't ready-made puff pastry great? You can get such great results in no time at all. This pie is simple to make and very impressive – and pears and chocolate are perfect partners.

Serves 6

2 medium eggs
100g softened butter
100g ground almonds
100g caster sugar
50g self-raising flour
½ tsp vanilla extract
100g plain dark chocolate
410g can pear halves, in juice or syrup, drained

pastry

375g ready-rolled puff pastry sheet

Preheat the oven to 220°C/Fan 200°C/Gas 7. Whisk the eggs until well combined. Set aside a tablespoon of the beaten egg in a small bowl to use for glazing the pie later.

Stir the butter, almonds, sugar and flour into the rest of the egg and beat hard with a wooden spoon until smooth. Add the vanilla extract and beat once more. Put the chocolate on a board and chop it roughly, then stir it into the almond mixture.

Unroll the pastry and place it on a baking tray lined with baking parchment. Spoon the chocolate and almond mixture down one long half of the pastry. Press the pears into the mixture and brush the pastry around the filling with beaten egg.

Bring the other half of the pastry over the filling to enclose it completely and press the edges together to seal. Brush with more egg and slash the pastry diagonally down its length.

Bake in the centre of the oven for 25–30 minutes or until the pastry is puffed up and golden brown. Serve in thick slices, with cream or vanilla ice cream.

posh salmon coulibiac

A spectacular centrepiece for any party, this is great served hot or cold. It's surprisingly straightforward to make – nothing difficult about it all.

Serves 6

2 x 1kg sides of fresh salmon fillet, skinned and pin-boned
½ fish stock cube
500ml just-boiled water
100g easy-cook long-grain rice
knob of butter
100g chestnut mushrooms, chopped
1 medium egg, beaten
200g cooked peeled prawns, drained
2 tbsp chopped fresh dill
2 tbsp chopped parsley leaves
2 tbsp finely sliced chives
finely grated zest of 1 lemon
1 tsp lemon juice
100g baby spinach leaves
flaked sea salt
freshly ground black pepper

pastry

2 x 500g blocks of ready-made puff pastry
plain flour for rolling
beaten egg, to glaze

Tip:

The coulibiac parcel can be made up to 8 hours before baking, then covered with clingfilm and chilled until needed.

Check that all the little pin bones have been removed from the salmon. Dissolve the stock cube in the 500ml water, then pour into a saucepan and return to the boil. Stir in the rice, return to the boil and cook for 5 minutes. Drain in a sieve and leave to cool, fluffing up the rice occasionally with a fork. Melt the butter in a small pan and fry the mushrooms over a high heat for 3–4 minutes until lightly browned. Leave to cool.

To make the stuffing, stir together the cold rice, mushrooms, egg, prawns, herbs, zest and juice in a large bowl. Season to taste, then work everything together well with your hands.

Roll out the puff pastry on a lightly floured surface. You need 2 rectangular sheets, at least 5cm larger all round than your salmon, to make the top and bottom of the coulibiac parcel. Place 1 sheet on a large baking tray lined with baking parchment.

Put a layer of spinach leaves down the centre of the pastry sheet and place a salmon fillet on top, inner side up. Spread the stuffing over the salmon – it will be about 2cm thick. Place the other fillet on top to make a sandwich, making sure the tail ends match.

Scatter the rest of the spinach leaves over the top and around the sides of the salmon and brush the pastry edge with beaten egg. Place the other sheet of puff pastry on top, pressing the pastry together firmly to seal. Trim away any excess and use it to craft whatever decoration takes your fancy to put on top of the coulibiac. Cut a couple of small steam holes into the top of the pastry.

Preheat the oven to 200°C/Fan 180°C/Gas 6. Brush the parcel with beaten egg and cook in the centre of the oven for 45–55 minutes or until the pastry is golden brown and the stuffing is hot throughout. Cover with foil if the pastry starts to get too brown. Delicious served with salad and some mayonnaise or hollandaise sauce.

salmon pastillas with salad & salmon roe

We cooked this dish on Saturday Kitchen, having been inspired by Moroccan pastillas. Bloomin' gorgeous we have to say and, once you get used to handling filo pastry, very easy to put together. A good show-off supper.

Serves 4

4 x 75g pieces of salmon fillet, trimmed to about the size of a thin matchbox
12 marinated anchovy fillets (boquerones)
4 tsp soured cream
4 tsp chopped fresh dill
1 tsp lemon juice
beaten egg, to glaze
vegetable oil, for shallow frying
rocket and watercress salad leaves
1 small jar of salmon roe
sea salt flakes
freshly ground black pepper

pastry
4 filo pastry sheets (each about 32 x 38cm), thawed if frozen
plain flour, for dusting

salad dressing
2 tbsp olive oil
1 tbsp white wine vinegar
2 tsp clear honey
a pinch of salt

Lay a sheet of filo pastry on a floured work surface. Cut a slit into 1 of the salmon portions and lay it on the edge of the pastry. Tuck 3 anchovies, a teaspoon of soured cream and a teaspoon of fresh dill into the salmon and close it up, then add a little lemon juice and a sprinkle of sea salt and black pepper. Roll the salmon and filo into a neat parcel, sealing it with beaten egg. Repeat to make 3 more parcels and brush them all with beaten egg.

Heat the oil in a frying pan and shallow fry the pastillas until golden. Be careful not to overcook them – the salmon should still be juicy.

Meanwhile, wash the salad leaves and make the dressing. Mix together the oil, vinegar, honey and salt to make the dressing. Put some salad leaves onto the plates and dress, then scatter some salmon roe on top of the leaves. Add a beautiful golden pastilla to each plate.

lamb cutlets in pastry

Would you believe it? A pie with a handle! The pastry crust around the cutlets keeps in all the flavour of the meat and the mint jelly and makes really succulent mouthfuls. You can make these a few hours ahead and keep them in the fridge.

Serves 8

1 well-trimmed rack of lamb or 8 lamb cutlets
1 tbsp sunflower oil
4 tsp mint jelly
flaked sea salt
freshly ground black pepper

red wine gravy
150ml red wine
200ml lamb stock (made with ½ lamb stock cube)
1 tbsp redcurrant jelly
1 tsp cornflour, mixed to a smooth paste with 2 tsp cold water
flaked sea salt
freshly ground black pepper

pastry
500g block of ready-made puff pastry
plain flour, for rolling
beaten egg, to glaze

Cut the rack of lamb into 8 cutlets and season well. Heat the oil in a large non-stick frying pan and brown the cutlets in batches for 2 minutes on each side. Transfer to a plate and leave to cool.

To make the gravy, return the frying pan to the heat and pour in the red wine. Stir to lift the sticky sediment from the bottom of the pan. Bubble for 30 seconds or so, then add the lamb stock and redcurrant jelly. Bring to the boil and cook for 2–3 minutes or until the liquid has reduced by half. Stir the cornflour paste into the pan, then add any juices from the lamb and cook the gravy for a minute more until thickened and glossy. Season and set aside.

Line a large baking tray with baking parchment. Roll out the pastry on a floured work surface until it is about 3mm thick. Cut out 8 squares of about 10–12cm, depending on the size of the lamb cutlets.

Place half a teaspoon of mint jelly just off centre on each square and put a cutlet on top, towards one of the corners. Brush the pastry edges lightly with the beaten egg and fold the remaining 3 corners of the pastry over the lamb. Wrap firmly around the meat, leaving the bone bare if possible. Turn the parcels over and place them on the lined tray. Preheat the oven to 200°C/Fan 180°C/Gas 6.

Bake the cutlets for 20 minutes until the pastry is risen and golden brown. Reheat the gravy until it's bubbling and simmer for a couple of minutes, while stirring. Check the seasoning and serve with the cutlets.

sausage & apple puff

The sausage roll goes supersize! This is a great treat, with little nuggets of apple flavouring every mouthful. We like Cumberland sausages, but use whatever is your favourite.

Serves 8

1 tsp sunflower oil
1 small onion, finely chopped
1 crisp eating apple, peeled, quartered, cored and diced
1 tbsp finely chopped fresh sage leaves or a good pinch of dried mixed herbs
450g good-quality sausages, skinned
50g fresh white breadcrumbs
flaked sea salt
freshly ground black pepper

pastry
2 x 375g ready-rolled puff pastry sheets
beaten egg, to glaze
¼ tsp poppy seeds

Heat the oil in a large non-stick frying pan and gently fry the onion for 5 minutes, stirring occasionally until softened. Add the apple pieces and cook for 2 minutes more. Tip the onion and apple into a large heatproof bowl, add the dried herbs, a pinch of salt and plenty of freshly ground back pepper. Leave to cool for 15 minutes.

Preheat the oven to 200°C/Fan 180°C/Gas 6. Mix the sausage meat and breadcrumbs with the vegetables. Unroll 1 of the pastry sheets and lay it on a large baking sheet lined with baking parchment.

Form the meat mixture into a long sausage shape and place it in the centre of the pastry. Trim the pastry, leaving a 3cm pastry border all around the filling, then brush the pastry border with beaten egg. Place the second puff pastry sheet over the first so that the filling is enclosed and press the edges firmly to seal. Trim with a sharp knife and knock up the edges (see page 367).

Slash through the pastry from side to side every couple of centimetres, all the way down the length of the pie. Glaze the pastry with beaten egg and sprinkle with poppy seeds. Bake for 35 minutes until the pastry is risen and golden brown and the sausage meat is cooked. Serve warm or cold in thick slices.

beef wellington
with marsala sauce

This is an absolute feast – one of the best British dishes. The secret of our recipe is in the herb pancakes, which stop the pastry going soggy, keep the mushrooms in place and add texture. There's quite a bit to do but nothing tricky so take it slowly and you'll have a supper to be proud of.

Serves 6

4–5 tbsp sunflower oil
900g beef fillet, trimmed
275g chestnut mushrooms, wiped
knob of butter
1 long shallot, finely chopped
2 garlic cloves, finely chopped
150g smooth duck pâté
2 tbsp plain flour,
flaked sea salt
freshly ground black pepper

herb pancakes
50g plain white flour, sifted
1 large egg
150ml semi-skimmed milk
1 tbsp finely chopped thyme leaves
1 tbsp finely chopped parsley
1 tbsp sunflower oil
flaked sea salt

marsala sauce
200ml Marsala wine
750ml good-quality fresh beef stock
1 tbsp cornflour, mixed to a smooth paste with 1 tbsp water

pastry
500g block ready-made puff pastry
plain flour, for rolling
beaten egg, to glaze

First make the pancakes. Put the flour, egg and milk in a food processor and blitz until smooth. Add the finely chopped thyme, parsley and a pinch of salt, then blitz again until combined. Transfer the mixture to a jug.

Drizzle a little of the sunflower oil into a large non-stick frying pan and wipe with a thick pad of folded kitchen roll to coat the pan lightly. Place over a medium-high heat. Pour a third of the pancake batter into the pan and swirl around until it covers the base evenly. Cook the pancake for 1–2 minutes, then flip over and cook on the other side. Transfer to a plate and leave to cool. Repeat to make 2 more pancakes.

Now for the beef. Heat a tablespoon of the oil in a large non-stick frying pan. Season the beef all over with sea salt and black pepper, then put it in the pan and cook over a medium-high heat for 7–9 minutes or until well browned on all sides, turning occasionally. Remove from the pan and set aside on a plate lined with kitchen roll. Once the beef is cool, cover and chill until ready to wrap.

Put the mushrooms in a food processor and blend on the pulse setting until they are finely chopped but not mushy. Return the frying pan to the heat and add 2 more tablespoons of the oil. Add the mushrooms and cook for 5–6 minutes, stirring regularly until they are lightly browned and any excess liquid has evaporated. Tip the mushrooms into a bowl.

Return the pan to the heat and add the remaining oil and the butter. Gently fry the shallot and garlic over a low heat until softened, stirring regularly. Increase the heat slightly and cook for a few minutes more until lightly browned, then return the mushrooms to the pan, season with black pepper and cook for a 1–2 minutes. Tip everything into a bowl and leave to cool.

Continued overleaf...

beef wellington continued...

To make the Marsala sauce, place the frying pan you used for the beef and mushrooms over a medium heat and pour in the Marsala. Cook until it is reduced by half, then add the beef stock and bring to the boil. Cook until the liquid has reduced to about 250ml, then stir in the cornflour paste and continue to stir for about 2 minutes, until the sauce is thick and glossy. Pour into a small saucepan and leave to cool. Chill until 10 minutes before serving.

To wrap the beef, place 2 of the pancakes side by side on a board, slightly overlapping each other. Fill any gaps with pieces of the remaining pancake to make a neat, almost rectangular shape. Stir the pâté into the cooled mushroom mixture until thoroughly combined. Spread the mushroom mixture evenly over the pancakes, leaving a 2cm gap around the edges. Sprinkle with the flour.

Pat the beef with kitchen roll until it is as dry as possible and place in the centre of the pancakes. Fold the ends and sides of the pancakes over the beef to cover. Trim away any excess.

Roll out the pastry on a lightly floured board into a rectangle that's large enough to cover the beef and overlap at the top and sides. Place the pancake-wrapped beef in the centre and tuck the short ends in over the fillet. Brush with beaten egg to seal the ends.

Bring the longer sides up and over the beef, overlapping in the middle and brushing with a little more egg to seal. Place the beef, with the folded pastry edges underneath, on a baking tray lined with baking parchment. Cover loosely with clingfilm and chill for at least 2 hours or overnight before baking. Cover and chill the egg for glazing the pastry later.

Preheat the oven to 200°C/Fan 180°C/Gas 6. Brush the pastry with the reserved egg. Bake the wellington in the centre of the oven for 40 minutes for rare beef, or longer if you prefer your beef well done. Remove it from the oven and leave to stand for 10 minutes before slicing. Bring the Marsala sauce to the boil over a medium heat, reduce the heat and simmer for 2–3 minutes, while stirring, until thickened and glossy.

To serve, put the rested beef on a board and trim away the thick pastry ends to reveal the meat. Carve into 6 pieces and serve immediately with the hot sauce.

steak & kidney pudding

This is the classic of classics and just the thing on a winter day. If you've never made a steamed pudding before, don't be scared – it's not hard, but may the force be with you when you turn it out! Just make sure you core the kidneys well.

Serves 6

700g braising steak, well marbled with fat
3 very fresh lambs' kidneys
3 tbsp plain flour
4–5 tbsp sunflower oil
1 medium onion, chopped
200ml red wine
4–5 sprigs of fresh thyme
1 bay leaf
500ml good beef stock
1 tbsp tomato purée
fine sea salt
freshly ground black pepper

suet pastry
350g self-raising flour, plus extra for rolling
175g shredded suet
½ tsp fine sea salt
300ml water
butter, for greasing

You'll need a 1.5-litre pudding basin

Tip:
A nice touch is to mix 2 teaspoons of dried mixed herbs into the suet pastry. As the pud steams, the herbs give the suet crust a lovely flavour.

Trim the beef of any hard fat or tough bits of gristle and cut into cubes of about 2.5cm. Rinse the kidneys and pat them dry with kitchen roll. Snip out the white cores and cut the kidneys into rough 1.5cm chunks. Put the steak and kidneys in a large, strong plastic bag. Add the flour, salt and plenty of black pepper. Knot the top of the bag and shake until the meat is well coated in the seasoned flour. Preheat the oven to 170°C/Fan 150°/Gas 3½.

Heat 2 tablespoons of the oil in a large non-stick frying pan and fry the steak and kidneys over a medium heat until well browned all over. You'll need to do this in a few batches so you don't overcrowd the pan, so add an extra tablespoon or 2 of oil if the pan gets dry. Transfer the meat to a flameproof casserole dish as it is browned. Return the pan to the heat and add the remaining oil, then the onion. Cook over a low heat for 5 minutes or until softened, stirring often. Stir the onion into the casserole dish with the steak and kidneys.

Deglaze the frying pan with the wine, bringing it to the boil while stirring hard to lift all the sediment from the bottom of the pan. Pour immediately over the meat and onions. Strip the thyme leaves from the stalks and add them to the casserole dish. Stir in the bay leaf, beef stock and tomato purée. Bring everything to the boil, then cover and cook in the oven for 1½–2 hours or until the meat is tender. Give it a stir halfway through the cooking time.

When the meat is done, take the dish out of the oven and place it on the hob. Take out 3 ladlefuls of the sauce and set aside to use for gravy later – once cool, this can be kept in the fridge until needed. Simmer the rest, uncovered, for 2–3 minutes or until the sauce is thick enough to coat the beef generously. The sauce needs to be thick enough not to run out over the plate when the pudding is cut, but not too thick or the pudding will taste dry. Take the dish off the heat and leave to cool.

Continued overleaf...

steak & kidney pudding continued...

Butter your pudding basin and line the base with a circle of baking parchment.

To make the suet pastry, put the flour in a large bowl and stir in the suet and salt. Stir in enough water to make a soft, spongy dough – you'll probably need about 300ml. Turn the dough out onto a floured surface and bring it together to form a ball. Knead lightly, then remove a generous quarter of the dough to make a lid for the pudding and roll the rest into a circle measuring about 25cm (the size of an average dinner plate). It should be about 1cm thick.

Use this circle of pastry to line the pudding basin, with the top resting about 1cm below the edge of the dish. Press the pastry well against the sides of the basin and trim neatly, then pile in the cooled steak and kidney mixture. Brush the top edge of the pastry with water. Roll the remaining pastry into a round just large enough to sit on top of the pastry edge and place over the filling. Trim into place and press the edges together to seal.

Cover the dish with a large circle of baking parchment, with a pleat in the middle to allow for expansion. Cover the parchment with a circle of foil, again with a pleat. Tie both tightly in place with string. Create a carrying handle by tying the excess string across the top of the basin – this will help you lift the pudding once it's cooked.

Place the basin on an upturned saucer or a small trivet in a large, deep saucepan and add enough just-boiled water to come halfway up the sides of the basin. Cover the pan with a tight-fitting lid and place over a medium heat. Allow to steam in simmering water for 2½ hours, topping up with more hot water when necessary. Alternatively, cook the pudding in a hob-top steamer.

When the pudding is done, turn off the heat and carefully lift the basin from the water. Leave it to stand for 5 minutes. Take the sauce that you set aside earlier and heat it in a small pan until bubbling – keep stirring it so it doesn't stick and burn. Strain the gravy through a small sieve into a warmed jug.

Cut the string, foil and paper off the basin. Loosen the sides of the pudding with a blunt-ended knife and turn the pudding out onto a deep plate. What a sight! Serve with the hot gravy.

roast chicken & mushroom puddings

There's life beyond steak and kidney for suet puddings so be imaginative with your fillings. Chicken and mushroom works brilliantly with the suet crust and you can make little individual puds or one big one.

Makes 6

1 medium onion, sliced
1 medium carrot, peeled and sliced
1 smallish chicken, around 1.3kg
2 bay leaves
few sprigs fresh thyme
2 rashers smoked back bacon
150ml red wine
450ml water
½ chicken stock cube
25g butter
1 tbsp sunflower oil
225g small chestnut mushrooms, sliced
2 heaped tbsp plain flour
1 tsp redcurrant jelly
flaked sea salt
freshly ground black pepper

suet pastry
butter, for greasing
350g self-raising flour
175g shredded suet
1 heaped tsp dried mixed herbs
½ tsp fine sea salt
300ml cold water

You'll need 6 x 200ml metal pudding basins, buttered and bases lined with circles of baking parchment

Preheat the oven to 200°C/Fan/180°C/Gas 6. Pile the onion and carrot into a roasting tin and sit the chicken on top. Put the herbs inside, season the chicken and place the bacon over the breast. Roast for 45 minutes, then pour the red wine into the tin. Cover the chicken with foil and return to the oven for 30 minutes. Take the chicken out, put it on a board and leave to cool. Place the tin on the hob and stir in the stock cube and water. Bring to the boil, stirring well. Pour the stock through a sieve into a jug and leave to stand.

When the chicken is cool enough to handle, remove the skin, then take off one breast and all the dark meat. Chop the chicken into small pieces. To make the gravy, spoon off any fat that has risen to the surface of the stock. Melt the butter in a frying pan and fry the mushrooms until golden. Stir in the flour, then gradually add the chicken stock, stirring well. Add the redcurrant jelly and simmer for 3–4 minutes until thickened, stirring. Leave to cool.

Preheat the oven to 190°C/Fan 170°C/Gas 5. Stir the chopped chicken into the cooled gravy. Make the pastry (see page 259) and divide into 6 balls. Take 1 ball and remove a third of the dough to make a lid. Roll out the rest into a circle and use to line the inside of 1 of the basins, leaving any excess overhanging.

Spoon some of the filling into the pastry-lined basin. Roll out the pastry for the lid. Brush the edges with water, place on top, then seal the edges and trim and put into a large roasting tin, lid side up. Repeat with the rest of the pastry and filling. Pour just-boiled water into the tin until it rises halfway up the sides of the puddings. Cover loosely with baking parchment and cover the tin with a sheet of foil pleated in the middle to allow the puddings to rise and pinched all the way around the edge to create a good seal (see page 259). Carry carefully to the oven and cook for about 1¼ hours until the pastry is done and the filling is hot. Holding with an oven cloth, loosen the edges of each pudding with a round-bladed knife and turn out onto warmed plates. Remove lining paper and serve.

Always measure your pastry ingredients carefully for best results.

rhubarb & orange pudding pie

Is it a pie or a pudding? This dish has a base made of bread soaked in a sweet vanilla custard and is topped with very pink poached rhubarb. Rhubarb and custard are the perfect combination and here they are in one delicious bowlful.

Serves 6

3 large eggs
100g caster sugar, plus
1 tsp extra for sprinkling
200ml double cream
200ml semi-skimmed milk
½ tsp vanilla extract
50g softened butter,
plus extra for greasing
8 slices white bread,
crusts removed
125g fine-cut orange marmalade

rhubarb topping

1 tbsp water
50g caster sugar
375g young rhubarb
(5–6 slender stalks), trimmed

You'll need a 1.2-litre pie dish

Beat the eggs with the 100g of sugar in a large jug until smooth. Stir in the cream, milk and vanilla extract and set aside.

Butter the slices of bread generously on one side and cut them in half diagonally to make triangles. Spread each triangle with a little marmalade. Butter your pie dish and line the base with about 12 of the bread triangles, butter side up. You should have about 3 layers.

Cut the remaining 4 triangles in half again and overlap them around the edge of the dish like the petals of a flower. Pour the custard slowly over the bread, including the small triangles around the sides. Leave to stand for 20 minutes to allow the bread to soak up the custard. You may think there is too much custard but don't worry, it's just what you need.

Preheat the oven to 190°C/Fan 170°C/Gas 5. Bake the pudding for 25–30 minutes until puffed up and beginning to brown. While the pudding is in the oven, make the rhubarb topping.

Dissolve the sugar in the water in a large non-stick frying pan over a low heat. Cut the rhubarb into 2cm lengths and add them to the pan in a single layer. Cook gently for 4 minutes, then turn them over with a spatula and cook on the other side for a further 3–4 minutes until just softened. Remove from the heat.

Take the part-cooked pudding out of the oven and spoon the rhubarb and any sugary juices into the centre. Sprinkle both the rhubarb and bread with reserved teaspoon of sugar. Put the pudding back in the oven for another 8–10 minutes until the bread is crisp and golden and the rhubarb topping is hot. Serve with some extra cream.

lemony pond pudding

Paddles at the ready! You'll need them when you breach the crust and the gorgeous lemony sauce comes flowing out of this pudding – an old-fashioned dish and none the worse for that.

Serves 6

1 medium unwaxed lemon
175g demerara sugar
175g cold butter, cut into 2cm cubes

suet pastry
butter, for greasing
250g self-raising flour, plus extra for rolling
50g fresh white breadcrumbs
150g shredded suet
1 tbsp demerara sugar
finely grated zest of 1 orange
freshly squeezed juice of 1 orange

You'll need a 900ml heatproof pudding basin

To make the pastry, put the flour, breadcrumbs, suet, sugar and orange zest in a large bowl and mix lightly. Measure the orange juice into a jug and add enough cold water to bring the level of liquid up to 200ml. Pour the liquid onto the suet mixture and stir with a wooden spoon until the dough comes together and forms a ball. Knead the dough very lightly on floured surface for a few seconds until it's soft and pliable. Butter your pudding basin and line the base with a circle of baking parchment.

Break off about two-thirds of the dough, shape it into a ball and roll it out into a circle around 5mm thick. Use the dough to line the inside of the buttered basin, leaving the excess overhanging the sides. Keep the remaining third of the dough for the lid.

Slice the lemon very thinly and discard the end pieces. Sprinkle a couple of tablespoons of the sugar into the lined basin and dot with a 4 or 5 cubes of butter. Top with a couple of the lemon slices. Repeat the layers until all the ingredients are used, adding a little extra to each layer as the basin becomes wider.

Roll out the reserved pastry on lightly floured surface. Brush with water and flip over on top of the pudding. Press the pastry edges together firmly to seal and trim neatly. Cover with pleated baking parchment and foil and tie with string (see page 259). Place on a trivet or upturned saucer in a very large saucepan and add enough just-boiled water to rise halfway up the sides of the basin. Cover and bring to the boil on the hob. Reduce the heat to a simmer and cook for 3½ hours, topping up with hot water when necessary.

Remove the basin carefully from the water and stand for 2 minutes. Snip off the string and remove the foil and paper. Loosen the sides of the pudding with a round-bladed knife. Invert the pudding onto a plate and allow it to drop gently down. The pudding will look slightly sunk on the top and the pastry should be golden.

galette des rois

Also known as King cake (or Kingy cake in Si's household), this puff pastry dessert is a traditional Christmas recipe, but delicious at any time of year.

Serves 8

125g butter, softened
125g caster sugar
1 tsp vanilla extract
or 1 tbsp brandy
2 medium eggs
125g ground almonds
2 tbsp plain flour,
4 tbsp raspberry jam (optional)

pastry
500g block of ready-made
puff pastry
plain flour, for rolling

Cut the pastry in half and roll out each piece on a lightly floured surface until they are large enough to cut out a 25cm round. Use a dinner plate as a template if you like. Put the pastry circles on flat baking trays and chill for 30 minutes.

Preheat the oven to 200°C/Fan 180°C/Gas 6. Cream the butter and sugar with the vanilla extract, or brandy, in a food processor until light and fluffy. Lightly beat the eggs, setting aside 2 tablespoons in a small bowl for brushing the pastry later.

With the processor on, add the remaining beaten egg to the sugar and butter mixture and blend until smooth. You may need to remove the lid and push the mixture down a couple of times with a spatula. Add the almonds and flour, then process again until the mixture is well combined.

Remove the pastry from the fridge and spread 1 of the roundswith the jam, if using, to within 4cm of the edge. Spoon the almond mixture on top and spread it gently over the jam. Brush the pastry edge with a little of the reserved egg and place the other round on top.

Press the edges together firmly to seal, then knock up with a sharp, horizontally held knife to help separate the layers so they puff up while the cake is cooking (see page 367). Score the surface with a sharp knife, then brush with beaten egg. Bake in the centre of the oven for 30–35 minutes or until puffed up and golden brown. Remove from the oven and serve warm or cold.

simple apple strudel

This is a proper apple strudel but it's made using filo pastry so very easy. Who would think such simple ingredients could be transformed into such a feathery, fruity delight?

Serves 6

500g Bramley cooking apples
100g caster sugar, plus a little extra to sprinkle
100g raisins or sultanas
50g fresh white breadcrumbs
1 tsp ground cinnamon
50g butter, melted
1 tbsp fresh lemon juice
finely grated zest of ½ lemon

pastry

4 filo pastry sheets (each about 32 x 38cm), thawed if frozen
40g butter, melted
icing sugar, to decorate

Peel, quarter and core the apples, then slice very thinly. Put them in a large bowl with the sugar, raisins, breadcrumbs, cinnamon, melted butter, lemon juice and zest. Toss everything together carefully but thoroughly until evenly mixed.

Preheat the oven to 180°C/Fan 160°C/Gas 4. Line a large baking tray with baking parchment. Place a sheet of filo pastry on the parchment and brush it with a little melted butter. Repeat with the remaining pastry sheets, brushing each layer with butter. If your pastry sheets are shorter than recommended, you may need to stagger them slightly, or add a couple of extras, as you need the final stack to be about 30 x 40cm.

Spoon the filling onto the pastry, leaving a 2cm border all around the edge. Carefully fold over the short sides to seal in the filling. Roll up the pastry firmly from one of the long sides, making sure the seam is placed underneath. Brush with more melted butter and use strips of spare pastry to repair any cracks. Brush again. Sprinkle with a little extra sugar.

Bake for 35–40 minutes until golden brown and crisp. Serve in thick slices, warm or cold, sprinkled with sifted icing sugar.

pecan & pistachio baklava

If you have a sweet tooth, you'll love baklava. We visited a baklava maker in Gaziantep in Turkey and watched them making these wonderfully sticky pastry morsels. Inspired, we created our own version, which we're sure you'll enjoy.

Makes 20

150g pecan nut halves
200g shelled pistachios
1 tsp ground cinnamon
½ tsp ground mixed spice
finely grated zest of ½ lemon
6 tbsp golden caster sugar

pastry
8 filo pastry sheets (each about 32 x 38cm), thawed if frozen
85g unsalted butter

syrup
250g golden caster sugar
freshly squeezed juice of ½ lemon (you need about 2 tbsp)
5 tbsp cold water
3–5 tsp rose water for cooking, to taste

You'll need a tin or ovenproof dish measuring about 20 x 30cm and 4cm deep

Put the nuts in a food processor and blitz on the pulse setting until they are coarsely chopped. Tip them into a bowl and mix with the spices, lemon zest and caster sugar.

Preheat the oven to 200°C/Fan 180°C/Gas 6. Melt the butter for the pastry in a small saucepan. Take the sheets of filo and put them in a stack. Cut the stack half through the middle to make 16 rectangles measuring 32 x 19cm. Take 1 of these, brush with a little butter and top with a second rectangle. Repeat until you have a stack of 6 rectangles.

Lightly butter your tin. Place the stack of pastry inside and cover with a third of the nut mixture. Place a rectangle of pastry on top, brush with melted butter and top with a second to make a layer of 2 sheets on top of the filling. Sprinkle with another third of the nut mixture and spread evenly. Top with 2 more sheets of filo as before and sprinkle over all the remaining nut mixture. Make a final stack of 6 sheets, buttering between the layers as before, and place on top of the filling. Use a round-bladed knife to tuck any excess pastry down the sides of the tin. Brush the remaining butter over the pie and, using a sharp knife, score into 20 squares, cutting just through the first 3 layers of filo. Bake for 25 minutes until the pastry is crisp and golden brown.

To make the syrup, put the sugar, lemon juice and water in a small saucepan and gently heat until the sugar dissolves completely and the syrup is clear, stirring regularly. This will take about 5 minutes. Remove from the heat and leave to cool for 8–10 minutes. Add the rose water a teaspoon at a time and carefully taste the syrup – making sure it is cool enough first. Continue adding the rose water until the syrup is to your liking. Take the baklava out of the oven and cut into portions, following the score lines. Slowly pour the syrup over, allowing it to gently drizzle between the layers. Stand for at least an hour before serving.

Tip:
If you can't get hold of any rose water, add a few tablespoons of fresh orange juice or orange flower water to the syrup instead.

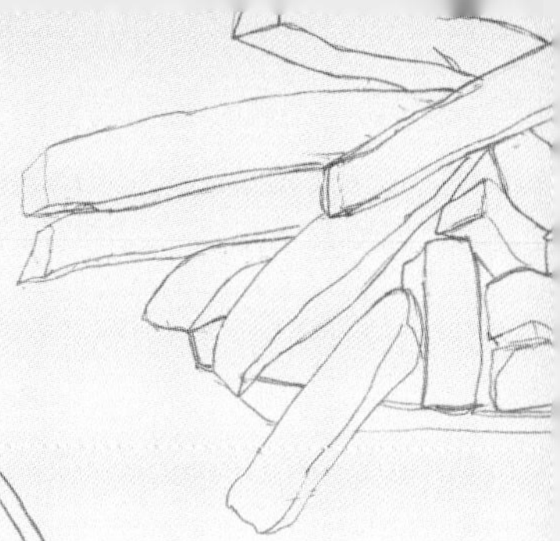

sides, salads & sauces

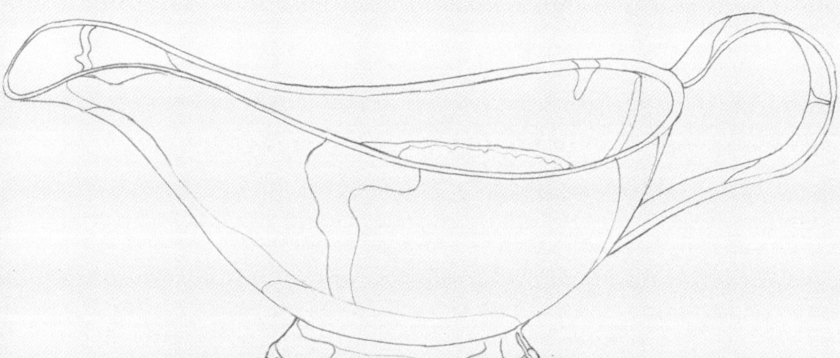

the best chips ever

For the best chips, always use floury potatoes with a good fibre content – that is, more potato and less water. Yukon Gold, Nadine and Maris Piper are all great, and Cyprus are also good.

Serves 4

4 large floury potatoes
2 litres sunflower oil, for deep frying
flaked sea salt
malt vinegar

Peel the potatoes and cut them into slices about 1cm thick. Cut each slice into fairly thick chips and rinse them in a colander under plenty of cold water to remove excess starch. If you have time, it's worth letting the chips soak in a bowl of cold water for several hours or overnight. Blot them dry on kitchen roll.

Ideally, use an electric deep-fat fryer for cooking your chips – the fire brigade are dead against people using an ordinary pan. But if you have to, half fill a large deep saucepan with sunflower oil and heat to 130°C. It's important to use a cooking thermometer and check the temperature regularly. Do not allow the oil to overheat and never leave hot oil unattended.

Gently drop half the chips into the hot oil and stir carefully with a large metal spoon. Leave to fry for 10 minutes until cooked through but not browned. Remove the chips with a slotted spoon and drain them on plenty of kitchen roll. Follow the same method with the rest of the chips and drain well. The chips can be left for several hours at this stage.

Now, here is the secret of success – cooking the chips for a second time at a higher temperature. Reheat the oil to 190°C. Lower all the chips gently into the pan and cook for 4–5 minutes until crisp and golden brown. Lift out with a slotted spoon and drain on kitchen roll. Tip the chips into a serving dish and sprinkle with salt and vinegar to serve.

a mashed potato for every pie!

Nothing goes better with a pie than some good old mashed potatoes. Here's our basic recipe, plus lots of ideas for getting more creative. Have fun!

Serves 6

1kg potatoes, peeled and quartered
75ml single cream or milk
50g butter
flaked sea salt
freshly ground pepper

Floury potatoes make the best mash and Desiree, King Edward or Maris Piper are all good options. Make sure your spuds are all cut about the same size so they cook evenly – nothing worse than lumpy mash.

Put the potatoes into a pan of salted water, bring to the boil, then reduce the heat and simmer for about 20 minutes until soft. Warm the cream or milk in a separate pan and melt the butter – it's really worth doing this as it will help the mash stay hot for longer.

When the potatoes are cooked, drain them well and return them to the pan to drive off any excess moisture, then mash. Really put your back into this and think of the good all that exercise is doing you. Add the warm cream or milk and the butter, then mix well. Season to taste. We often use white pepper with mash as it seems to make it more potatoey.

Once you've got your mash perfect, keep it warm in an ovenproof bowl covered with foil.

sage & onion mash

Blanch a few sage leaves in hot water for a minute or so (this helps to take the bitterness out of the sage leaves). Chop the leaves finely and set aside. Boil 2 onions until tender, but not soft, and drain well. Chop the cooked onions, add the sage and mix well. Add the sage and onion mix to the mash and stir through. Season to taste.

garlic mash

Crush a couple of raw garlic cloves with the back of a knife and add them to the butter as you melt it. Leave to infuse over a very low heat for 5 minutes or so. Remove the garlic and stir the butter into the mash.

roast garlic mash

Place the garlic on large square of foil, drizzle it with oil and wrap it up. Bake the garlic at 190°C/Fan 170°C/Gas 5 for about 30 minutes until soft, then cool. Melt 50g of butter. Separate the cloves of garlic and pop the flesh out of the skins into the melted butter. Leave to infuse for a good 5 minutes over a low heat. Remove the garlic cloves from the butter and stir the garlicky butter through the mash and serve. If you like a stronger garlic flavour, squash some of the garlic cloves into the butter and stir into the mash.

roast garlic & truffle oil mash

Use the method for the roast garlic mash and add half a teaspoon of truffle oil to the butter as you melt it.

black pudding mash

Remove the skin and dice the black pudding into small pieces. Fry these in a little butter and then stir through your mash. Heaven!

mustard mash

Add 2 teaspoons of Dijon mustard and a dessertspoon of whole grain mustard to every 1kg of mashed potatoes.

parsley & chive mash

This mash is perfect for topping a fish pie. Stir a couple of tablespoons of chopped parsley and chives through your mash.

thyme mash

Great with chicken. Finely chop a few sprigs of lemon thyme, then soften in the melted butter before stirring into the mash.

pancetta mash

Fry some chopped pancetta or streaky bacon and stir into your mash.

best-ever roast potatoes

Adding semolina is a clever little tip we learned in Ireland and goose fat is a must for really crispy roasties. These are the tastiest roast potatoes ever.

Serves 4–6

1.5kg good spuds (Maris Pipers are great for roasting)
100g goose fat
2 tbsp semolina
flaked sea salt
freshly ground black pepper

Peel the potatoes and cut them into chunks – whatever size you fancy, according to how you like your roasties.

Put the potatoes in a saucepan of cold, salted water, bring to the boil and boil for about 5 minutes. Drain well and then put the potatoes back in the saucepan and shake them to scuff up the surfaces. This helps to give you lovely crispy potatoes.

Meanwhile, preheat the oven to 200–220°C/Fan 180–200°C/Gas 6–7 and melt the goose fat in a roasting tin. Sprinkle the semolina over the potatoes and carefully tip them into the sizzling goose fat. Season liberally and roast until golden – this will take about 45–50 minutes, depending on the size of the potatoes.

dauphinoise potatoes

This is a recipe that's often mucked about with – people add cheese and other bits and pieces. Simple is best, we reckon, and when a dauphinoise is done well, there's nothing to touch it.

Serves 6

300ml double cream
300ml whole or semi-skimmed milk
3 large garlic cloves, crushed
1 tsp flaked sea salt
2–3 sprigs of fresh thyme (optional)
knob of butter, for greasing
1kg potatoes (preferably Maris Pipers)
freshly ground black pepper

You'll need a 2-litre ovenproof dish – a lasagne dish is ideal

Put the cream, milk, garlic, salt and lots of freshly ground black pepper in a jug and whisk lightly until combined. Strip the leaves from the thyme, if using, and stir them into the milk mixture.

Preheat the oven to 190°C/Fan 180°C/Gas 5. Butter your ovenproof dish. Peel the potatoes and cut them into very thin slices, no more than 3mm thick. Arrange a layer of potatoes in the base of the dish. Stir the cream mixture and pour a little over the potatoes.

Cover with another layer of potatoes, then add some more cream. Repeat the layers until all the potatoes and cream are used. Season with a little more pepper and bake for 35–45 minutes or until the potatoes are softened and the top is lightly browned. You can test the potatoes are ready by sliding a knife into the centre.

honey-roasted parsnips

Adding honey towards the end of the cooking time makes roast parsnips extra delicious. Maple syrup is also good. Just take care that you don't cook them for too long or the honey or syrup will turn black and taste bitter.

Serves 6

1kg parsnips
2 tbsp goose fat or vegetable oil
lots of cracked black pepper
sprinkling of flaked sea salt
½ tsp dried chilli flakes
2 tbsp clear honey

Preheat the oven to 180°C/Fan 160°C/Gas 4. Peel and cut the parsnips into chunks. We tend to cut off the pointy end and then cut the stouter top into pieces of roughly the same size so that they roast evenly. Heat the goose fat or oil in a roasting tin until it is smoking.

Toss the parsnip pieces in the hot fat or oil until they are nicely coated, then sprinkle them with the black pepper and sea salt. Place them in the oven and roast for about 45 minutes or until cooked and starting to turn golden. The exact cooking time will depend on how big you cut the chunks, so keep an eye on them.

Add the chilli flakes and honey, then roll the parsnips in the sticky juices. Return them to the oven for about 10 minutes and continue cooking until golden. Keep a close eye on them so they don't overcook.

creamed celeriac

Celeriac is an ugly-looking brute, but beat it about a bit and you can produce something beautiful. You can also mix celeriac fifty-fifty with potato to make a tasty mash or mix in some Jerusalem artichokes to make three-root mash.

Serves 4

1 celeriac (about 750g)
100ml double cream
50g butter
½–1 tsp fresh lemon juice
flaked sea salt
freshly ground black pepper

Fill a medium saucepan just under half full with cold water and bring to the boil. While the water is coming to the boil, put the celeriac on a board and, using a sharp knife, carefully cut off all the skin and any damaged areas. Cut the celeriac in half – these veg can be very hard, so watch your fingers – and then into chunks of about 4cm.

Drop the celeriac gently into the bubbling water and return to the boil. Cook for 15–20 minutes until very soft, checking for tenderness with the tip of a knife. Drain in a sieve and leave to cool for 5 minutes.

While the celeriac is cooling, warm the cream and butter in a small saucepan over a low heat, stirring occasionally, until the butter has melted. Add a good pinch of salt and plenty of ground black pepper. Pile the celeriac into a food processor and blend to a rough mash.

With the motor running, pour the warm cream mixture in a steady stream onto the celeriac mash and blend to a very smooth purée. Adjust the seasoning to taste, adding lemon juice to sharpen the flavour slightly. Spoon the creamed celeriac into a warmed serving dish and serve at once.

You can also use this method to make creamed parsnips or sweet potatoes.

creamy colcannon

This mixture of creamy mash and tender green cabbage is a fab accompaniment to a home-made pie. We like to add a bit of bacon for extra flavour, but you can leave it out if you prefer.

Serves 6

1kg medium potatoes (preferably Maris Pipers or King Edwards)
1 small green cabbage, such as savoy
75g butter
100g rindless, smoked streaky bacon rashers, cut into 2cm pieces
5 spring onions, trimmed and finely sliced
200ml double cream
flaked sea salt
freshly ground black pepper

Peel the potatoes and cut them into even-sized chunks. Put them in a large saucepan and cover with cold water, then bring to the boil and cook for about 15 minutes or until very tender. Test with the tip of a knife.

While the potatoes are cooking, remove any damaged leaves from the cabbage and cut it in half. Cut out the tough central core and thinly shred the leaves. Heat 25g of the butter in a large non-stick frying pan and fry the bacon and cabbage for 4 minutes, stirring regularly. Add the spring onions and cook for 1 minute more.

Drain the potatoes in a large colander, return them to the saucepan and leave to stand for a couple of minutes. Warm the cream and the remaining butter in a small pan. Mash the cooked potatoes with the cream and butter until smooth and season to taste. You can use a set of electric beaters if you want your mash to be really fluffy and light.

Tip the cabbage and bacon mixture into the pan with the mash and stir together until lightly combined. Pile into a warmed dish and serve.

Tip:
Curly kale leaves make a great alternative to the cabbage and add lovely deep green streaks to the mash.

peas with bacon & lettuce

Fabulous with fresh or frozen peas, this juicy dish is good with any pie or a butch quiche. Bacon and peas work really well together and the lettuce hearts add extra crunch and sweetness. Lovely!

Serves 4–6

25g butter
4 rashers of smoked, rindless streaky bacon
½ small onion, finely chopped
2 baby gem lettuces
400g frozen peas
150ml hot chicken stock (made with ½ chicken stock cube)
1 tbsp crème fraiche or double cream
flaked sea salt
freshly ground black pepper

Melt the butter in a large frying pan over a low heat. Cut the bacon rashers into 2cm pieces and add them to the pan. Increase the heat a little and cook for 3–4 minutes or until the fat begins to brown, stirring regularly.

Add the onion, reduce the heat and cook gently for 2–3 minutes until softened. Trim the lettuces and remove any damaged leaves, then cut the lettuces into quarters lengthways and add them to the pan. Fry for 2 minutes, turning once or twice until they are very lightly browned.

Tip the peas into the pan, add the chicken stock and bring to a simmer. Cook for a couple of minutes or until the peas are tender, stirring occasionally. Season, stir in the crème fraiche or cream and bubble for a few seconds more. Serve hot.

green beans
with chilli & garlic butter

This flavoured butter works well with freshly cooked runner beans and broccoli too. Or try putting a couple on a fried steak or chicken breast or even wedge a bit into a fluffy baked potato.

Serves 4

350g green beans

chilli & garlic butter
1 plump red chilli
150g softened butter
good pinch of dried chilli flakes
2 garlic cloves, crushed
1 tbsp finely chopped parsley
freshly ground black pepper

To make the flavoured butter, cut the chilli in half lengthways and discard the seeds. Cut the chilli into tiny dice and put it in a bowl with the softened butter, chilli flakes, crushed garlic and parsley. Season with lots of freshly ground pepper, then beat with a wooden spoon until thoroughly combined. Don't forget to wash your hands thoroughly after handling the fresh chilli.

Place a sheet of non-PVC clingfilm, about 20cm long, on the work surface. Spoon the flavoured butter into a fat sausage shape in the centre, about 5cm up from one long side. Roll up like a Swiss roll to enclose the butter and twist the ends of the parcel to seal. Freeze for at least an hour and up to a month.

To prepare the beans, trim off the stalks but leave the tops intact as they will make the beans look a bit more glamorous. Bring a medium pan of water to the boil, then add the beans and bring back to the boil. Cook for 5 minutes or until tender, then drain the beans in a colander and put them back in the pan.

Take the flavoured butter from the freezer and unwrap one end. Cut 3 slices, about 1cm thick, and add them to the beans. Rewrap the rest of the butter and return it to the freezer to use another time. Toss the beans with the butter over a low heat until the butter melts and lightly coats the beans. Tip into a warmed dish and serve.

broad beans
with pancetta & shallots

This rocks with a fish pie, and frozen broad beans are so good you can make this at any time of the year. Lots of supermarkets now sell ready-diced pancetta, so that makes life easy.

Serves 6

400g frozen broad beans, defrosted
4 tbsp olive oil
150g pancetta, finely diced
4 shallots, finely chopped
flaked sea salt
freshly ground black pepper

Defrost the beans and remove the tough outer skins. This is a bit of a job, but it's well worth the effort, believe us, and defrosted beans are easier to peel than fresh ones.

Warm the olive oil in a non-stick frying pan and sauté the pancetta until golden. Add the shallots and cook for a couple of minutes more until soft. Then tip in the beans and fry gently over a low heat for a further 2 minutes. Season and serve.

mushy green peas

The large marrowfat peas used for making mushy peas aren't readily available all over the UK, so we've made a variation of this delicious pea purée with green split peas instead.

Serves 4

200g green split peas
1.5 litres water
1 medium onion, finely chopped
1 bay leaf
25g butter
good pinch of caster sugar
flaked sea salt
freshly ground black pepper

Rinse the peas in lots of cold water and drain. Tip them into a large saucepan and stir in the 1.5 litres of cold water, then bring to the boil and skim any scum off the surface. Stir in the chopped onion, add the bay leaf and bring back to the boil. Reduce the heat and simmer for about 1½ hours or until the peas are very soft. Stir regularly, especially towards the end of the cooking time when the peas can begin to stick.

The peas are ready when they are completely soft and tender and look thick and mushy. If they are still a little tough after the recommended cooking time, add some extra water and continue cooking until tender. If the peas are ready but there's too much water remaining in the pan, continue cooking at a slightly higher temperature, stirring constantly until thickened. You'll need to use a long-handled spoon and watch out for splashes, as the peas will bubble like hot lava.

Remove the bay leaf, and stir in the butter, sugar, a good pinch of salt and plenty of ground black pepper. Eat hot.

How long the peas take to cook will depend on the length of time they have been stored and can vary enormously. It's best to stick around while they are cooking and be ready to top up with water when necessary. If you want to cut the cooking time, soak the peas in lots of cold water for a few hours before cooking, then drain and cook as above.

perfect cauliflower cheese

We've always loved cauli cheese and this is our special version with mushrooms and a touch of nutmeg to spice it up. Great with a pie, great on its own for supper.

Serves 4

1 large cauliflower
2 tbsp olive oil
250g chestnut mushrooms, wiped and finely sliced
25g butter
2 tbsp plain flour
250ml whole milk
½ tsp English mustard powder
200g Gruyère cheese, grated
pinch of freshly grated nutmeg
50g ciabatta breadcrumbs
50g Parmesan cheese, finely grated
flaked sea salt
freshly ground black pepper

Trim the cauliflower and break it into florets. Bring a big saucepan of water to the boil, add the florets and boil for about 10 minutes until just soft. Drain and set aside.

Heat the oil in a frying pan and sauté the mushrooms until they are just starting to take on a bit of colour. Set aside.

Melt the butter in a saucepan and beat in the flour. Add the milk, stirring all the time, to make a thick white sauce. Add the mustard powder and grated Gruyère, while still stirring, and season. Fold in the mushrooms.

Preheat the oven to 180°C/Fan 160°C/Gas 4. Put the cauliflower florets in an oven dish, pour in the cheesy mushroom sauce and add a sprinkling of freshly grated nutmeg. Mix the ciabatta crumbs with the grated Parmesan and spread them over the top. Place in the preheated oven and bake for about 15 minutes until the sauce is bubbling and the crumb and Parmesan topping is golden.

A blast of citrus is a great way of adding extra zing to a simple veg dish or salad.

glazed carrots

Carrots are naturally sweet and a glaze of butter and sugar makes them extra scrumptious.

Serves 6

750g chantenay carrots
or 6 medium carrots
25g butter
1 tsp caster sugar
2 tbsp finely chopped parsley
flaked sea salt
freshly ground black pepper

Wash and peel the carrots. Chantenay carrots can be left whole but if you're using larger ones, cut them into batons about 5mm thick. Put them in a pan of water, bring to the boil and cook for 8–10 minutes, depending on their size.

Drain the carrots and return them to the pan. Add the butter, sugar and parsley and toss over a medium heat for a couple of minutes. Season with salt and pepper.

pan-roasted vegetables

No trouble to make, these veggies pack a big flavour punch.

Serves 6

1 medium aubergine,
cut into 2cm chunks
2 medium red onions, cut into wedges
2 medium courgettes,
cut into 1.5cm diagonal slices
1 red pepper and 1 yellow pepper,
deseeded and cut into 4cm chunks
4 tbsp olive oil
4–5 sprigs of thyme
4 large, ripe tomatoes,
skinned and quartered
2 garlic cloves, finely sliced
2–3 tsp red wine vinegar
handful of fresh basil leaves,
roughly torn (optional)
flaked sea salt
freshly ground black pepper

Preheat the oven to 220°C/Fan 200°C/Gas 7. Put the aubergine, onions, courgettes and peppers in a roasting tin that's large enough to hold the vegetables in one layer, then add the oil. Strip the thyme leaves from the stalks and scatter over the vegetables. Season with salt and plenty of freshly ground black pepper, then give everything a good old toss with your hands.

Roast the vegetables for about 30 minutes until lightly browned, turning them with a spatula halfway through. Remove from the oven, add the tomatoes and garlic and toss them with the other vegetables. Return to the oven for a further 10 minutes or until all the vegetables are tender.

Season with more salt and pepper and add a dash of red wine vinegar to taste. Serve warm or cold, garnished with fresh basil leaves if you like.

spicy red cabbage

Spicy, warm and hearty, this cabbage dish is real comfort food that any pie would be happy to see on the same plate. Reheats well so keep any leftovers to serve up the next day.

Serves 6

1 small red cabbage
40g butter
1 large onion, finely sliced
2 star anise
1 cinnamon stick
¼ tsp freshly grated nutmeg
1 bay leaf
150ml cider
3 tbsp cider vinegar
2 tbsp light muscovado sugar
2 tbsp sunflower oil
1 red eating apple, peeled, quartered, cored and sliced
2 tbsp redcurrant jelly
flaked sea salt
freshly ground black pepper

Finely slice the cabbage, chucking out the core and any tough pieces. Use a pan that has a tight-fitting lid and is large enough to hold all the cabbage. Melt 25g of the butter in the pan and cook the onion, uncovered, for 5 minutes until it is soft but not browned.

Add the star anise, cinnamon stick, nutmeg and bay leaf, then the cabbage, cider, cider vinegar and sugar. Stir until everything is thoroughly mixed and the sugar has dissolved. Season generously. Bring to the boil, then cover the pan tightly and simmer gently for about 45–50 minutes, stirring occasionally, until the cabbage is very tender and the liquid has evaporated.

When the cabbage has been cooking for about 30 minutes, melt the remaining butter with the oil in a small non-stick frying pan. Fry the apple slices for 2–3 minutes until lightly browned on both sides. Add them to the cabbage for the last 10 minutes of the cooking time. Stir in the redcurrant jelly and allow it to melt. Remove the star anise and cinnamon stick before serving.

creamy potato salad

This is the warlord of the salad world. If you want a salad with a bit substance, this is for you. Just the thing with a home-made quiche (see page 115).

Serves 6

1kg new potatoes, well scrubbed
3 large free-range egg yolks
2 tbsp white wine vinegar
1 tbsp Dijon mustard
1 tsp caster sugar
½ tsp sea salt flakes
300ml sunflower oil
200ml tub of crème fraiche
2–3 tbsp cold water
1 bunch of spring onions, trimmed and finely sliced
1 tsp caraway seeds (optional)
freshly ground black pepper

Tip:
If you don't want to make your own mayonnaise, use about 400ml of ready-made.

Put the potatoes in a large pan of salted water and bring to the boil. Reduce the heat to a fast simmer and cook the potatoes for 18–20 minutes, or until tender but not breaking apart. Rinse the potatoes in a colander under cold running water for a couple of minutes, then leave to drain thoroughly. Cut the potatoes in half, or into thick slices if large.

To make the creamy mayonnaise, put the egg yolks, vinegar, mustard and sugar in a food processor. Season with the salt and some ground black pepper. Blitz until smooth, then, with the motor running, gradually add the oil and blend until smooth and thick. Add the crème fraiche and the cold water. Blend for a few seconds longer, adding more water if necessary, until the mayonnaise has a soft, dropping consistency.

Tip the potatoes into a bowl and mix with the mayonnaise and spring onions. Check the seasoning. Scatter the caraway seeds, if using, into a dry frying pan and toast over a medium heat for 2–3 minutes, shaking the pan regularly. Sprinkle the seeds over the salad and add a little black pepper before serving.

rainbow coleslaw

Crunchy, colourful and packed with flavour. Take some on a picnic or serve with a quiche or savoury tart – a salad for all seasons.

Serves 6–8

½ medium red cabbage
2 medium carrots, peeled
6 spring onions,
trimmed and finely sliced
50g sultanas
1 apple, peeled, quartered, cored and cut into small chunks

dressing
150g mayonnaise
150ml natural yoghurt
1 small garlic clove, crushed
flaked sea salt
freshly ground black pepper

Remove any damaged outer leaves from the cabbage and cut out the tough central core. Shred the cabbage as finely as possible and put it in a large bowl. Coarsely grate the carrots lengthways into long, thin shreds and finely slice the pepper.

Add the carrots, spring onions and sultanas to the bowl with the cabbage. Add the apple and toss lightly.

To make the dressing, mix the mayonnaise, yoghurt and garlic and season with a little salt and plenty of ground black pepper. Pour the dressing over the vegetables and toss lightly.

green salad

It's all in the dressing. Get that right and your green salad will be the perfect partner for any pie.

Serves 6

2 romaine lettuces, trimmed
½ cucumber, finely sliced

simple vinaigrette
2 tbsp sunflower oil
2 tbsp extra virgin olive oil
1 tbsp white wine vinegar
½ tsp caster sugar
1 tsp Dijon mustard
flaked sea salt
freshly ground black pepper

Separate the lettuce leaves and discard the stalk and any damaged parts. Wash the leaves and drain them very well. Tear the leaves into pieces, put them in a serving bowl and scatter with the cucumber slices.

To make the vinaigrette, mix the oils in a small jug. Put the white wine vinegar, sugar and mustard in a small bowl and add a pinch of salt and a little freshly ground black pepper. Whisk until smooth. Slowly whisk the oils into the vinegar mixture until the dressing is slightly thickened. Adjust the seasoning to taste and toss with the salad.

lovely home-made gravy

Pies need gravy. That glorious filling, that crumbly crust just needs the lubrication of rich tasty gravy to make a mouthful of perfection. Match the stock cube to your pie filling and follow our simple steps.

Serves 4–6

1 tbsp sunflower oil
1 medium onion, finely sliced
3–4 sprigs of fresh thyme (optional)
75ml red or white wine
2 tbsp plain flour
450ml hot stock (made with the appropriate stock cube)
flaked sea salt
freshly ground black pepper

Tips:

Add a teaspoon or 2 of redcurrant jelly to chicken or lamb gravy.

Make pork gravy with 200ml of apple juice and 200ml pork stock.

Cook a couple of rashers of bacon with the onions for a delicious chicken gravy.

Heat the oil in a large non-stick frying pan. Gently fry the onion with the thyme, if using, for about 10 minutes until softened and lightly browned, stirring regularly. Then pour the wine into the pan and allow to bubble until reduced by half.

Sprinkle the flour over the onion and cook for about a minute, while stirring. Slowly add the stock, stirring constantly, until the gravy thickens. Continue to cook and stir for 3–4 minutes.

Pass the liquid through a sieve and into a clean pan. Return to the hob, add seasoning to taste and simmer for a couple of minutes more, while stirring.

home-made tomato ketchup

It's time to get saucy. And there's no better sauce for a pie than home-made tomato ketchup. Yes, we know you can buy it in bottles and squeezy tubs, but try this and you'll be converted.

Makes 2 litres

3.75kg ripe tomatoes, roughly chopped
3 medium onions, roughly chopped
6 garlic cloves, sliced
200ml cider vinegar
200ml malt vinegar
200g light brown muscovado sugar
1 tbsp flaked sea salt
1 tsp English mustard powder
1 tsp ground cloves
1½ tsp ground allspice
1 tsp ground ginger
2 cinnamon sticks
2tsp celery salt
1 tsp ground white pepper

You'll need 4 x 500ml Kilner jars or some bottles or jars with lids

Put the tomatoes, onions and garlic into a large, heavy-based saucepan. Pour in both vinegars, then add the sugar, sea salt, mustard powder, spices, celery salt and pepper. Place over a medium heat and slowly bring to the boil, stirring constantly until the sugar has dissolved. Reduce the heat, cover the pan loosely with a lid and leave to simmer gently for 3–3½ hours. Watch the ketchup carefully and stir often, particularly towards the end of the cooking time, as the mixture could begin to stick.

When the ketchup is cooked, the liquid should be reduced and the tomatoes pulpy. Remove the pan from the heat and take out the cinnamon sticks. Cool for 10 minutes, then blitz with a hand blender until as smooth as possible.

Place a large fine sieve over a clean saucepan. Working in batches, ladle the mixture into the sieve and force it through with the bowl of the ladle. Push and press as hard as you can to extract every bit of the precious liquid. When you're done, discard the tomato seeds and skin.

Place the pan over a medium heat and add extra salt or pepper if necessary. Bring to a simmer, stirring constantly. Watch out for splashes, as the sauce will bubble up and it will be scalding hot. Cook for 2–3 minutes, then remove from the heat.

Meanwhile, sterilise your bottles or jars. Preheat the oven to 180°C/ Fan 160°/Gas 4. Wash the bottles and stoppers really well and put them on a baking sheet in the oven for 10 minutes – remove any rubber seals first. Leave to cool slightly.

Pour the hot sauce through a large funnel into the sterilised bottles or jars. Tap the bottles on your work surface a couple of times to get rid of any air bubbles and leave them open for about 30 minutes before sealing. Store for at least a month before using and keep in the fridge once open.

chilli & green apple chutney

This chutney has a tangy fruit flavour with a hit of spice and is bound to tickle your tastebuds. It's easy to make, keeps well and goes down a treat with our wonderful home-made pork pie (see page 225).

Makes about 1.5 litres

4 crisp green eating apples
2 long red chillies
4 medium red onions, roughly chopped
4 garlic cloves, finely chopped
4 tbsp finely chopped fresh root ginger
250g ready-to-eat dried apricots, quartered
250g sultanas
1 tsp ground allspice
1 cinnamon stick
400ml red wine vinegar
400g light muscovado sugar
1 tsp flaked sea salt

You'll need about average jam jars with glass or plastic-coated lids

Peel the apples, cut them into quarters and remove the cores. Cut the apples into small chunks and put them in a large saucepan. Cut the chillies in half and scrape out the seeds – or leave them in if you like a really spicy chutney. Finely chop the chilli and add it to the pan with the apple.

Add the onions, garlic, ginger, apricots, sultanas, allspice and cinnamon stick. Pour the vinegar into the pan and stir in the sugar. Bring the vinegar to a gentle simmer and cook over a low heat for 1½ hours, stirring occasionally until the fruit is plump and most of the liquid has evaporated.

Just before the chutney is ready, wash the jars thoroughly. Rinse in hot water, drain well upside down on a rack and leave to dry. To sterilise the jars, place them on a baking tray and heat in a preheated oven at 180°C/Fan 160°C/Gas 4 for 10 minutes. Remove and leave to cool for 10 minutes before using. Don't let them cool completely and remember that they will still be hot when you come to use them, so handle them with an oven cloth.

Spoon the chutney into the warm jars and leave to cool. Cover with lids, label and keep in a cool, dark place for at least 2 weeks before using.

hot mustard pickle

This is our version of the classic piccallili, jazzed up with English mustard. Try it with a ham and egg pie. You know it makes sense.

Makes 2 litres

- 250g green beans
- 500g small cauliflower florets
- 250g courgettes (2 medium courgettes)
- 100g fine sea salt
- 3 medium onions, chopped
- 300ml malt vinegar
- 300ml white wine vinegar
- 1 heaped tbsp English mustard powder
- 1 heaped tbsp ground turmeric
- 1 tsp ground ginger
- 1 tsp dried chilli flakes
- 25g cornflour
- 250g granulated sugar

You'll need about 5 average jam jars with glass or plastic-coated lids

Trim the green beans and cut them into lengths of about 1.5cm. Divide the cauliflower into small florets, then cut them into quarters. Trim the courgettes and cut lengthways into 4, then into 1cm slices. Put the vegetables in a non-metallic mixing bowl, sprinkling salt between the layers. Cover with a plate and leave to stand for 24 hours.

The next day, tip the vegetables into a colander and rinse off the salt, then put them in a large bowl, cover with cold water and swirl around a few times. Tip them back into the colander and leave to drain. Put the onions in a large saucepan and stir in the malt vinegar. Bring to a gentle simmer and cook for 15 minutes, stirring every now and then.

Mix 5 tablespoons of the white wine vinegar with the mustard powder, turmeric, ginger, chilli flakes and cornflour. Stir the remaining white wine vinegar and the sugar into the malt vinegar and onions until dissolved. Tip the drained vegetables into the same pan, return to a simmer and cook for 10 minutes, stirring occasionally. Stir the cornflour and spice mixture, then pour it into the pan with the vegetables and stir briskly. Cook for 8–10 minutes more, stirring regularly, until the vegetables are tender but crisp and the pickle is thick. Wash and sterilise the jars (see opposite page).

Pour the pickle into warm sterilised jars, making sure that all the vegetables are as evenly distributed as possible, and leave to cool. Cover with glass or plastic-coated metal lids and seal. Label and store in a cool, dark place for at least a month before eating.

farmhouse pickle

This is a beautiful pickle that goes perfectly with all cold pies. It's dead easy to make too and keeps really well.

Makes 2 litres

2 tbsp finely chopped fresh root ginger
2 tsp flaked sea salt
1 tsp freshly ground black pepper
1 tsp ground mixed spice
½ tsp ground allspice
2 medium onions, chopped
150g sultanas
500g soft brown sugar
500ml malt vinegar
500g Bramley cooking apples, peeled, quartered, cored and roughly chopped
500g dark purple plums, stoned and cut into chunky pieces
1 medium swede (about 725g)
2 medium carrots, peeled and cut into rough 1cm dice
4 tsp ground arrowroot

You'll need about 5 average jam jars with glass or plastic-coated lids

Put the ginger, salt, pepper and spices in a large saucepan or flameproof casserole dish and add the onions, sultanas, sugar and 450ml of the vinegar. Bring to the boil, then reduce the heat and simmer for 20 minutes. Add the apples and plums and cook for 20 minutes more, stirring occasionally.

While the onions and fruits are simmering, prepare the swede. Put it on a board, carefully cut off the thick skin and discard. Cut the swede into thin slices – about 75mm thick – then cut the slices into small cubes. Watch your fingers because swede can be tricky to slice.

Tip the swede and carrots into the pan with the other ingredients. Return to a simmer and cook for 20 minutes, stirring regularly until the swede and carrots are only just tender but the apples and plums have almost completely turned to mush. Blend the arrowroot with the remaining vinegar until smooth and stir into the pan. Cook for 3 minutes more, stirring constantly, or until the pickle looks thick and glossy.

While the pickle is cooking, wash the jars and lids thoroughly and rinse in hot water. Drain well upside down on a rack and leave to dry. To sterilise the jars, place them on a baking tray and heat in a preheated oven at 180°C/Fan 160°C/Gas 4 for 10 minutes. Remove and leave to cool for 10 minutes before using. Do not let them cool completely. They should still be hot when you come to use them, so handle with an oven glove.

Spoon the pickle into the warm jars and leave to cool. Cover with lids, label the jars and keep in a cool, dark place for about a month before using.

home-made vanilla custard

There is nothing more luxurious than home-made custard. If you've taken the trouble to make a sweet pie, it's worth giving it this final flourish of vanilla-scented gorgeousness.

Serves 6

250ml whole milk
250ml double cream
1 vanilla pod, split, or
½ tsp vanilla extract
4 large egg yolks
50g caster sugar
2 heaped tsp cornflour

Pour the milk and cream into a medium saucepan. Split the vanilla pod in half lengthways, if using, and scrape the seeds into the pan. Drop the pod in too. Place the pan over a low heat and bring to a gentle simmer. Watch carefully so it doesn't have a chance to boil over and stir occasionally. Remove from the heat.

Put the egg yolks, sugar and cornflour in a heatproof bowl and beat with a metal whisk until pale and creamy. Remove the vanilla pod from the warm milk and cream and pour the mixture over the eggs, whisking constantly until smooth.

Return the mixture to the saucepan and cook over a low heat for 4–5 minutes, stirring constantly with a wooden spoon until the custard is thick and creamy. Do not allow it to overheat. Serve immediately.

boozy cream

Go on – spoil yourself for once and worry about your cholesterol levels another day.

Serves 6

300ml fresh double cream, well chilled
2 tbsp caster sugar
2 tbsp brandy, rum or Cointreau (orange liqueur)
finely grated zest of ½ orange (optional)

Pour the cream into a large bowl and stir in the sugar, booze and orange zest, if using.

Using an electric whisk, whip the cream until soft peaks form. Transfer to a pretty bowl for serving.

You can make this ahead, then cover the bowl with clingfilm and chill until needed. Bear in mind that you may need to give it a quick whisk again before serving.

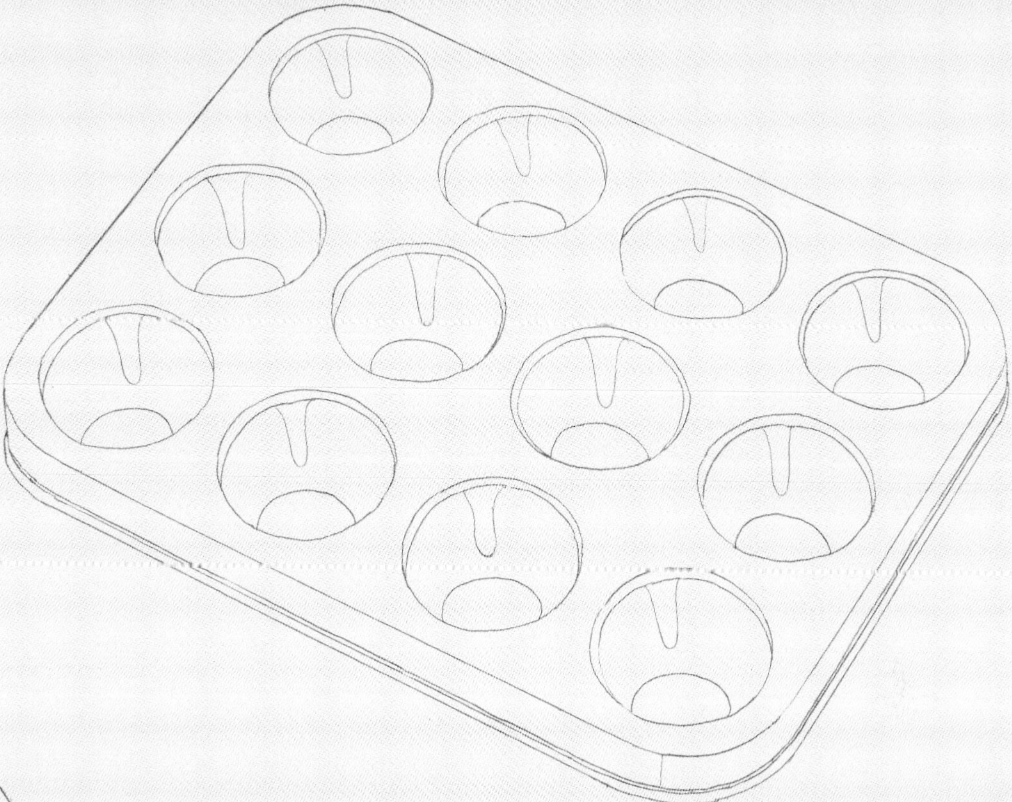

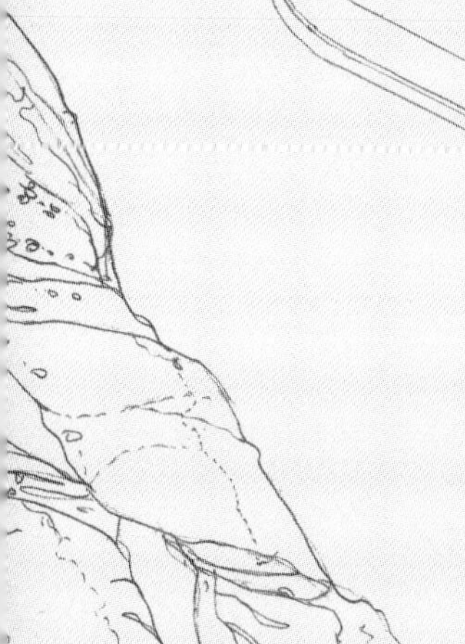

leftovers

simple sausage bites

Even leftover puff pastry can be used again. You just need to be careful to keep the layers, so gather the pastry up without kneading and roll it out on a floured surface. It might not rise quite as much but it will still taste good.

Makes 6–8

about 250g leftover puff pastry
plain flour, for rolling
2–3 good-quality sausages, skinned
beaten egg, to glaze
¼ tsp poppy seeds (optional)

Tip:
You can use any leftover pastry to make this recipe. Shortcrust works well when rolled around the sausage meat to make mini sausage rolls.

Preheat the oven to 200°C/Fan 180°C/Gas 6. Gather the leftover pastry together and put it in a heap without kneading or squeezing too much. You need to try to keep the layers intact so that the pastry still puffs up as it cooks. Don't worry if your pile looks a bit of a mess.

Roll the pastry out on a lightly floured surface until it is about 4mm thick. Use a 6cm straight-edged biscuit cutter to cut out 6–8 rounds, then place them on a baking tray lined with baking parchment.

Squeeze the sausage meat out of the skins and place a tablespoon in the centre of each round. Brush around the sausage meat with a little beaten egg. Gather the pastry trimmings again, then cut them into strips and make a lattice pattern, or cut more rounds and place them on top of the sausage meat. Brush with more egg and sprinkle with poppy seeds if you have some.

Bake for 25 minutes or until the pastry is golden brown and the sausage meat is cooked. Serve warm or cold.

cheese straws

Everyone loves a cheese straw and they're the perfect thing to make with scraps of puff pastry. We like Parmesan on these, but use any cheese you have handy – Gruyère is good.

Makes about 12

150g leftover puff pastry
plain flour, for rolling
20g Parmesan cheese, grated
beaten egg, to glaze

Roll out the puff pastry on a lightly floured surface into a rectangle measuring about 20 x 22cm and trim the edges neatly. Preheat the oven to 200°C/Fan 180°C/Gas 6.

Cut into the pastry into strips of about 1.5cm wide and brush with beaten egg. Take each strip and twist it into a spiral, then lay it onto a baking tray and sprinkle with grated Parmesan. Press down the ends slightly to make sure the cheese straws don't uncurl.

Bake for 15–20 minutes until golden. Leave to cool slightly if you can manage to hold people back!

little biscuits for cheese

These are just right to serve with cheese at the end of a meal and you can have fun making different shapes. Store in an airtight tin.

Makes 15

200g leftover pastry, ideally cheese or chilli pastry
plain flour, for rolling
beaten egg, to glaze
freshly ground black pepper
poppy seeds
Parmesan cheese, finely grated

Preheat the oven to 200°C/Fan 180°C/Gas 6 and line a baking tray with baking parchment.

Roll out the pastry on a lightly floured surface until it's about the thickness of a £1 coin. Cut out rounds with a 6cm biscuit cutter, or any other shape you want, and place them on the baking tray.

Brush the biscuits with beaten egg. Sprinkle lightly with some freshly ground black pepper, poppy seeds or finely grated Parmesan. Bake for 12–15 minutes or until crisp and golden brown. Store the biscuits in an airtight tin and eat them up within 5 days.

If you like, you can freshen up the biscuits by warming them in a hot oven for 5 minutes.

deli tomato & cheese filo tartlets

Make these little tartlets with leftover filo pastry and a tub of sun-blush tomatoes with mini mozzarella balls. They make a great party snack or can serve 3 or 4 as a starter with salad.

Makes 12

25g butter
3 filo pastry sheets
(each about 38 x 32cm)
3 tbsp pesto sauce
200g tub of sun-blush tomatoes
with mini mozzarella balls or feta
tiny fresh oregano or basil leaves
(optional)

You'll need a 12-hole mini muffin or mini-cupcake tin

Melt the butter in a small pan over a low heat. Cut each sheet of filo pastry into 16 evenly sized rectangles. Brush 1 of the rectangles very lightly with butter and cover with another square at a right-angle to the first. Brush with a little more butter and cover with a third and fourth pastry rectangle, both at slightly different angles to give lots of pointy ends.

Transfer the stack of pastry to 1 of the holes in the mini muffin tin, pressing well into the base and sides. There is no need to grease the tin first. Repeat with the remaining pastry until all 12 holes are filled with tartlet cases.

Preheat the oven to 200°C/Fan 180°C/Gas 6. Divide the pesto sauce between the tartlets, adding a little dab to each one. Drain the tomatoes and cheese in a sieve and cut the mini mozzarellas in half. Put 2 halves of mozzarella or 2 chunks of feta in each tartlet with a couple of pieces of sun-blush tomato.

Bake for 10 minutes or until the pastry is golden and crisp and the filling is hot. Garnish with tiny oregano or basil leaves and serve.

Tip:
You can put lots of other deli ingredients into these tartlets. Try adding a little canned tuna, some anchovies, olives, strips of ham or even prawns.

GRAND PRIX
and the Holiday too!

Keep a bun tin
in the freezer
and add tart
cases whenever
you have
leftover pastry.

colourful jam tarts

Jam tarts are the first thing most kids learn to cook so let them loose with some pastry scraps and a pot of jam. Make sure they call you when it's time to take the tarts out of the oven, though – hot jam is very hot and can burn.

Makes 12

250g leftover shortcrust or sweet shortcrust pastry
plain flour, for rolling
12 heaped tsp jam, marmalade or lemon curd

You'll need a 12-hole, fairly shallow bun tin

Preheat the oven to 200°C/Fan 180°C/Gas 6. Roll out the pastry on a floured surface until it is about 3mm thick and cut out rounds of about 7–9cm, depending on your tin. Use the pastry rounds to line a 12-hole bun tin.

Spoon the jam, marmalade or lemon curd into the pastry cases. Bake for 15–20 minutes until the pastry is pale golden brown. Cool for 5 minutes in the tin. Using a dessertspoon, carefully lift out each jam tart, and place on a wire rack. Leave for a few more minutes before serving as the jam will remain scalding hot for quite a while.

Place the tarts on some folded kitchen roll to absorb any moisture and store in an airtight tin for up to 3 days.

the five-minute fruit tart

This is a breeze to put together – the easiest pud ever. Keep your pastry trimmings in the freezer and sprinkle them over any fruit you have handy. You can use frozen fruit in the winter.

Serves 4–6

300g fresh strawberries
300g Bramley cooking apple
200g fresh raspberries
350–400g frozen pastry trimmings
4 tbsp golden caster sugar

You'll need a 1.2-litre pie dish

Whenever you have scraps of leftover shortcrust pastry after making tarts or pies, scatter them in an even layer on a baking tray lined with baking parchment. Cover the pastry with clingfilm and freeze for 1–2 hours until solid. Transfer the pieces to a plastic bag and use from frozen.

Here's one way of using the scraps in a super-quick pie. Preheat the oven to 200°C/Fan 180°C/Gas 6. Hull the strawberries and cut them in half – or quarters if large. Peel the apple, then core, quarter and cut it into rough 2cm chunks. Put the strawberries, raspberries and apple chunks in the pie dish and toss lightly together. Scatter the frozen pastry pieces on top and sprinkle with the sugar.

Bake for 35 minutes or until the pastry is golden brown and the filling is bubbling.

If you don't have any home-made pastry trimmings, you can make this quick pie by breaking up a packet of frozen, ready-rolled shortcrust pastry and dropping the pieces on top of the pie. Sprinkle with sugar as above.

min
max
min

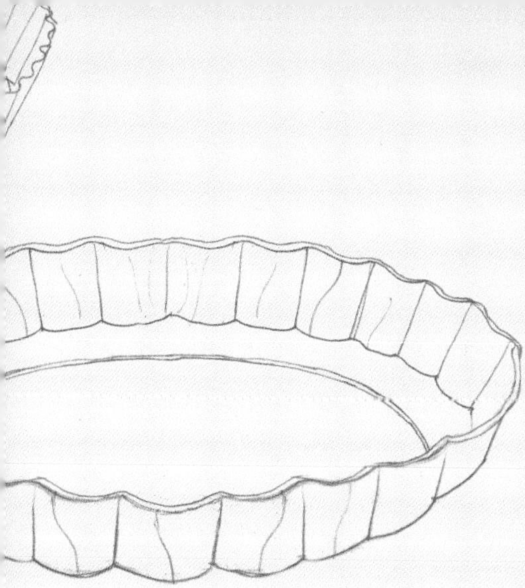

the basics

1
2
3
4
5
6
7
8
9
10
11

tins, dishes & pie plates

1. tart tins

We like using metal tins, as metal conducts the heat to the pastry well. Choose sturdy tins with loose bases that make it easier to remove the tart after baking. Tins of about 3–3.5cm deep are ideal, as this allows a good filling to pastry ratio and helps compensate for any shrinkage.

2. ceramic dishes

Great for serving your tart but it's more difficult to get a good crisp base with these. Put the dish on a hot baking tray to help conduct the heat through the bottom.

3. individual pie dishes

We like the metal dishes with wide rims. The most useful hold about 200ml liquid for a good filling to pastry ratio.

4. springclip cake tin

Ideal for making deep pies, as you can pack your pie with a hearty filling. And the pie will be really easy to remove after cooking.

5. individual tart tins

Choose tins with loose bases and deep sides. Look for a depth of at least 2.5cm to contain a good deep filling.

6. metal pie dish

Nothing beats a metal pie dish for a double-crust pie, as the metal conducts the heat well and helps ensure perfectly cooked pastry. Look for a pie dish with a nice wide rim for crimping the pastry. We've found that a tin with a 23cm base is the most useful size.

7. 12-hole bun tins

Good for mini tarts and pies, 12-hole bun tins should have sloping sides. The shallow ones are about 1.5cm and are good for anything that doesn't need a deep filling, such as mini canapés or jam tarts. For other tarts, use a tin with holes about 2.5cm deep.

8. ceramic pie dish

Pie dishes come in a variety of sizes and shapes. Ceramic dishes are best for top-crust pies and crumbles (anything with a really juicy filling) and look good for serving. The most useful size is about 1.2 litres.

9. Victoria sandwich tin

Just what you need for making a deep-filled custard tart or any double-crust pie that doesn't need a crimped edge and would look good served from the tin. The loose bottom helps you remove the pie, ready to slide onto a serving plate.

10. rectangular cake tin

Square and rectangular cake tins and small roasting tins are great for making double-crust pies that you might want to transport or serve in squares. The metal conducts the heat very well and the pies are easy to cut into portions.

11. pie plates

Metal pie plates conduct heat brilliantly, but we've also used Pyrex glass or ovenproof ceramic plates. In this book, we suggest using a pie plate that's 23–25cm – so as long as it can go in the oven the choice is yours.

essential baking equipment

1. pie funnel

Not always necessary, but we find these most useful when we have a dish that's a bit too big for our filling. The pie funnel helps stop the pastry drooping into the filling and getting soggy. Also useful with a loose fruit filling, as the hollow funnel helps the steam escape.

2. sieve

Most modern flours don't need sifting, but, if you have time, sifting flour before you start rubbing in the butter can help to add air to the mix and make it even lighter. Don't sift wholemeal flour or you'll sift out all the grainy bits.

3. baking beans

A necessity for baking blind but you don't have to buy the posh ceramic variety. Some dried beans or chickpeas work just as well – and you'll need about 600g for a 25cm tart tin. Cooled after use and kept in a jar, they'll last for ages.

4. pastry brush

A must for glazing pastry with egg before baking. Choose one with heat-resistant bristles if possible.

5. baking parchment

Essential for lining tins and trays and for baking blind. Sometimes called baking paper, the ones we like are made from unbleached paper with a silicone coating. Don't use greaseproof paper – it doesn't have the same non-stick qualities.

6. whisk

Fantastic for beating eggs before adding to the flour and fat and also for helping guarantee a smooth sauce. Treat yourself to a heat-resistant silicone-coated whisk if you use non-stick pans.

7. cook's knife

A decent cook's knife (with a 16–18cm blade) is a must. Should have a good sharp blade and a comfortable handle. You'll need one for trimming pastry and knocking up puff pastry.

8. measuring spoons

A proper set of measuring spoons is absolutely vital for following the recipes in this book.

9. pastry cutters

We like the double-sided ones with a crinkly cut on one side and a straight edge on the other.

10. measuring jug

A good heatproof measuring jug will help you make sure your liquid quantities are spot on.

11. pasta & pastry wheel

Fantastic for giving a lovely scalloped edge to your lattice pastry and other decorations.

12. ruler

Important for checking the size of your tart and pie tins – we always measure across the base – and for checking the size of your rolled pastry.

13. scissors

Good kitchen scissors have long, sharp blades. Look out for ones that are dishwasher-safe.

14. rolling pin

A decent rolling pin is a lifelong investment. Choose a long, fairly slender one with rounded ends that feels comfortable in your hands and rolls smoothly.

1
2
3
4
5
6
7
8
9
10
11
12
13
14
FLEXIBLE

ingredients

1 & 2. flour

We usually use plain white flour (1) for our pastry recipes. Wholemeal flour (2) is good when you want a nuttier flavour but we find it is best to mix it with white flour as it can be difficult to roll. Be prepared to fiddle with the liquid quantities too, as it will soak up water very quickly. You'll also need flour for dusting your work surface to prevent the pastry sticking.

3, 4 & 5. fat

Fat gives pastry its flaky texture. We tend to use salted butter (3) which adds a rich flavour and means you don't need to add additional salt to your dough. If you like using lard (4) in your pastry for its short, silky texture, feel free to make up half the butter quantity with it. Use cold fat, straight from the fridge and cut it into small cubes. Shredded suet (5) is perfect for dumplings and suet pastries. We've tested our recipes with beef suet but you can also buy vegetarian suet.

6, 7 & 8. sugar

We use caster sugar (6) for most of our sweet pastries. Golden caster sugar (7) is lovely for sprinkling onto pies before baking, and icing sugar (8) gives a smoother, more silky crust.

9. eggs

Use fresh free-range eggs of the size recommended, as this affects the total amount of liquid in pastry and fillings. Egg makes the pastry richer and tastier and we've found the additional protein makes the pastry easier to roll and less likely to shrink.

10. biscuits

Crushed biscuits make a great base for sweet tarts. Mix with melted butter to make glossy crumbs that are easy to press into a tart tin and set to a crisp base.

11. potatoes

For the fluffiest mash toppings, make sure you choose a good floury potato such as Maris Pipers or King Edwards. Waxy potatoes, such as Cara, are much less likely to give you a smooth mash.

12. cornflour

Cornflour thickens the juices that flow from berries and helps to ensure your meat fillings don't soak into pastry bases and make them soggy. We mix equal amounts of cornflour and water for thickening meat fillings, and we toss cornflour with sugar and fruit for sweet ones.

13. oats

Porridge oats make a delicious crunchy addition to crumbles. They are less likely to soak up the fruity juices, so your crumble will stay crisper longer. Jumbo oats have the best texture.

14. water

Water binds the other ingredients together to make dough. If you have too much water in your pastry it will be stretchy and will shrink back or crack when it cooks. Always use cold water unless hot water is recommended. Warm water will begin to melt the fat and make the pastry greasy. Dumplings, cobblers and hot water crust pastries need a higher proportion of water.

4
2
5
3
1
7
6
11
10
8
9
12
13
14

making shortcrust by hand

Pastry is basically made from flour blended with fat and some egg or water. We like to use egg as we think it gives a richer pastry and it's also easier to use – simpler just to pop in an egg than measure spoonfuls of water. Some people like to make pastry by hand while others prefer to use a food processor. We often take the food processor route, but there's something very satisfying about hand-made pastry and it's good to know how to do it.

You'll see the quantities for all the different pies in the recipes, but the basic proportions are as follows: ***double-crust pie:*** *350g flour and 200g butter;* ***top-crust pie:*** *250g flour and 150g butter;* ***open tart:*** *250g flour and 150g butter;* ***plate pie:*** *300g flour and 175g butter.*

this is what you do:

1. Measure out your ingredients and put the flour in a bowl. Cut the cold butter into small pieces or cubes and add them to the flour. Rub the butter into the flour with your fingertips until the mixture resembles coarse breadcrumbs. Cutting the butter into small cubes helps you rub the fat into the flour quickly, before it has a chance to melt. Using your fingertips helps to keep everything cool for a lighter, flakier pastry. The idea is to coat all the little pieces of hard butter in flour. Keep lifting the mixture out of the bowl as you rub in the fat to get as much as air into the pastry as possible.

2. Now add the egg, water or milk, depending on the recipe. You can break the egg straight into the mixture – saves washing up – but it's probably best to beat it in a small bowl first. Add the liquid with one hand while stirring with a round-bladed knife until the dough comes together and the sides of the bowl are clean.

3. Form the dough into a flattened ball because it will be much easier to roll, but bear in mind the shape of your pie. If you're going to be making a square pie, shape the pastry into a square rather than a disc. This makes it easier to roll out and you'll have loads less waste.

4. Most recipes tell you to chill the pastry at this stage, but this can make it harder to roll later. For tarts of all sizes, we find it's better to roll out the pastry and line your tin first, THEN chill the pastry in the tin.

Our top tip:

Keep everything as cool as possible. Your butter should be well chilled and straight from the fridge. If you have time, pop the butter back in the fridge for 30 minutes after you've cut it into cubes. Use eggs from the fridge too, and make sure the water has run very cold before using.

making shortcrust in a food processor

If you're nervous about pastry making, try this method. It's so easy to do and you don't have to worry about melting the pastry with warm hands. Even better, your pastry will be ready in minutes. You can't go wrong.

this is what you do:

1. Measure out your ingredients and put the flour in the bowl of the food processor. Add the cubes of cold butter, then blitz on the pulse setting until the mixture resembles coarse breadcrumbs. Take care not over-process or the mixture will start to come together before you add the egg or water. We've carefully worked out how much egg or other liquid is required for the recipes in this book, but the quantities you need can vary according to the brand of butter and flour you use, the size of your food processor – and even the time of year.

2. With the motor running, add the egg in a slow but constant stream. Stop processing as the mixture starts to come together and is beginning to form a ball. You may not need all the egg or water. If you keep processing the dough for too long you'll see it forms a firm ball that whizzes round and round the bowl. Try not to let this happen, as it could stretch the pastry too much and it might shrink when you bake it.

3. Remove the sharp blade before gathering the dough with your fingertips and taking it out of the food processor. Shape the dough into a flattened ball or roughly the shape you plan to roll it into.

Our top tip:

Use the pulse setting for mixing the flour and butter. Pulsing means that the mixture is lifted up and dropped down each time, which helps to incorporate air and keeps the pastry light.

variations on basic shortcrust

We've given you some brilliant basic pastry recipes in this book that cook up a treat. Don't think that you have to stick with just the basics though. If you are making one of our pie recipes, why not experiment with some other varieties of pastry. Here are some of our favourites:

cornmeal shortcrust

This has a lovely, slightly crunchy texture and works well for handheld pies and for lining tart tins. The addition of grated Parmesan brings heaps of flavour to the pastry. ***You need:*** *200g quick-cook polenta, 100g plain flour (plus extra for rolling), 150g cold butter, 75ml just-boiled water, 50g finely grated Parmesan cheese.*

Put the flour and polenta in a large bowl and rub in the butter until the mixture resembles coarse breadcrumbs. Make a well in the centre and pour in the just-boiled water. Stir well with a wooden spoon until the mixture comes together and forms a soft dough. Leave to cool, then wrap in clingfilm and chill for an hour or until firm enough to handle. Knead in the Parmesan until thoroughly combined and then roll out the pastry. Makes enough to line a 25cm tart tin.

wholemeal shortcrust

Gives a great, slightly nutty flavour and makes delicious tarts and pie crusts. The wholemeal flour does soak up liquid quickly when you make it, so it's best to roll and use immediately. We've combined it with plain flour so it's a bit easier to work. ***You need:*** *125g plain flour (plus extra for rolling), 125g wholemeal flour, 150g cold butter, cubed, 1 large beaten egg.*

Put both flours into the bowl and make the pastry in the usual way (see pages 336–339). Enough for a 25cm tart tin.

sweet shortcrust

Perfect for desserts such as fresh fruit pies and deep-filled tarts. ***You need:*** *400g plain flour (plus extra for rolling), 250g cold butter, cubed, 2 tbsp caster sugar and 1 large egg beaten with 2 tbsp of cold water.*

Put the flour and sugar in a bowl and make the pastry in the usual way (see pages 336-339). Enough for a double-crust pie made in a 1.2-litre round pie dish.

gluten-free pastry

A must for people who suffer from an intolerance to gluten. Gluten-free flour is much softer than wheat flour, so won't bake blind without cracking. ***You need:*** *250g gluten-free flour (plus extra for rolling), 150g cold butter, cubed, 1 medium egg beaten with 3 tbsp of cold water.*

Make the pastry in the usual way (see pages 336-339). Chill for 1 hour before rolling and don't bake blind. Enough for a 25cm tart tin.

flavoured pastries

Once you feel confident with basic shortcrust, try these variations. The method is the same but you add extra ingredients. One warning – these pastries can be a little harder to roll out so you might prefer to use them for small pies and tarts, particularly at first. Here are some ideas:

citrus shortcrust

Gives a lovely zingy taste. Choose unblemished and preferably unwaxed lemons, oranges and limes and make sure you scrub them well. Pat them dry with kitchen roll before you begin to grate. We like using a fine grater that makes thin shreds rather than tiny pieces.

For citrus shortcrust, *add finely grated lemon, orange or lime zest to the flour and fat mixture before you begin rubbing it in.* Match the flavour to your pie or use a combination of fruit.

chocolate shortcrust

Goes particularly well with soft berry tarts and pies. We've found that sweetening the basic shortcrust with icing sugar and using a good-quality cocoa powder gives the best results. Do sift your icing sugar and cocoa powder before you add them though, or your pastry will be lumpy. This pastry may be a bit tricker to roll out, so roll on floured baking parchment and turn the paper rather than the pastry. Flip gently over into your tart tin and peel off the paper. This pastry is best baked blind with overhanging pastry to prevent shrinkage (see page 358).

For chocolate shortcrust, you will need: *250g plain flour (plus extra for rolling), 175g cold unsalted butter, cubed, 2 tbsp sifted icing sugar, 2 tbsp sifted cocoa powder and 1 large beaten egg.* Make the pastry in the usual way (see pages 336–339), adding cocoa powder to the flour before mixing in the butter. Makes enough for a 25cm tart tin.

herby shortcrust

Wonderful on a savoury pie. You can use any herbs you like but we think that the woody ones, such as thyme and rosemary, work best. You'll need to chop your herbs finely before you use them and discard any twiggy bits.

For herby shortcrust, *add 1 tbsp finely chopped fresh thyme or rosemary leaves to the flour before rubbing in the fat.*

spicy shortcrust

A great favourite of ours. We've found that a combination of paprika and dried chilli flakes offers the best flavour and a rosy red colour too.

For spicy shortcrust, *add 1½ tsp paprika, ½ tsp dried chilli flakes to the flour before rubbing in the fat.*

rough puff pastry

You can buy good puff pastry but it's fairly tricky to make your own from scratch, so try our rough puff pastry instead. It rises beautifully, is flaky and golden and it tastes great. You need strong white bread flour for making rough puff pastry, as the extra gluten makes the pastry more elastic for rolling and folding. ***To make enough puff for a top-crust pie to feed 4–6, you'll need 225g strong white bread flour, a pinch of fine sea salt. 185g cold butter*** *(cut into cubes),* ***125ml cold water and 2 teaspoons of fresh lemon juice****.*

this is what you do:

1. Put the flour and salt into a large bowl. Add the butter and then using a round-bladed knife, gently cut the butter down to mix it into the flour. Keep cutting the butter into smaller and smaller pieces, tossing them with the flour until lightly coated.

2. Add the lemon juice to the water and pour it into the bowl. Keep working the mixture with your knife until the dough comes together and the bowl is almost clean, then remove it from the bowl and place on a floured surface. Roll the dough out into a rectangle with a well-floured rolling pin. Your rectangle should be about 3 times as long as it is wide.

3. Fold down the top third of the pastry, then fold up the bottom third and press the edges with the rolling pin. Rotate the pastry a quarter turn. Use the rolling pin to make 3 shallow depressions across the pastry – this helps to keep the edges straight. Roll into a rectangle again.

4. Repeat the process 5 more times, rolling the pastry to a rectangle, folding the ends into the middle, pressing, making a quarter turn each time. Be sure to keep the work surface and rolling pin well floured. Don't worry if some of the softened butter escapes – just dust heavily with flour and continue. Wrap the pastry in clingfilm and chill for at least an hour, or overnight if you prefer, before using, then allow to stand at room temperature for a few minutes before rolling.

Our top tip:

This pastry freezes well. Wrap in clingfilm, then in foil and freeze for up to 2 months. To use, thaw overnight in the fridge or at room temperature for 2–3 hours.

flaky freezer pastry

This is a great pastry for small pies and tarts and gives a light, flaky crust that's stable enough to hold the pie together once it is out of its tin. You can make a large amount of good pastry very easily by this method. Just remember to put your butter in the freezer for an hour or two before you use it. ***You'll need 400g plain flour*** *(plus extra for rolling),* ***½ teaspoon of fine sea salt, 250g butter that's been frozen for at least 1 hour, and about 125ml cold water.***

this is what you do:

1. For the pastry, sift the flour into a large bowl and stir in the salt – we don't usually sift the flour but it helps for this kind of pastry. Coarsely grate a third of the butter into the flour and toss lightly. Frozen butter can be brittle, so grate it onto a board before adding to the bowl if you are nervous about grating your fingertips! Repeat twice more, tossing the butter through the flour mixture with a round-bladed table knife, until all the butter strands are lightly dusted with the flour. This will help ensure that the pastry bakes into lovely flaky layers.

2. Slowly pour very cold water into the flour mixture, stirring constantly until it all comes together and makes a light dough. Add a little extra water if necessary until the dough feels soft and pliable. Do not knead the dough as it will become tough when baked. Shape into a ball or block and place on a floured surface ready to roll.

Our top tip:

Wrap your butter in a couple of layers of baking parchment before you start grating so the heat from your hands doesn't melt it.

pâte sucrée

This is a lovely sweet pastry that has a fine crumb and silky texture. It has a high fat and sugar content, so good for sweet French patisserie-style tarts of all sizes. The initial chilling really makes a difference to the rolling and lining, so don't forget to rest the pastry in the fridge for at least an hour before you use it. ***You'll need 250g softened butter, 100g caster sugar, 3 large egg yolks, 375g plain flour****, plus extra for rolling,* ***and 2 tbsp cold water.*** *Makes enough for a 28cm tin.*

this is what you do:

1. Cream the butter and sugar together in a large mixing bowl with electric beaters until smooth and light. Beat the egg yolks in a separate bowl and add a little at a time to the creamed mixture, beating well between each addition.

2. Slowly start adding the flour, a heaped tablespoon at a time, alternating with the water until the pastry forms a stiff paste. Scoop out of the bowl with a spatula and shape into a ball or block, then flatten until it's about 3cm deep. Wrap in clingfilm and pop into the fridge for an hour.

3. Roll the pastry out on a sheet of baking parchment lightly dusted with flour. Turn the pastry on the paper every couple of rolls until it reaches the right size for your tin. Lift the pastry on the paper and gently flip it over and into the tin. Peel off the baking parchment and press the pastry into the base and sides of the tin, leaving the excess overhanging the sides. Mend any cracks or tears with a little of the excess pastry.

4. Place on a baking tray and prick the base with a fork. Chill for a further 30 minutes before baking blind (page 358).

Our top tip:

This pastry benefits from being trimmed in the tin after baking. You'll find it easier to trim the pastry when it is still warm, so only stand for 5 minutes before you start. Brush out any crumbs that fall into the crust with a pastry brush.

hot-water crust

This is used for raised pies, such as pork pie. Some hot-water crust recipes use just lard, but ours contains butter as well which we think makes it extra good. You can't buy this pastry, you have to make it which means it's really special. The pastry is rolled thicker than usual so it makes a sturdy, water-tight case for the filling. You can either make the pies in a tin or mould the pastry around jam jars for a homely touch. ***For 4 pork pies, you'll need 475g flour****, plus a bit extra for dusting,* ***½ teaspoon of ground black pepper, 50g of cold butter, cut into cubes, 150g lard, cut into cubes, 125ml water, 2 tsp of flaked sea salt and 1 beaten egg****.*

this is what you do:

1. Sift the flour into a large bowl and stir in the pepper. Rub in the butter and 50g of the lard until the mixture resembles coarse breadcrumbs. Make a well in the centre.

2. Put the remaining lard, water and salt in a small saucepan. Bring to a simmer, then stir into the flour mixture with a wooden spoon. This will turn the mixture into a thick, hot paste that will quickly begin to thicken from the heat of the water. When it is cool enough to handle, mix with your fingers to make a smooth, pliable dough. Cover the dough with clingfilm and set aside for 30 minutes until the pastry has cooled enough to work with. Do not put it in the fridge or it may go rock hard and crumbly.

3. When you line your tin with this pastry it's important to make sure there are no cracks. The pie needs to be completely watertight when you pour the stock for the jelly into the pie.

4. If you do find a crack, take a bit of leftover pastry, smooth it into the crack and brush with beaten egg. You can even do this from the outside once the pastry is part-baked because it is so resilient. So don't worry if your crust isn't perfect first time around. As long as you mend any tears, your pie will be a triumph.

crumble toppings

Crumble toppings are easy to make and can be used for sweet or savoury pies. You can mix your ingredients in a food processor if you like, but it's really just as quick to do it by hand and you'll end up with a much better texture. Here are the basics, plus our ideas for special crumble mixes which you can mix and match as you like.

For a basic crumble, mix 175g plain flour, 50g jumbo oats and 125g demerara sugar in a bowl. Add 125g cold butter, cut into cubes, and rub it into the dry ingredients with your fingertips until the mixture has the texture of coarse breadcrumbs. Makes enough topping for a crumble to serve 6.

For a coconut crumble topping, mix 125g plain flour, 50g desiccated coconut and 75g demerara sugar in a large bowl. Add 75g of butter, cut into cubes, and rub it into the dry ingredients with your fingertips until the mixture has the texture of coarse breadcrumbs.

For a spicy crumble topping, mix 175g plain flour, 50g jumbo oats, 125g demerara sugar and 1 tsp ground cinnamon in a large bowl. Add 150g of butter, cut into cubes, and rub it into the dry ingredients with your fingertips until the mixture has the texture of coarse breadcrumbs.

For an almond crumble topping, mix 150g plain flour and 100g golden caster sugar in a large bowl. Add 100g of butter, cut into cubes, and rub it into the dry ingredients with your fingertips until the mixture has the texture of coarse breadcrumbs. Then add 50g of flaked almonds and mix well.

Our top tip:

If you're using a very juicy filling for your crumble, such as blackcurrants or gooseberries, toss the fruit with sugar and a spoonful of cornflour to absorb some of the moisture. This will help to keep your crumble from getting too soggy. Crumble mixture also freezes well.

rolling out pastry

Rolling out a bit of pastry might sound like child's play but it's surprising what a difference it makes if you take some care and do it properly. It makes life a bit easier if you start rolling with your pastry roughly the same shape as you want it when you've finished. So, form your pastry into a round, square or rectangle and flatten it slightly with your hands before you begin to roll – you'll be amazed at how much easier it is and you'll have much less waste.

this is what you do:

1. Flour your work surface and rolling pin but not the pastry. If you flour the pastry, it may get too dry and crack. Have a palette knife to hand that you can slide under the pastry if it begins to stick.

2. Start rolling and **roll only in one direction** – always turn the pastry, not your arms and body. Keep an even pressure over the dough – you want to flatten the pastry not stretch it. If you do stretch the pastry as you roll, it will shrink back when it's baked and ruin your pie.

3. Every 2 or 3 rolls, move the pastry a quarter turn before it has a chance to stick to the work surface. Lift it gently over the rolling pin and sprinkle a bit more flour on the work surface before you put it down again. Don't flip the pastry over if you can help it, as the additional flour can cause it to become extra dry and crack.

4. Always bear in mind what shape tin or dish you are using and roll the pastry out accordingly. When you are making a square or rectangle pie, turn the pastry less frequently and knock in the sides every now and then with the rolling pin.

5. For tarts, roll the pastry until it is about the thickness of a £1 coin. We keep a coin in the kitchen for checking – much easier than using a measuring tape. Some recipes require thicker pastry, up to just under a centimetre for raised pies and about 5mm for double crust. You are looking for a good balance between pastry and filling when your dish is finished.

Our top tip:

Sweet pastry can be difficult to roll, so place it onto a piece of floured baking parchment and then turn the parchment rather than the pastry. You'll need to flip it over gently to line the dish or tin and then peel off the paper.

2005

rolling out ready-made pastry

There's nothing like pastry you've made yourself, but sometimes ready-made saves the day, allowing you to put together a pie in no time. Puff pastry is harder than shortcrust to make at home, and you can buy excellent all-butter puff now. We've found that ready-made shortcrust seems to shrink more as it cooks than our own home-made pastry does, so we'd recommend it for pies rather than tarts.

this is what you do:

1. Most ready-made shortcrust pastry comes as a block. You'll make rolling much easier if you start by forming the pastry into the shape you're going to want at the end. So if you're going to be lining a round pie tin, shape the block into a round before rolling. You can do this easily by pressing in the corners with your hands.

2. When rolling ready-made puff pastry, always start by making 3 indentations across the block with your rolling pin. This makes it easier to roll the pastry out straight and flat, without stretching it. The same goes for home-made puff and rough puff pastry.

3. Some puff pastry comes ready rolled and interleaved with plastic sheets. We find it best to take this out of the fridge about 5 minutes before unrolling – any longer and it can get a bit sticky. We've also found it best to use it as soon as possible after purchase. If it is close to its use-by date or has been previously frozen, it can become unworkable. Unroll very gently and trim off the edges before using – this gives a better finish. Sprinkle flour under and over the pastry and use as soon as possible. If any cracks appear, smooth them out with your finger.

Our top tip:

Watch out for the sizes on different packs as they can vary. If you do find you've bought two 250g blocks instead of a 500g block, simply brush one portion with a little cold water and pop the other on top. Leave them for a few minutes and then roll out together. It works a treat.

lining a tart tin

You've made your beautiful pastry, you've rolled it out carefully and now it's time to put it in the tin. There is nothing worse than baking your tart only to discover that the pastry has shrunk back down into the tin, leaving you hardly any room for your filling. To avoid this, you need to be careful not to stretch the pastry, so take it slowly and follow our tips below.

this is what you do:

1. Once the pastry is rolled out to the right thickness, lift it on your rolling pin. Try to work quickly or the pastry will stretch as it hangs over the rolling pin. Hold it over the tin and gently flop it in. Keep the rolling pin off the sides of the tin or its weight will cut the pastry.

2. Using your fingers, push the pastry first into the base and then the sides of the tin, making sure you press into the flutes if using a fluted tin. If your tin has sharp edges, you'll need to make sure that they don't cut through the pastry as you work.

3. Instead of trimming with a knife or rolling pin, press your fingers against the inside edge of the pastry to push it up about 3–4mm above the rim of the tin. Push with one hand and pinch off the excess with the other, keeping those precious few millimetres of pastry poking up above the rim. This will help counteract any shrinkage that may occur.

4. If you are making a very sweet or rich pastry tart, or lining a particularly deep tin, you may want to leave the excess pastry overhanging the sides and then trim it after baking. This prevents shrinkage and gives a neat finish to your tart.

5. Prick the base very lightly to stop the pastry rising, but be careful not to make holes right through the pastry or the filling could escape. Chill for 30 minutes before baking.

Our top tip:

We usually use tins for baking tarts and quiches. You can also use ceramic dishes if you prefer which look pretty, but they don't conduct heat so well. The trick with these is to put a baking tray into the oven to heat up, then pop your quiche dish onto the hot tray so the heat gets to the pastry right away.

blind baking

Baking blind is simply baking a pastry case before adding the filling. This is important when making pies or tarts with a soft or liquid filling, such as quiches and custards, as it stops the pastry base going soggy. And we don't want a soggy bottom, do we? There's nothing difficult about it, but you will need some non-stick baking parchment to put over the pastry and some baking beans (see pages 332–333) to help it keep its shape as it cooks.

this is what you do:

1. Preheat the oven to 200°C/Fan 180°C/Gas 6. Tear a square of baking parchment slightly larger than your tin, scrunch it up, then unfurl it. This helps it fit into the corners better.

2. Roll out your pastry and use it to line your tart tin in the usual way (see pages 356–57). Prick the base lightly with a fork. Place the baking parchment over the pastry, then add a layer of beans, about 2.5cm deep depending on the height of your tin. These keep the pastry flat and support the sides as it bakes. The beans don't need to reach the top of the tin but they should be in a fairly deep and even layer.

3. Put the tin on a baking tray in the preheated oven and bake for about 25 minutes, or the time given in the recipe.

4. Take the tin on the tray out of the oven and gently remove the parchment and beans – be careful as they will be very hot. The pastry should be set but pale and a little damp looking. Put the pastry on the tray back into the oven for 5–10 minutes more, according to the time given in the recipe. (For a cold filling, you will need to cook your pastry fully.)

5. The pastry is ready when the base is pale golden brown and looks dry. If you see any cracks, brush them with a little beaten egg and put the pastry back in the oven for a few minutes until the egg hardens. Leave to cool before adding the filling.

Our top tip:

If you notice any cracks in your pastry after it's cooled, use a little of the reserved pastry trimmings to patch the holes and brush them lightly with beaten egg. There's no need to return the pastry to the oven unless you are putting a cold filling into the tart, as any patches will bake at the same time as the filling.

putting on the top crust

The secret to a really stunning pie is a lovely, chunky rim. It just makes the pie look more luscious somehow. And it is very easy to achieve – it's all about having two layers of pastry running around the edge. You don't need to worry about this for a double-crust pie because you'll always have a bottom and top crust meeting, but for a pie with lots of gravy or juicy fruit when a pastry lid is all you need, an extra layer of pastry makes all the difference. You can use this technique with puff or shortcrust.

this is what you do:

1. Put your pastry on the work surface and roll it out until at least 5cm larger than the dish you are planning to cover with your pastry lid. Fill your pie before you roll the pastry and make sure the filling is completely cold before it is covered.

2. Cut 3 or 4 strips of pastry, about 3cm wide, from around the edge of your rolled pastry. It doesn't matter if they are different lengths but they need to be about 1cm wider than the rim of your dish.

3. Brush the rim of the dish with a little beaten egg. Don't be too generous or the pastry can slide off when the lid is added. Stick the pastry strips to the rim, leaving a little hanging over the edge on both the inside and the outside. You will need to overlap the pastry occasionally, so brush with a little egg to fix in place and press the pieces together to seal. Brush the pastry rim with more egg.

4. Lift the rolled pastry over a rolling pin and place gently over the filling, leaving the excess hanging over the edge. Make sure there isn't too much excess pastry before you place the lid on the pie or it will stretch over the sides and then shrink back as it bakes. Press the rim firmly to seal the pastry together, then trim with a sharp knife. Chill before baking if you have time.

Our top tip:

Choose a pie dish with a nice wide rim to make a good-looking pie. It will help hold the lid in place and give you plenty of room for a decent crimp.

The secret of successful cooking: clean up as you go along.

trimming and crimping

When you put the top crust on your pie it's important to have too much pastry, rather than too little. Be generous and then trim your top to fit. For a perfectly finished pie, crimp or flute the edges as neatly as you can and it'll look the real deal.

this is what you do:

1. To trim your pie, hold the dish from underneath with one hand and take a sharp cook's knife in the other hand. Cutting away from you, trim away the excess so it drops down onto the work surface – watch your fingers! And remember, clean cuts mean a neat edge for your pie. If the pie is too heavy to hold in one hand, trim on the work surface instead or place the pie on an upturned bowl. Just remember always to cut in a downwards motion and work quickly before the pastry has a chance to stretch.

2. To crimp your pie, pinch the pastry edge with the thumb and forefinger of one hand, while pushing in with the forefinger of the other hand. It's much easier than you'd think and gives a lovely finish. For puff pastry pies, you can use the tip of a knife to draw the pastry back either side of your finger to give a fluted finish. Chill for at least 30 minutes before baking. This will give the fat in the pastry time to harden and set in its shape more securely before it is cooked.

3. For most pies, it's a good idea to cut a small hole in the top to let out the steam – particularly if there's a wet filling, which will create lots of steam and make the pastry soggy. We do this after the pie has had a chance to chill. Brush the pie with beaten egg to glaze just before you bake it.

Our top tip:

When trimming pastry, always be sure to use a sharp knife. A blunt or serrated knife will stretch your pastry and the finish will not be so good. This is especially important for puff pastry – a blunt knife would drag through the layers and prevent them from rising at the edges.

If you have any spare beaten egg, tip it into an ice cube tray and freeze, then add any more when you have it. These little cubes of beaten egg can then be thawed when you need them for making and glazing pastry.

knocking up

This is something you do to a puff pastry crust after it has been trimmed. It helps to allow air in between a few of the layers around the edge so they separate and puff up in the oven. To make a truly glorious crust, you'll also need to start with a double layer of puff pastry all the way around the rim (see page 361).

this is what you do:

1. Trim off any excess pastry neatly (see page 364) using a sharp knife. A blunt knife will crush the layers together and prevent the pastry from rising properly. It's worth giving your knife a quick sharpen before you use it, but make sure you wipe the blade clean afterwards or it may stain the pastry.

2. Take the knife and hold it horizontally against the cut edge. Gently tap the knife into the pastry edge and separate into several layers. As you do this, press the pastry outwards with the forefinger of your other hand to prevent it being pushed off the rim and back onto the filling. (Watch your fingers.) Decorate your pastry if you like and chill for at least 30 minutes before baking.

3. Brush the top of the pie evenly with beaten egg to glaze, but be very careful not to drip egg onto the knocked-up sides or they will stick together and not rise properly. If you brush the pie with beaten egg before you chill it, you may find the egg dries and cracks giving an uneven finish.

Our top tip:

Make sure you cook puff pastry at 220°C/Fan 200°C/Gas 7 as the moisture in the dough needs a hot oven to turn into steam and make the pastry layers rise.

decorating pies

There are always some scraps of pastry left over and it's fun to use some of these to make little decorations for your pie. Leaves are a classic but you can make anything you like – fruit, hearts, lattice strips, highland terriers, whatever you want! See the previous pages for some ideas. Here's how to make one of the most popular decorations – pastry leaves.

this is what you do:

1. Gather your scraps together and knead lightly if necessary – don't handle them any more than you have to, or the pastry will be tough. Roll the pastry out to the thickness of a £1 coin.

2. Cut out your leaves, or whatever you're making. You could even try cutting strips of pastry and plait them to place around the edge or down the centre of your pie. Cut shapes slightly bigger than you want them to be as they will shrink as they cook – particularly if you're using puff pastry. Add little marks for the leaf veins if you're feeling really creative.

3. Brush the part of the pie that you are going to decorate with a little beaten egg. Brush your decoration with a little more egg and place it on the pie. It will look even better if you curl it up slightly rather than laying it flat, and the heat from the oven will reach the pie lid more efficiently too. Repeat for your other decorations.

4. Chill the pastry for at least 30 minutes, then brush with beaten egg before baking. It's nice to sprinkle sweet pies with a little caster sugar before baking for a gorgeous glistening top.

Our top tips:

If you use lots of pastry trimmings to decorate your pie, you'll be adding what is almost an extra layer of pastry, so may need to increase your cooking time slightly. If the decorations begin to get too brown before the rest of the pie is ready, cover them with small pieces of foil.

Fruit pies look great with leaves on top, but you can also cut out small holes with a pastry or cookie cutter to reveal the colourful filling beneath. A little of the juice may escape as the pie cooks, but it will look all the better for it.

our top tips for perfect pies

Keep everything cool

Probably the most important tip of all because if the fat melts and becomes greasy it will coat the flour granules and they won't absorb the liquid properly. This will make your pastry tough and could cause it to shrink.

Handle the pastry as little as possible

Handling the pastry too much can cause it to warm up and become oily. You mustn't knead it for long either – just gather it up into a ball once it's made. Pastry that is handled too much stretches and will shrink when baked.

Use only a little flour for rolling

Don't put too much flour on your work surface or your pastry will become dry and could crack. It's best to keep moving your pastry and dust with flour underneath every now and then.

Roll in one direction

Always roll the pastry in one direction, forward and back, pressing gently and turning regularly to make the shape you want. By moving your pastry regularly, you'll keep an even shape and prevent it sticking. Rolling in the same direction will stop you stretching the pastry.

Use your rolling pin to lift pastry

The best way to lift pastry that you are rolling, or about to use to line a tin, is to place it over a rolling pin. This helps prevent the pastry stretching and avoids finger holes. If you are rolling a very large piece of pastry, a flat baking sheet can also be slid under for lifting the pastry.

Roll out on baking parchment

If you are rolling a very rich or sweet pastry, try rolling it out on a sheet of baking parchment dusted with flour. This way you can move the paper rather than the pastry itself as you roll. Make sure you keep your rolling pin lightly dusted with flour too. You can move your pastry on the paper to its tin and then gently flip it over and peel off the paper.

Choose a tin or dish as close as possible to the ones we've recommended

Tart tins and pie dishes vary enormously, so we've allowed a little extra pastry in our recipes to help compensate for the differences (and to make it easier to roll to the right size). Try to match your own tins and dishes as closely as possible to the ones we've recommended in the recipes. We've measured ours across the bottom, but some manufacturers take their measurements across the top, so watch out.

Chill the pastry before you bake

Chilling your pastry in its tin or dish before you bake it allows it to relax, helps set the pastry in its shape and prevents shrinkage. An uncooked tart case or a filled pie can be chilled over night if you like. If you're baking a pie straight from the fridge, it's best to increase the cooking time by a few minutes.

Bake sweet pastry blind before you trim

Some pastries are best suited to baking blind without trimming first. The overhanging pastry cooks at the same time as the pastry case and can be trimmed off while it is still warm. This method is particularly useful for very rich or sweet pastry that can tend to fold back on itself in the tin when baked. It also gives a very professional looking finish.

Always reserve some pastry trimmings for mending cracks

No matter how carefully you make and bake your pastry, sometimes you simply can't avoid cracks or tears. If you keep some of the pastry trimmings to hand, you can always mend the holes. This works before baking and after blind baking. Be very gentle and almost smear the new pastry over the crack, a bit like putting plaster in a hole in the wall. A dab of beaten egg and you are ready to go again.

Beat your eggs well before glazing

Beat the egg for glazing your pastry well before using. Ideally, beat it quickly with a whisk rather than a fork which can leave eggy strands.

Freeze unused beaten egg

To save having to crack a new egg each time you need to glaze your pastry, pour any leftover beaten egg into an ice cube tray and freeze. Next time you want to glaze some pastry, remove a cube and allow it to thaw at room temperature before using – it should only take 15 minutes.

Use a sharp knife to trim pastry

Always use a sharp knife to trim your pastry to give a good, clean edge. This is very important for puff pastry, as a blunt or serrated knife will pinch the layers and prevent them rising.

Freeze tart cases unbaked

Uncooked pastry freezes very well, so think about lining a tin and popping it in the freezer so it's ready next time you want to make a tart. Cover with clingfilm or foil once it's solid and freeze for up to 2 months. Bake blind from frozen, adding an extra 5 minutes to the cooking time.

Cook ceramic quiche dishes on a hot baking tray

If you are using a ceramic quiche or pie dish for a tart or double crust pie, put a baking tray in the oven to warm first. The heat from the tray will help cook the base of the pie and prevent it becoming soggy.

Make sure your filling is completely cold before using

Fillings must be completely cold before you use them or the fat in the pastry will soften and the pastry will stretch. This is particularly important for puff pastry pies which have a higher proportion of fat. If puff pastry softens too much it won't rise. If you are using a filling that has been in the fridge for a while, you may need to increase the cooking time of your pie to heat it thoroughly.

index